The Coward

Robert Hugh Benson

Printing Statement:

Due to the very old age and scarcity of this book, many of the pages may be hard to read due to the blurring of the original text, possible missing pages, missing text, dark backgrounds and other issues beyond our control.

Because this is such an important and rare work, we believe it is best to reproduce this book regardless of its original condition.

Thank you for your understanding.

THE COWARD

BY

ROBERT HUGH BENSON

AUTHOR OF "THE CONVENTIONALISTS," "THE NECROMANCERS,"
"A WINNOWING," "NONE OTHER GODS," "THE DAWN
OF ALL,' "CHRIST IN THE CHURCH," ETC.

ST. LOUIS, MO., 1912
PUBLISHED BY B. HERDER
17 SOUTH BROADWAY

Copyright, 1912, by Joseph Gummersbach

PART I

THE COWARD

CHAPTER I

(1)

JIMBO, the old fox-terrier, suddenly appeared
in the doorway, stood for a moment blinking
with something of a surly air at the golden level
sunlight that struck straight down upon him from
the west, across the sloping park; then he wheezed
once or twice, and with a long sigh lay down half
across the threshold, his head on his paws, to watch
for the return of the riders. He was aware that the
dressing-bell would ring presently.

The view he looked upon is probably as well
known to house-worshippers as any in England; for
he lay in the central doorway of Medhurst. Before
him, on an exact level with his nose, stretched the
platform-like wide paved space, enclosed by the two
wings and the front of the Caroline house, broken
only by the carefully planted saxifrages and small
weed-like plants that burst out of every line between
the great grey stones, and ending in the low terrace

I

approached by two or three steps from the drive.
It was extraordinarily inconvenient, this separation
of the main entrance from the drive, on wet nights;
but this lordly indifference to comfort had something of dignity about it. (Besides, the door in the
south wing could always be used, if the rain were
very heavy.) For the rest, the house is almost pure
Caroline, except for a few rooms in the south wing
that are Tudor. It is of grey weather-stained stone,
of an extremely correct and rich architecture, restrained and grave, except where, over Jimbo's
head, the lintel breaks out into triumphant and flam-
boyant carving — two griffins clawing at one another over the Medd shield, surmounted again by
wreaths and lines vaguely suggestive of incoherent
glory. To the north of the north wing stand the
great stables, crowned by a turret where a bell rings
out for the servants' breakfast, dinner, and tea; to
the south of the south wing, the laundry, buried in
gloomy cypresses and resembling a small pagan
temple.

Altogether it is a tremendous place, utterly complete in itself, with an immemorial air about it; the
great oaks of the park seem, and indeed are, *nou-
veaux riches,* beside its splendid and silent aristocracy, for Medhurst has stood here, built and inhab-
ited by Medds, pulled down and rebuilt by Medds
again and again, centuries before these oaks were

acorns. For, as Herald's College knows very well,
though the Medds never speak of it, it is reasonably
probable that a Medd lived here — after what fashion archæological historians only can relate — long
before Saxon blood became tainted and debased by
Norman.

It is remarkable that they have never become
peers (a baronetcy has always, of course, been out of
the question); but the serious fact seems to be that
they have consistently refused this honour. It is
not likely that they would have accepted such a
thing from the upstart Conqueror; and after such
a refusal as this, any later acceptance was of course
impossible. In Henry VIII's reign they remained
faithful to the old religion, and consequently in
Elizabeth's reign were one of the few families in
whose house their sovereign did not sleep at least
one night of her existence; in fact they went abroad
at that time and produced a priest or two, prudently
handing over their property to a Protestant second
cousin, whose heir, very honourably, handed it back
when Charles I came to the throne. And then,
when danger seemed more or less over, Austin
Medd, about the time of the Oates Plot, in which he
seems to have believed, solemnly changed his religion with as much dignity as that with which his
grandfather had maintained it on a certain famous
occasion which it would be irrelevant to describe.

Now when a Medd has done a thing, deliberately
and strongly, it naturally becomes impious for later
Medds to question the propriety of his action; and
from thenceforth two or three traditions — moral
heirlooms, so to speak — have been handed down
at Medhurst. The objective reality of the Oates
Plot, the essential disloyalty of Catholicism, the
sacrosanctity of the National Church as a consti-
tutional fact — these things are not to be doubted
by any who bears legitimately the name of Medd.

And so the great family has lived, coming down
through the centuries solemnly and graciously, each
generation rising among the associations of a house
and tradition whose equal is scarcely to be found in
England, and each generation passing away again
with the same dignity, and ending down there in the
Norman church at the foot of the park, where
Medds have filled long since the vaults of the south
chapel, among whose dusty rafters a hundred hatchments have hung and dropped to pieces again. In
the village itself — Medhurst Village, jealously so
called, lest the House should lose the honour of the
original name — the Medds are treated with the
same kind of inevitable respect and familiarity as
that which kings and gods obtain from their subjects and worshippers. Dynasties rise and pass
away again; but the Medds go on. There are various kinds of pride — the noisy pride of the self-

made man, the eloquent pride of the enthusiast,
the steady assertive pride of the sovereign — but
there is no pride in the universe such as that of
the Medds, dead silent, claiming nothing, yet certain of everything. They have produced soldiers,
priests, judges, statesmen, bishops, clergymen, and
the portraits of these worthies throng the hall and
the parlours; they have consented to hold the Garter
three times, and have, more recently, refused it
twice; a Medd has governed a certain Dominion,
under pressure, in spite of his commoner rank;
they have spent two fortunes on kings; a Medd
has, twice at least, turned the fortune of a battle
on whose issue hung the possession of a crown;
there are relics at Medhurst which I simply dare
not describe, because I should be frankly disbe-
lieved — relics whose mention does not occur in
any guide-book. Yet all these things are, honestly,
but as dust in the scale to the Medd mind, compared
with the fact of legitimate Medd blood . . .
And, indeed, it is something to be proud of . . .

(II)

The dressing-bell rang from the turret; and as if
answer, a great cawing burst out of the high elms
beyond the stables, as the rooks, settling for the
night, rose and circled again, either as if taken by
surprise, or, as seems more likely, following some

immemorial ritual handed down to them through the mist of centuries. Then they settled again; and Jimbo, who had raised an enquiring face, dropped it once more upon his paws. This delay to return from the ride, seemed highly unusual; but it still remained his duty to be here until the soft thunder of hoofs sounded beyond the terrace. It was then his business to bark three or four times with closed eyes, then to waddle to the head of the steps, where he would wag his short tail as General Medd came up them; he would then accompany him to the door of the house, going immediately in front of him, slightly on the right side; enter the hall-door, go straight to the white mat before the hearth; and remain there till all came down and dinner was announced. Then, once more, he would precede the entire party into the dining-room.

He seemed to be dozing, not an eyebrow lifted each time that a sound came from the house behind. Finally, he lifted his head altogether as a tall woman came out, leaning on a stick.

"Well, where are they, Jimbo?" she said.

He grunted a little, and replaced his head on his paws.

She looked this way and that, and presently saw through the open bedroom window behind her an old face, wrinkled, and capped with white, smiling and nodding. She waved a hand.

"Not come home yet, Benty," she cried.

The old nurse said something.

"Can't hear," she said again. "Never mind; they'll be back soon."

She was a very fine figure as she stood there in the level sunlight — close on fifty years old, but as upright as a girl. There was a little grey in her dark hair, and several lines in her clear face; her lips and brows were level and well-marked, and her eyes steady and kind. She was in black from head to foot, and she wore a single string of diamonds on her breast, and a small star in her hair. But she used a rubber-shod stick as she walked, and limped even with that, from the effect of an old fall out hunting ten or twelve years before.

Of course she could not for one instant compare with a Medd; but she came, for all that, from a quite respectable family in the next county, whose head had been ennobled a hundred and fifty years ago; and she had been chosen after a good deal of deliberation for John Medd, then of lieutenant's rank, by his father, old John Austin Medd, who himself had left the army soon after the battle of Waterloo. Her father, Lord Debenham, had been perfectly satisfied with the arrangement — he had scarcely, indeed, with his great family of daughters, hoped for such an excellent alliance for Beatrice, his third; and so young Lady Beatrice had come with her small income, her nurse, Mrs. Bentham, and her quiet beauty, twenty-five years ago, to begin her education as a mother of Medds. She had borne four children, two sons and two daughters, of whom three remained alive, two sons and one daughter. She had educated them excellently, by means of governesses, until the boys went to school; and she had retained her daughter's last governess — a poor relation of her own — as a companion ever since. She was a lady of an extraordinarily unobtrusive personality.

Miss Deverell, in fact, came out as the great lady stood there.

"Are they not come back yet?" she said, and so stood, fussing gently, and trying to look in the face of the setting sun.

"It's twenty minutes to eight, yet. Ah! there they are."

The soft thunder of hoofs, so familiar to her on these summer evenings, and so reminiscent of her own riding days, made itself audible somewhere round to the right from the direction of the long glade that ran up into the park; grew to a crescendo, and so, yet louder. A groom, whose waiting figure Lady Beatrice had made out two minutes before standing at the corner of the shrubbery, darted across the drive to be in readiness; and the next instant three or four riders came suddenly into sight, checked at the gravel, and then trotted on, vanishing again beneath the terrace at which they would dismount. Then, as the heads of two girls appeared above the level, again came the soft thunder, and two tall boys came at a gallop round the corner. The procession was closed by another groom running desperately from the stables to be in time.

" Well, my dears; you're late."

John Medd, coming up behind, preceded, according to etiquette, by Jimbo, who had duly uttered his ceremonial barks, took the question to himself.

" Val had a fall," he said, " and we couldn't catch Quentin."

" Not hurt at all? " she asked, with just a shade of anxiety.

" Who? Val . . . Strained a leg, I think; but he's all right. We must hurry and dress. Now then, girls. . . ."

And he drove them fussily and kindly before him into the house.

She still stood, waiting for her sons. Miss Deverell had hurried in after the girls, adjuring them from behind to make haste.

" Well, Val, had a fall? " asked his mother, looking at him as he came, limping a little, across the terrace.

He was a pleasant looking boy, about sixteen;

not handsome in any way, but with the long Medd face, with its slightly flattened profile and straight hair. He looked rather pale, and his mother noticed that he limped as he came. He stopped to beat off the dust from his knees, as he answered:

"Strained myself a bit, mother. It was simply ridiculous. Quentin simply bucked me off."

"Well, have a hot bath to-night. I'll get some stuff from Benty . . . Well, Austin?"

Her elder son saluted her solemnly. He was a couple of years older than his brother; but absurdly like him.

"Yes, mother; Quentin bucked him off. It was scandalous. And we couldn't catch the brute." He had a slightly superior manner about him. (Val found it annoying sometimes, and said so.) She laughed.

"Well, go make haste and dress, my son. It's ten to eight. We'll hear about it at dinner." She patted him on his shoulder as he went past her. She was extraordinarily proud of him, though she took great care not to show it.

She still stood an instant in the sunshine, till she heard the horses' hoofs ring out on the stones of the stable yard; then, as the sun finally dipped beyond the hill and the grass grew shadowed, she turned and went in.

(III)

She sat a little apart after dinner, as her manner was, in the tall chair by the wide fire-place, gently embroidering a piece of *appliqué* work in a fashion which she believed herself to have invented, and looking up tranquilly from time to time. There was no need to talk much; the girls were at the piano, and her husband dozed unobtrusively opposite her, over a book dealing with Afghanistan from a military point of view.

It is worth while describing the place in which she sat, as this hall was, so to speak, the essential framework of that Medd spirit which she had learned so completely to live.

It was Caroline, not Tudor (as has been said), but it was none the worse for that; it was some sixty feet long by twenty wide, and the roof rose high and stately overhead. Opposite her was the gallery, where glimmered gilded orpan-pipes among a riot of fat cherubs, resting on the great screen that shut off the approach to the dining-room at one end and the kitchens on the other. (She caught a glimpse of Val once or twice, leaning over the gallery, and nodded to him to come down and sit by her, but he seemed not to notice. She had learned well the supreme art of the mother of sons, and made no more of it.) The hall itself was panelled with dark Jacobean oak up some sixteen feet of its sides, lit by candles in sconces that projected below the cornice; and above, in a dignified row, hung the splendid collection of portraits, tilted slightly forward — that collection which is one of the first things for which the instructed sightseer asks. Between these, here and there, hung tattered colours; and, higher yet, the trophies of Royalist arms once worn by the Medhurst troop of horse at Naseby. (Hitherto the General had entirely refused to allow all these to be lighted by those shaded electric lamps just then coming into use.)

The floor of the hall was furnished extremely suitably. Against the walls stood, of course, the heavy shining tables and the stiff chairs of state; but the couches and the little dark tables and the deep leather chairs made the rest of it completely habitable. Great bowls of roses stood here and there — a delight to smell and sight; there were carpets, skins, standing candles, and all the other unnoticeable things that make the difference between comfort and bleakness. The tall windows still stood open to the summer air that breathed in, fragrant with the evergreen mignonette that bordered the narrow beds outside.

There then she sat, contented and soothed by that

atmosphere to which she herself largely contributed
— that atmosphere of dignity and comfort and,
above all, of stately beauty. It had been compounded year by year, distilled, refined seventy
times seven; and hung as heavy and as sweet and
as delicate as that of the old pot-pourri in the great
china jars on the side-tables. . . .

Now and again she looked up at the girls. Her
daughter May was accompanying now, while Gertie
sang — Gertrude Marjoribanks that is, the friend
her daughter had made out at Mentone last year.

The two girls looked charming — real *jeunes filles*
— the one fair, as became a traditional Medd, the
other startlingly dark, olive-skinned, and black
eyed. The piano-playing of the second was really
remarkable too, considering her age, in its extraordinary delicacy of feeling. It was her single accomplishment or, rather, it was the accomplishment
into which she put all her energy; for she did other
things sufficiently well: she rode, she talked a couple
of languages besides her own, she sketched a little,
and she was beginning to act. But her piano-playing was her real passion; she practised a couple
of hours a day; she continually hung round the
piano at odd times.

"Gertie," said the great lady when the last
rippling chord died on the upper octave, "Gertie,
have you ever met Father Maple?"

"No; who is he?"

(To see this girl look up suddenly was a real pleasure. Her face was still alight with the pathos of the music.)

"He's the Roman Catholic priest here. He's a great musician, I believe."

The girl got up and came round the piano.

"I think May told me about him. He's quite old, isn't he?"

The other smiled, as she fitted her needle into the stuff.

"He's about fifty," she said.

Gertie sat down, clasping her knees with her two slender hands. She still wore frocks above her ankles, and a thick pigtail of hair; but she had no trace of the adolescent clumsiness that May occasionally showed.

"Does he play, Lady Beatrice?"

"Oh! I think so. But he's composer too, you know. Ecclesiastical music, I expect."

Gertie said nothing. Ecclesiastical music seemed to her tiresome.

"We'll ask him to dinner before you go. We'll ask him when Professor Macintosh is here."

Lady Beatrice laid her embroidery resolutely aside and reached for her stick.

"Well, my dears, bed. Where are the boys?"

Austin rose from a deep couch in the corner behind.

" Here, mother."

" You've been asleep, my son."

He shook his head.

" I've been listening to the music."

" And Val?"

" Val went out ten minutes ago."

Then the General opened his eyes with a start, and rose briskly from his chair as Miss Deverell began to clink about the bedroom candlesticks.

(IV)

Austin went upstairs with his candle, whistling softly ten minutes later.

He had reached that age when it seemed to him proper to go in to the smoking-room and stand about for a few minutes while his father settled down to his cigar. He was going up to Cambridge in October, and until that event it had been decided that he was not to smoke. But it was necessary for him to begin to break the ice; and these holidays he had begun to visit the smoking-room, and, indeed, to keep himself a little ostentatiously to soda-water, at the great silver tray on which the tantalus and siphons stood. It all served as a kind of preface to the next Christmas holidays; when he

would drink whisky and smoke cigarettes with his
father.

The old nurse peeped through a baize-door at the
head of the stairs.

"Well, Benty?" (Somehow everybody greeted
her in genial fashion.)

"Master Val's hurt himself," she said. "I'm
going to take him some liniment."

Austin laughed.

"Take care he doesn't drink it by mistake. Good
night, Benty."

He kissed her.

Austin was a nice boy; that must be understood;
but he was just a little pompous. He had gone
through his four years at Eton with credit, if not
with distinction. He had always behaved himself
well; he had played cricket for his house for the last
two years; he had played football for the school
three or four times; and during his last year he had
hunted the beagles. He was so respectable that he
had been permitted to rise to the dignity of sixth
form, and for his last two halves to walk into
chapel in stuck-up collar with his hands at his sides
and his face deprived of all expression, in that
stupendously august little procession that enters as
the bell ceases. Finally, he had been elected to
"Pop" last Easter, and had enjoyed the privilege
of carrying a knotted cane on certain occasions,

sitting on the wall in front of schoolyard during vacant hours on Sunday,[1] and of having his umbrella tightly rolled up.

All these distinctions had had their effect on him. They had rendered him pompous; and further, acting upon a character that was really blameless, they had even made him something of a prig. For, not only had he Eton on one side to foster self-respect, but he had Medhurst on the other, and the knowledge that he was the eldest son. And these two forces acting upon his high standard alternately had had their practically inevitable results. The consequence (that consequence at least which is of importance for the purpose of the story) was that he did not get on very well with Val, who, besides being his younger brother at Medhurst, had only reached the Upper Division at Eton, and was distinguished by no cap other than that of the Lower Boats. The brothers would scarcely have been human if their relations had been really cordial.

The two had their rooms here, in the north wing, communicating from the passage outside with the old nurseries where Mrs. Bentham, once the presiding deity of them, now reigned in splendour. The sitting-room common to them both was at the western end, and looked out three ways,—on to the

[1] I note with regret that this privilege has recently been abolished by the present Headmaster.

front, on to the park, and on to the stable shrubbery; and their bedrooms adjoined — Austin's immediately, with a communicating door, and Val's
next to it, down the passage. The whole floor of
this wing was practically theirs, as the two other
rooms in it were spare bedrooms, only used when
the house was full.

These three rooms were exactly what might be
expected. The sitting-room had been their schoolroom a few years ago, where a crushed tutor (who
had since gained great distinction as a war-cor-
respondent) had administered to the two boys the
Latin *Principia,* Part I, and the works of Mr. Tod-
hunter, so there still remained in it a big baize-
clothed table, and three or four standing book-
shelves, as well as a small hanging cupboard with
glazed doors where little red-labelled bottles had
stood, representing "chemistry." But Temple
Grove and Eton had transformed the rest. There
was a row of caricatures from *Vanity Fair* upon
one wall, a yellow-varnished cupboard with little
drawers full of powdering butterflies and moths,
with boxes on the top, made of a pithy-looking
wood, in another corner; another wall was covered
with photographs of groups by Hills and Saunders,
with gay caps balanced upon the corners of the
frames; and finally and most splendid of all, above

the low glass upon the mantelpiece hung now the
rules of "Pop" enclosed in light blue silk ribbon.
There were also one or two minute silver cups standing upon blue velvet, beneath glass domes, recording the victories of J. A. Medd at fives. The curtains and furniture were of cheerful chintz; and a
trophy of fencing-masks and foils filled the space
between the west windows. These were Austin's:
Val had taken up the sport and dropped it again.
Austin was too good for him altogether.

As Austin came in carrying his candle, still
whistling gently, he expected to see Val in a deep
chair. But there was no Val. He went through
into his own room, and changed his dress-coat for a
house-blazer of brilliant pink and white, and came
out again; but there was still no Val.

"Val!"

There was no answer.

"*Val!*"

A door opened and Val came in, in shirt and
trousers. He looked rather sulky, and limped as he
came in.

"What's up? Why the deuce are you yelling?"

Austin sniffed contemptuously.

"Lord!" he said, "I don't want you. I didn't
know where you were."

"I'm going to have a bath, if you want to know."

"Oh, well, go on and have a bath, then. Jolly sociable, isn't it?"

Val writhed his lips ironically. (This kind of thing was fairly common between the two.)

"If you want to know," he said bitterly, "I've strained myself rather badly. That's all."

"Strained yourself! Why, good Lord, you only came down on your hands and feet, on the grass!"

"I've strained myself rather badly," explained Val with deadly politeness. "I thought I'd said so. And I'm going to have a bath."

Austin looked at him with eyelids deliberately half-lowered. Then he took up a "Badminton" volume in silence.

Val went out of the room and banged the door. Then his bedroom door also banged.

This kind of thing, as has been said, happened fairly frequently between these two brothers, and neither exactly knew why. Each would have said that it was the other's fault. Austin thought Val impertinent and complacent and unsubmissive; and Val thought Austin overbearing and pompous. There were regular rules in the game, of course, and Rule I was that no engagement of arms must take place in the presence of anyone else. If relations were strained, the worst that was permitted in public was a deathly and polite silence. This one had been worked up ever since Val's fall this afternoon. Austin had jeered delicately, and Val had excused himself. As a result, Austin had sat silent on a sofa after dinner, and Val had absented himself in the music-gallery, and had gone upstairs without wishing anyone good night. There were other rules as well. Another was that physical force must never under any circumstances be resorted to; no actual bodily struggle had taken place for the last six years, when Austin had attempted to apply a newly learned torture to Val, and Val had hit Austin as hard as he could on the chin. But any other weapon, except lying and complaining to the authorities, was permissible; and these included insults of almost any kind, though the more poignant were veiled under a deadly kind of courtesy. Such engagements as these would last perhaps a day or two; then a *rapprochement* was made by the one who happened to feel most generous at the moment, and peace returned.

Austin's thoughts ran on, in spite of "Badminton," for some while in the vein of the quarrel. He saw, once more, for the fiftieth time, with extraordinary clarity of vision, that he had tolerated this kind of thing much too long, and that the fact was that he was a great deal too condescending to this offensive young brother of his. Why, there were the rules of " Pop " hanging before his very eyes, to symbolise the enormous gulf that existed between himself and Val. Strictly speaking, he could cane Val, if he wished to — at least he could have caned him last half at Eton. Certainly it would not have been proper for him to do so, but the right had been there, and Val ought to be made to recognise it. Why, the young ass couldn't even ride decently! He had been kicked off ignominiously, that very afternoon, by Quentin — Quentin, the most docile of cobs! — in the middle of a grass field. As for the strain, that was sheer nonsense. No one could possibly be strained by such a mild fall. It was all just an excuse to cover his own incompetence. . . .

CHAPTER II

(1)

VAL was extraordinarily miserable the very instant he awoke next morning, and he awoke very early indeed, to find the room already grey with the dawn.

For the moment he did not know whence this misery came; it rushed on him and enveloped him, or, as psychologists would say, surged up from his subconscious self, almost before he was aware of anything else. He lay a minute or two collecting data. Then he perceived that the thing must be settled at once. He had a great deal to review and analyse, and he set about it immediately with that pitilessly strenuous and clear logic that offers itself at such wakeful hours — that logic that, at such times, escapes the control and the criticism of the wider reason.

I suppose that the storm had been gathering for the last year or two — ever since he had been called a " funk " openly and loudly in the middle of football. Of course he had repelled that accusation vehemently, and had, indeed, silenced criticism by his subsequent almost desperate play. A hint of it, however, reappeared a few months later, when, as it had appeared to him, he had avoided a fight with extreme dignity and self-restraint. And now, once again, the problem was presented.

The emotion of which he had been conscious when, after his fall, he had remounted to ride home, was one of a furious hatred against Quentin —not fear, he had told himself repeatedly during the ride and during his silences after dinner, but just hatred. He had even cut Quentin viciously with his whip once or twice to prove that to himself. It was ignominious to be kicked off Quentin. And this hatred had been succeeded by a sense of extreme relief as he dismounted at last and limped into the house. And then a still small voice had haunted him all the evening with the suggestion that he was really afraid of riding Quentin again, and that he was simulating a strain which was quite negligible in order to avoid doing so.

To the settling of this question, then, he arranged his mind. He turned over on to his back, feeling with a pang of pleasure that his left thigh was really stiff, clasped his hands behind his head, and closed his eyes.

The moment he really faced it, in the clear mental light that comes with the dawn, it seemed to him simply absurd ever to have suspected his own courage. Every single reasonable argument was against such a conclusion.

First, he had ridden Quentin for the last three years; he had had fall after fall, one or two of them really dangerous. . . . Why, he had actually been rolled on by the horse on one occasion when they had both come down together! And he had never before had the slightest hesitation in riding him again.

"*What about that jumping?*" whispered his inner monitor.

The jumping! Why, that had been absurd, he snapped back furiously. Austin, mounted on old Trumpeter, who had followed the hounds for years, had challenged Val, mounted on Quentin, who never yet had been known to jump anything higher than a sloped hurdle, to follow him over a low post and rails. Val, very properly, had refused; and Austin, on telling the story at dinner, had been rebuked by his father, who said that he ought to have known better than to have suggested such a thing for Quentin. Yes, said Val to himself now; he has been perfectly right.

"*Was that the reason why you refused?*"

Of course it was. He wasn't going to risk Quentin over nonsense like that.

"*Well then; what about that funking at Eton?*"

He hadn't funked. He had been hovering on

the outside in order to get a run down. Besides, hadn't he been applauded later for his pluck?

"Well then; come down to the present. Are you going to ride this evening?"

He would see, said Val. Certainly he wasn't going to ride if his thigh was really strained. (He felt it gingerly.) What was the fun of that? Certainly he wasn't going to ride simply to show himself that he wasn't afraid. That would be a practical acknowledgment that he was. No, if the others rode, and his thigh was all right, and . . . and he didn't want to do anything else, of course he would ride just as usual. It was absurd even to think of himself as afraid. The fall yesterday was nothing at all, he had just been kicked off — certainly rather ridiculously — just because he wasn't attending and hadn't been expecting that sudden joyous up-kicking of heels as the horse felt the firm turf under him. Why, if he had been afraid, he would have shown fear then, wouldn't he? He wouldn't have mounted again so quickly, if there had been the slightest touch of funk about the affair.

"You're . . . you're quite sure?"

Yes. Perfectly sure. . . . That was decided again. He would go to sleep. He unclasped his hands and turned over on his side, and instantly the voice began *da capo.*

"You're . . . you're quite sure you're not a funk?" . . .

As the stable clock struck six he got up in despair, threw his legs over the side of the bed, entirely forgetful of the strained thigh (though he remembered it quickly five minutes later), and went to look for " Badminton " on riding. He remembered it was in the bookshelf on the left of the fire-place in the sitting-room. He was going to be entirely dispassionate about it, and just do what " Badminton " advised. That would settle once and for all whether he was a funk or not. If, under circumstances of a strained thigh and a triumphant horse, and . . . and a faint, though really negligible feeling of apprehension, it said, Ride: he would ride that evening, anyhow, whether the others did or not. If not, not.

As he took down " Badminton," after a glance round the room that looked simultaneously familiar and unfamiliar in this cold morning light, he noticed another book on riding, and took that down too; and half an hour later, perfectly reassured, he put both the books on the table by his bed, and went tranquilly to sleep. He had found that even a slight strain in . . . in the lower part of the thigh ought not to be neglected, or serious mischief might result. He had dismissed as not in the least applicable to his case a little discussion on the curious fact that a fall, if it takes place slowly enough, and if the rider has plenty of time to consider it, will often produce such nervousness as that a really dangerous swift fall fails to effect. That was only in a footnote, and of course was unimportant.

(II)

It was at breakfast-time that the affairs of the day were arranged — usually towards the end, as by that time the whole party was arrived.

Very subtle laws seemed to govern the order and hour of these arrivals. Lady Beatrice was, as is proper, down first, and she could usually be observed from upper windows, five minutes before the gong sounded, dawdling gracefully on the terrace with her stick. (This was called " giving Jimbo a run," and usually ended in Jimbo's entire disappearance, by stages, in the direction of the stables, each protruding angle of balustrade and step and mounting-block having been carefully smelled *en route.*) Then she came indoors and made tea in an enormous silver teapot. Five minutes later the General came in, in tweeds, carrying the *Westminster Gazette* of the night before — tall, thin, hook-nosed, and fresh-faced. He kissed his wife and went to the sideboard, and this morning consulted her about a letter he had just opened, calling, on his return journey, for his tea. About five minutes later the girls appeared, apologising. (I forgot to say that Miss Deverell had been present throughout. She was always present at all engagements punctually, and was always forgotten, except when she suddenly made a small, shrewd, and often cynical remark, that made everyone wonder why they had not attended to her before. She sat on the General's right hand, in black; and he always put her plate back on the sideboard with his own, and asked her whether he could give her any cold bird.)

At a quarter to ten Austin came down, silent and respectable, and slipped into the company unnoticed; he ate swiftly and unhesitatingly, and had finished before the others. Finally Val appeared between ten minutes and five minutes to ten, also silent, but with an air of slight irritability; he fumbled about between the dishes, and usually ate a good deal in the long run.

This morning he was later than usual, but he limped so noticeably that the General, who had glanced up at the clock, which began to strike ten at that moment, spared him and said nothing. Besides, he had something else to say.

"And what about plans for to-day?" said his wife. "Why, Val, are you limping?"

There was a murmur of remarks interrupting Val in his careful explanations, and it became plain that riding after tea would be arranged. It was too hot this morning; this afternoon the girls had promised to do something in the village.

"Then ——" began the General.

"I don't think I'll ride to-day, mother," observed Val, eating omelette composedly. "I've strained myself rather badly."

"Is it bad, Val?" said his father.

"What about a doctor?" said his mother.

"No, not bad; but it hurts rather. . . . No, thanks. There's no need for a doctor, unless ——"

"Then ——"

But again the General was interrupted.

"Doctors say it's better to ride again at once," put in May.

"Thanks very much," remarked Val, with an altogether disproportionate bitterness. "But I'd rather not."

The General flapped the table with an open letter. He had reached the limits of his patience.

"Boys," he said, "I've got an invitation for you. And I think you'd better go. You must get your leg well, Val. It's from the Merediths, and it's to go to Switzerland for a fortnight."

Austin looked up.

" When is it for, father? "

" First of September. It'll just fit in before Val goes back to Eton. Eh? "

" Climbing? "

His father nodded.

" That's it. I want you boys to learn. You'll have plenty of time to get your things together."

The girls broke out into exclamatory envy. May determined to talk to her mother afterwards.

" I had an uncle who was killed in Switzerland," said Gertie tranquilly. " He was ——"

" My dear! " put in May. " Don't say such ——"

" But I had! He fell two thousand feet."

Val was conscious of a curious sense of relief, in spite of his reassurances to himself in his bedroom. It was scarcely more than a week to the first of September; and it was exceedingly likely that his strained leg would continue strained. Besides, even if it didn't, it would surely be rash to risk straining it again just before going to Switzerland. And when he came back there would be Eton again.

Austin was asking for details, in that dispassionate and uninterested manner which superior young gentlemen of eighteen years think proper to assume.

It appeared that the Riffel was the place; that "the Merediths" meant father and mother and a son; and that the son, aged twenty-two, was already a candidate for the Alpine Club.

Val listened. It seemed to him all very pleasant, and, somehow, appropriate that a new sport should present itself just at the moment when riding had begun to bore him. He had not an idea about climbing beyond what the smoking-room library told him; but he was quite confident, of course, that he would acquit himself creditably. It occurred to him as even possible that he might get level with Austin, towards whom he did not feel very favourably disposed this morning.

His father got up presently.

"You'll see about boots and clothes," he said to his wife. "And I'll write to the Stores about the other things."

"What things, father? Axes and ropes?" asked Val excitedly.

"Well — axes, at any rate."

When Austin came upstairs ten minutes later to get "Badminton," he was, very properly, annoyed to find Val already in the best chair, with the book on his knee. He searched, a little ostentatiously, through the shelves, as if unconscious of this, whistling in the manner that Val found peculiarly annoying, and proceeded further to turn over all the books on the table.

"Looking for anything?" asked Val at last, unable to bear it any longer.

"Yes, 'Badminton.' . . . Oh! I see you've got it."

"Didn't you see I'd got it as soon as you came in?"

"Well, when you've quite done with it," said Austin in a high voice, ignoring this pointed question, "perhaps I may have it. It happens to be my book."

"It isn't."

"It is."

Val, with an indulgent air, as if humouring a child, turned to the first page, while Austin smiled bitterly. Val's face changed. He stood up abruptly and tossed the book on to the table.

"There's your book," he said, with elaborate sarcasm. "I didn't know it was yours. I beg your pardon for using it."

"Oh! you can keep it till you've done," said Austin, his voice higher than ever. "I only wanted ——"

"I wouldn't deprive you of it for the world," said Val, his face working with anger. "I'll . . . I'll go and sit in the smoking-room. I don't want to disturb you."

He strode towards the door.

"Your leg seems better," remarked Austin, outwardly still calm.

Val cast a glance of venom at his brother, and faced about.

"My dear chap," he said, "you'd be howling in bed if you were me."

Austin simulated a genial and indulgent smile with extraordinary success. A sound burst forth from Val's mouth, which must be printed "Psha!" Then the door closed sharply.

(III)

It was really a bad day with Val. Boys of sixteen experience them sometimes, especially if their nervous centres are rather overstrung, and in such a state the faintest touch sets all a-jangle. He was so angry that he became completely and finally reassured as to his own courage. It seemed to him extraordinary that he had ever doubted it, and by noon he was almost determined to ride. But he saw this would never do, since it was conceded by all (as the theologians say), including himself, that the single reason for his not riding was his strained leg.

He spent the morning in a completely morbid manner, as his habit was at such times. He took a crutched stick, since his leg required it, and limped, even when he was entirely out of sight of the windows, out through the garden and into the woods. And there he sat down.

It was one of those breathless August days in which summer seems eternal and final. Every single, visible, living thing was at full stretch of its being. Over his head towered giant beeches, a world of greenery, with here and there a tiny patch of sky, blue and hot. About him was the bracken, every frond and vessel extended to bursting; beneath him the feathery moss. High up, somewhere in the motionless towers of leaf, meditated a wood-pigeon aloud, interrupting himself (as their manner is) as if startled at the beginning of a sentence. And the essence and significance of all was in the warm summer air — fragrant, translucent, a-sparkle with myriad lives, musical with ten thousand flies, as if a far-off pedal note began to speak.

Val had the vivid imagination which goes with such natures as his — an imagination that never grows weary of rehearsal; and in that realm, lulled externally by the perfect balance of life without him and within, leaning back at last on the bank as on a bed, with his hands clasped behind his head as usual, he began to construct the discomfiture of his brother.

His material, so to speak, consisted of two ele-

ments — Austin's superiority, and Switzerland.
He had caught on to the idea of climbing, and, as
has been said, was convinced (as would be every
wholesome boy of his age) that he would presently
excel in this. It would be the one thing, he had
determined, in which Austin would have to confess
himself beaten. (He remembered, for his comfort, that Austin had once refused to follow him —
some six years previously — along the ridged wall
leading to the stable roof.)

Very well, then; that was settled.

Then he began to construct his scenes.

The earlier ones were almost vindictive. They
represented Austin, a tiny figure, gazing up at him,
pallid and apprehensive, as he rose swiftly in the
air over the lip of an inconceivable precipice;
Austin, with shaking hands, being pulled up by a
rope, while he, Valentine, stood, detached and unperturbed, watching him from on high; Austin,
collapsed and inert with terror, while he himself
straddled, a second Napoleon, gazing out for suc-
cour from an inaccessible ledge. The final scene
of the series was staged in the hotel dining-room,
whose occupants rose to their feet and cheered as
he, Valentine, with a stern, set face, strode in, with
his paraphernalia jingling about him, after the conquest of a hitherto unclimbed peak.

He grew generous at last as he contemplated

his future. Austin was no longer to collapse, but simply to remain mediocre, while bearded men, browned with sun and exposure, discussed the brilliant younger brother who had swept all before him. There was a final scene, which for an instant brought tears to his eyes and a lump to his throat, in which an explanation took place between the two: Austin, reverent and humble at last, was to grasp his hand and say that he had never understood or appreciated him; while he, magnanimous and conciliatory, was to remind the other that in lawn tennis, riding, and fencing — all manly sports — Austin was unquestionably the superior. (Gertie Marjoribanks, he settled parenthetically, was to be present at this interview.)

Indeed Val was not a fool. He had a nervous system, it must be remembered, and an imagination; and he was nearly seventeen years old.

(IV)

He was silent at lunch; but no longer with irritation. It was rather a pregnant and a genial silence, warmed and perfumed by his imaginings. For to those who live largely in the imagination — who create rather than receive — reassurance, as well as apprehensiveness and depression, is always at their command. He had reconstructed his world now, by his earnest endeavours of the morning, and looked even upon Austin with benignity.

His geniality flowed out into words as he limped into the smoking-room afterwards and found Austin knocking the balls about.

"I'll play you fifty up," he said.

Austin nodded.

By the end of the game, which, although Austin won it by a final undeniable fluke, stood at "forty-eight all" before the balls, wandering about, happened to cannon, the two were talking freely again; and it was Switzerland of which they talked.

"Do tell me when you've done with 'Badminton,'" said Val. "By the way, I'm beastly sorry about this morning. I really didn't know it was yours, or I'd have asked you."

"That's all right," murmured Austin, touched in spite of his dignity. "You can have it all to-day." Val took his stick, helped himself to a leather couch, and curled upon it.

"Thanks awfully. I really do want to get an idea of the thing. Tom Meredith's a regular pro., I believe. . . . I say, do you think we shall do the Matterhorn?"

"Matterhorn! Good Lord, no. Why ——"

"I don't see why we shouldn't. Why, even ladies do it."

There was a pause, while Austin made a careful stroke with the balls, and missed. He put his cue up.

"I'm going up. I'll bring the book down if you like, if you're lame."

"Right. Thanks awfully."

Tea was under the cedar in the eastern gardens, and about ten minutes past five there was still no Val. Austin shouted once or twice under the windows; and at last the other appeared, reading as he came, and carrying his crutched stick under his arm. He remembered, however, to use it coming down the steps from the house.

Conversation was extremely genial. Val now joined in it, now sat silent and smiling, with bright eyes. His imagination had been vividly inspired by his three hours' reading; and he talked already familiarly of *arêtes* and *chimneys* and *couloirs*. May joined in enviously, with loud sighs; she had had her conversation, and it had proved unsatisfactory; the utmost she could get out of her mother was that if the Marjoribanks asked her for next year, and if there was nothing else particular to do, and if it was thought suitable when the time came — well, then perhaps she would be allowed to go. Meanwhile she was to remember that it was only natural that boys could do things that girls couldn't.

Val stood, a little ostentatiously leaning on his stick, with a smiling melancholy to see the riders start. He even laid his stick aside to mount Gertie, who was riding Quentin to-day by her own special request. Then he observed the usual caperings of the horses as they set their feet on the springy grass on the other side of the drive, and presently saw them vanish one by one over the near sky-line, in a cloud of flying turfs. He noticed how extremely well Gertie sat the cob.

Then he went back again to " Badminton."

CHAPTER III

(1)

THE dinner-party of which Lady Beatrice had spoken took place the night before the boys went abroad — if that can be called a dinner-party at which there are but two guests; and when Val came down, still rather out of breath with the desperation with which he had dressed, he found the two being entertained by the girls, while Austin looked picturesque on the hearth-rug. He said the proper things and retired to a window-seat.

Of the two there was no choice as to which was the most impassive. He had met Professor Macintosh once or twice before (the Professor was a college friend of his father's, he knew), but his appearance never failed to strike awe into the beholder.

For, first of all, he was a tall man, much bent, who grew his white hair and beard very long, and wore spectacles; and secondly, his costume marked him out evidently as a genius of the highest rank. (It was supposed, by Professor Macintosh's admirers, that he was unaware of any startling

41

difference between his dress and that of others, or, at the very least, was unaware that evening dress was usually governed by any code but that of individual taste.) He wore a brown velvet jacket and waistcoat, loose black trousers, and, most supreme of all, a crimson skull-cap not unlike those of the Renaissance Popes. His waistcoat was, of course, only slit down the front, disclosing a hemmed shirt held together by three pearl buttons. He wore square-toed, blacked boots upon his feet.

It was a tradition in the Medd family that the Professor was a man of gigantic knowledge. He did not actually occupy a Chair in any known University of the British Isles; but he had once, many years before, been an assistant lecturer at Owen's College, Manchester. There his startling views and his unorthodoxy had, it was understood, aroused the jealousy of the scientific world generally; and it had been left for Chicago to honour a man of whom his own country was not worthy. As regards the particular line in which he was eminent, General Medd could certainly have been evasive, if he had been questioned exactly on the point. The General was himself a man who laid no claim at all to learning, but he had always understood that " Science " was the Professor's subject. Further than that he could not penetrate. It is uncertain whence he had learned even these particulars; but

the Professor's critics did not hesitate to assert
that the only serious advocate of Professor Macintosh's claim to eminence was Professor Macintosh.
All this, however, was to the General's mind only
one more proof of his friend's greatness, since none
but a great man could be such a storm-centre in the
scientific world, or the occasion of such extraordinary bitterness. The Professor lived in Hendon,
in a small villa, with his wife, and was believed to
pass the greater part of his life in the reading-
rooms of the British Museum. He had issued two
or three pamphlets, printed without a publisher's
name; and was understood to be engaged upon a
gigantic work which was to be the monument of
his misunderstood life — subject unspecified.

Val, in the window-seat, therefore, looked upon
him with a proper awe.

The second guest, to whom he gave scarcely a
glance, was Father Maple — a smallish man, also
grey-haired, with a palish face and bright grey
eyes. He was disappointing, thought Val to himself, for he was dressed like an ordinary clergyman
in long frock-coat and trousers. He had expected
something more sensational. The priest at this
instant was turning over the books on the table.

" So you boys are off to Switzerland to-morrow,
I hear," said the Professor in his hearty voice.

(Val was not quite old enough to know why he
disliked this heartiness, or even the fact that he
did so.)

Austin said that that was so. They were to
catch the seven-fifteen, which would take them
up to town in time for the eleven o'clock train from
Victoria.

"Ah, ha," mused the Professor, "my climbing
days were over ten years ago. . . . Dear old
Tyndall! Many's the walk and talk I've had with
him."

"Professor Tyndall?" asked May, who was a
confirmed worshipper at the shrine, and would as
soon have doubted the existence of God as the
eminence of Dr. Macintosh.

"Yes, my dear. . . . Dear old Tyndall. I
remember on the Aletsch glacier once ——"

Then Lady Beatrice rustled in, apologetic but
perfectly dignified, followed by her husband. It
appeared that her maid was responsible.

Val for the last fortnight had, so to speak, eaten,
drunk, tasted, and smelt Switzerland and Switzerland only. The thing had seized on his imagination, as such things will at such an age; and even
Austin had been inspired. So it seemed to him
an extraordinary opportunity that the Professor
had come to stay at such a moment, and by the

time that the fish was removed, under the fire of the boys' enthusiasm, the subject had taken possession of the table and the Professor of the subject.

This was rather his way. It was said amongst his friends that he was a conversationalist, and that is always a fatal incentive to prolonged soliloquy. It was his habit therefore, positively forced on him by such a reputation and by the hushed silence that fell among his admirers, to use such social occasions as these to deliver a discourse on whatever subject had come up. (His friends used to say to one another, after such an evening, that " the Professor had been in great form.")

The impression diffused this evening was that the little band of scientists who for so long were associated with the Alps had by now positively been reduced to the Professor himself. Tyndall was gone, Huxley was gone, Hardy was gone; Macintosh only remained. He did not actually say this outright, but it was impossible to draw any other conclusion, and he was regarded with an ever deeper and more affectionate awe as the minutes passed by this extremely simple country-house party. A second impression made upon the company was to the effect that, in his younger days, there was scarcely an expedition of note with which he had not been closely connected. It appeared that he had been among the first to meet the diminished party that returned from the first ascent of the Matterhorn; that he had watched Hardy's conquest of the Finsteraarhorn through a telescope; and that there was not a peak or pass of any notoriety which he had not himself, at some time or another, ascended. Again, he did not say these things. . . .

He grew very eloquent at the end of his soliloquy, which was delivered in the form of a paternal lecture to the boys on the subject of a mountaineer's mental and moral equipment.

"You can take it from me, boys," he said impressively, "that it's nothing but foolhardiness to climb unless you've got the head and the nerves for it. There's nothing to be proud of in possessing them; there's nothing to be ashamed of in being without them. For myself, I'm as happy on an *arête* as on the king's highway; but that's neither here nor there. And if you'll take my advice, if you find that you haven't the head for it, why, be courageous and don't attempt to climb. It needs more courage to refuse to climb than to be foolhardy. Remember that."

He paused to put a spoonful of vanilla ice into his mouth; and the priest, who had been listening attentively with downcast eyes, looked up.

"You think, then, that the nerve for climbing can't be gained by effort, Professor?"

"Certainly not, Father, certainly not. It's a purely physical matter. I remember myself having to blindfold a young officer — it was on the Jungfraujoch, I remember — and to lead him by the hand before he could move. And I'm not talking of mere physical giddiness: I mean that nerve, as it's called, which many folks seem to think is a moral matter, is nothing of the sort. It's as physical as anything else. I should no more blame a man for . . . for funking a bad descent than I should blame him for falling over a precipice if I pushed him over."

"Do you hold that all the so-called virtues — I know no other word to use, I am afraid — are merely the result of physical conditions?"

A large, kindly smile beamed out on the Professor's face.

"Ah, ha, Father, we're touching on delicate ground there." (He glanced round at the faces of the young persons who were watching him.) "I'm a shocking materialist, you know — a shocking materialist."

He finished his ice in silence, with an air of extraordinary discretion.

"And what do you think about it all — er — Mr. Maple," said the General after a moment. (He was a humble and rather stupid man, and thought all these questions very important and very con-

fusing. He was also intensely full of his traditional contempt for a Papist, but veiled it admirably under courteous attentions.) "A cur's a cur,
it seems to me." (He stroked his grey moustache.)

The priest, who had dropped his eyes, looked up
again, smiling.

"I entirely disagree with the Professor, I am
afraid," he said. "I hold that a man is what his
will is; or, rather, that he will become so; and that
qualities like nerve and fortitude can certainly be
acquired."

Val fidgeted suddenly. It seemed to him an
extraordinarily tiresome conversation.

"Do tell us more about step-cutting," he said
shyly to the Professor.

(II)

. The last evening before a day on which something
pleasurable and exciting is going to happen has
always a peculiarly stimulating effect upon imaginative persons, and the two boys were in a state very
nearly approaching exaltation as they came out into
the hall after dinner.

Val vanished immediately, to take one more look
at the delightful luggage that already lay nearly
packed, in the joint sitting-room upstairs. He went
up three steps at a time, tore along the passages, and

then stood, eyeing it all once more: the sheaf of
axes, each with its little leather head-dress, umbrellas and sticks; the two portmanteaux, still open to
receive last touches and additions in the morning;
the roll of rugs, in the midst of which (as he knew)
reposed the coil of rope with its red-thread centre.
It seemed to him amazing that the eve of the journey was really come. . . .

He came down more slowly, once, indeed, turning back to reassure himself that his boots were
really packed — those boots which, heavy now with
the mutton-fat he had reverently administered to
them with his own hands after tea, he had worn, in
accordance with the directions of " Badminton,"
already for two or three days. As he came towards the hall he heard the piano. This was a
nuisance; he would not be able to talk to the Professor about *couloirs;* but at least he could think in
peace, so he slipped in noiselessly, tiptoed down the
length of the hall, and sat down on the couch behind his mother's chair.

In times of exaltation, external things take upon
them a value out of all proportion to their intrinsic
weight; and perfectly ordinary and familiar things
appear in a wholly new light. And so it came
about that Val, looking upon a scene which he could
remember so long as he could remember anything,

discovered in one or two trifling modifications of it
a significance that really bore no relation at all to
their essence.

It was the priest who was playing — a man of
whom a certain profane musician had said twenty
years before that the Church had only gained a
sacrament-monger while the world had lost an
artist; and though Val knew nothing at all of music,
it was impossible that he should not be enormously
affected, all circumstances considered, by the atmosphere generated by the really exquisite performance. For a time he watched the player's face, thin,
quiet, and intent, with the candlelight falling on it
and turning to pure silver the grey hairs about his
ears and temples, and thought only of rock-climbing. It crossed his mind with a kind of marvel
that any man should be as contented, as this priest
obviously looked, who was not going to Switzerland next day. And meanwhile the music did its
work.

Val knew neither then nor afterwards what music
it was that was being played. One phrase in it,
however — a *motif*, if he had only known it — began little by little to colour his thoughts. He began
almost to look for it, as it insisted upon itself gently
from time to time, like a wise friend intervening
with infinite tact. It was simple and clear now,
as if speaking alone; it inserted itself a moment

or two later across a tangle of controversy; it shouted suddenly across a raging sea; then once again it spoke gently. . . .

So the music began to do its work.

Val scarcely knew afterwards at what instant he first noticed Gertie Marjoribanks from the new angle. They were all very still. His mother's feather fan lay on her knee; he could see the jewelled fingers, perfectly motionless, clasping it. His father sat opposite, one long leg cocked over the other, one long foot outstretched in the air, with a shoe dangling from its toe; his hands were clasped behind his head, and his face was grave and still. Austin was in the shadow of a window-seat, all but invisible. Miss Deverell was beyond him again, seated beneath a lamp; but her work was lying unheeded in her lap as she leaned back and listened. . . . Above and about them all was the darkening beauty of this great old room.

And presently Val perceived that he was staring at Gertie Marjoribanks as if he had never seen her before.

This girl was sitting with her profile towards him, rather forward on her chair, in a pose that seemed to the boy one of the most beautiful things he had ever seen. (Naturally he would not have called it this.) She sat forward in her chair, with her slender white hands clasped round her knee, her face, shadowed in her dark hair, thrown forward and up, with her lips slightly parted, and her breath coming evenly between them. But it was that, so far as he could see it, which he saw on her face that gave such an amazing sense of beauty to the boy as he looked at her — an expression of absolutely real, rapturous attention, as if the sweetness and delicacy of the music had entered into her very life and transformed her altogether. These initiations are mysterious things, and it was Val's first experience of them. Only, he was aware that something had happened which somehow altered the relations of everything. He went on looking at this slender dark-haired girl, a year younger than himself, in her white frock; at her round arms clasped about her knee — this girl who, to do her justice, had lost during these minutes every ounce of that self-consciousness which girls can rarely evade; and who was actually, as she seemed to be, for the time being entirely absorbed in the astonishing sweetness of sound that was filling the room. . . . He looked carefully and minutely at her, at her face, again and again, at her hands, her arms, her feet, her thick hair; and suddenly and vividly a perfectly perceptible pang shot through him at the memory that the brougham was ordered for his departure at half-past six next morning.

As he turned a little restlessly in his seat, the music ended.

(III)

The cruellest nickname ever given to a really beautiful thing is that of calf-love. Certainly it has its clumsinesses and its crudenesses, but these result simply from the fact that the instruments of expression are not adequate. A boy in his first falling in love is of course awkward and spasmodic externally, and mentally he is usually sentimental and fatuous; but these defects no more detract from the amazing simplicity and gallantry and purity of the passion itself, than a creaky harmonium affects the beauty of a sonata played upon it.

Val's first clumsy moment fell at the handing out of bedroom candles that same night.

The priest had received the thanks of everybody (the Professor, indeed, had been kind enough to say that himself in his own musical days had never heard the piece played better), and had been ultimately seen as far as the porch by the General and as far as the terrace steps by Austin. Then, after a little talk, a move had been made towards the table under the gallery where the silver candlesticks stood. This was Val's moment. He had rehearsed it to himself while the priest had played for the second time; and he was there with a promptitude that made his mother smile at him approvingly. (Lady Beatrice had had a lot of difficulty about such matters with her younger son.)

Gertie came second in the queue for candles, and he had already set aside one for her with a glass that did not rattle. Then he gave it her before lighting it, that he might have the pleasure of holding it on one side while she held it on the other. Then he applied the taper to the wick, and simultaneously his fingers touched hers. The shock was so great that he dropped his side abruptly, and the entire candlestick, fortunately without the glass, fell crashing to the floor. Then, as he groped for it, he laid hold of her shoe by mistake, which was his second shock.

"My dear Val," said his mother.

"Very sorry, mother."

He stood up, and, to his horror, became aware that he was turning scarlet in the face.

"You've forgotten the glass, my boy," said his father behind.

This was remedied. And then Val fired off the sentence he had rehearsed, all in a breath.

"Good night, Miss Gertie, and good-bye. Shan't see you in the morning unless you're up by half-past six." He knew it was hopeless, but he had determined to say it. It would be exquisite to say good-bye to her again in the summer morning. It seemed to him an exceedingly daring suggestion to make.

"Half-past six! Why, good gracious, my dear boy——" began May explosively.

"Well, good-bye, Miss Gertie," said Val again. And for one vibrating instant their eyes met.

(IV)

The conflict of emotions was indescribable that night; for a boy, in the exaltation of a falling in love, will pose and attitudinise interiorly in a manner almost inconceivable to a maturer mind. He will, that is to say, group himself and his beloved, rehearse conversations, enact dramas — all in a scenery which the imagination contrives out of the material at its disposal — with a vividness and a dramatic power wholly unattainable by him in less emotional moods. Curiously enough, too, these dramas usually end in tragedy so moving and so poignant as to bring tears to the creator's eyes; and Val was no exception. More than once that night, before he fell asleep, he was on the point of an actual sob, as he lingered over some exquisite parting scene between himself and Gertie — or over some meeting, years hence, between himself as a homeless, stern-faced wanderer and her as a rich and important personage. These, however, came later, when the simpler situations had been exhausted — when he had perished of cold in the high Alps, after having covered her with his coat and waistcoat; when he had toiled homewards, bearing her inanimate form on his shoulders, himself to fall dead as the applauding crowds gathered round in the moonlight. . . .

He awoke with a start, to find the man in his room and the daylight streaming in.

" It's half-past five, Master Val; and Mr. Austin's in the bathroom," said fresh-faced Charles, who waited on the boys.

He still lay a minute or two re-sorting his emotions.

There had been something almost dramatic and appealing, last night, in the thought of his departure this morning (while she still lay sleeping in her beauty) to face the perils of the high Alps; but the drama seemed gone now, and dreariness to have taken its place. It suddenly seemed to him that it was by a peculiarly malevolent stroke of Providence that he had made the discovery that she was so lovable, only last night. Why, what a blind ass he had been not to have seen it before! What might not those past three weeks have been . . . those long afternoons, those rides? And he had let Austin open gates, and May walk with her in the woods. . . . And he had actually not ridden at all, for this last fortnight.

Then, with a pang, he remembered again the catastrophe of last night — the dropped candlestick, the clumsy gestures. . . .

It was a stern and moody Val who strode down to the early breakfast, who went into his mother's room as requested, on the way down, to wish her good-bye, who made rather more noise than he need on going past the door of the beloved. At the corner of the passage he even turned for one instant to watch that door. What if it were to open, and a sleep-flushed face look out! . . .

"You must buck up," said Austin, with his mouth full of kidney. " Brougham'll be round in ten minutes."

Val said nothing. He inspected the cold ham with the frown of a truculent despot. What did he want with ham?

He was, however, interiorly, slowly arranging the situation; and he saw himself now, once again, as a romantic lover whom severe duty called away to face dangers unspeakable. He was to go out and conquer; he was to return a fortnight hence, brown and determined and infinitely modest, to . . . to find her, no doubt, detained by some unforeseen accident, and still in his home. And if not? Well,

if not, she should see the newspapers, that by that
time would have some startling news from Switzerland.

"There are the wheels," said Austin. "Got your
things down?"

"I suppose so," said Val. "Charles said ——"

"Good Lord! don't trust to Charles."

"Better see after your own, hadn't you?" said
Val offensively.

Well, the impossible happened.

He stood in his tweed suit, bare-headed, on the
steps by the carriage, in something of an attitude,
it must be confessed; while Austin, practical and
efficient, as always, counted the pieces of luggage
which Charles was setting on the top of the brougham. Val's left leg was advanced a little; his right
hand was on his hip, grasping his hat; his left hand
held a walking-stick. He was aware that the morning sunlight fell on him from over the shrubbery
by the house, and that he stood, with a faint re-
semblance to a youthful Napoleon, exactly at that
point where his figure showed to the best advantage.
It was at this moment that the immense poignancy
of his situation struck him again with renewed
force. She was sleeping; he was taking his last
look — and all the rest — before setting out to meet

in a hand-to-hand struggle the elemental forces of
nature.

He turned then for one last look at the sleeping
house, carrying his eye slowly along the front, from
the north wing where his own room was to the
south wing where the girls slept. And as his eyes
rested there the impossible happened — that which
was now his last hope. The curtain drew back and
dropped again; but not before he had time to see,
as in a flash, a face crowned with dark hair tumbling
about the shoulders and a glimmer of white. . . .

"When you've done looking like a stuck pig,"
said Austin with peculiar vehemence from within
the brougham (it must be remembered that he had
had to do all the overseeing), "perhaps you'll get in
and let us go. We're ten minutes late already."

The brothers did not speak after that until they
reached the station.

CHAPTER IV

(1)

"BY George, you chaps!" said Tom Meredith, "but this is hot."

He sat down hastily above the angle of the path and wiped his face hard all over.

It was almost impossible to believe that forty-eight hours ago, at this very time, they had been struggling in the luggage-room of Victoria Station, between charging porters and half-hysterical women and furious vindictive-looking men in tweeds, all at other times civilised beings, but in the midst of this anxiety once more barbarous individualists. And now the three young men were on their way up from Zermatt to the Riffel. The elders were somewhere behind, on mules.

They had come out with as much speed as these days permitted. All the previous afternoon they had wound through the Rhone valley, passing hot little stations with green-shuttered official residences abutting on to the platform, looking up almost continually from the sweltering valley to the great hummocky hills on this side and that — hills that, in their turn, aspired here and there to vast crags of brown and black, and even to spires and towers, beyond which, now and again, looked down the serene snows, dazzling bright against the intense blue. Then, by haste, they had arrived at Zermatt the same evening.

Tom Meredith was the kind of young man with whom boys inevitably make friends almost immediately. In physical build he was impressive; in his short, jerky sentences he was even more impressive, for his speech was full of allusiveness and vivid detail, singularly unlike the periods of Professor Macintosh, who had held forth three days ago on the same subject. In appearance he was a lean, well made young man, hard and strenuous, thin-faced, with projecting cheek-bones, and extremely keen blue eyes beneath rather prominent brows. He was the proper colour, too, for a young man of his age and vocation, browned even with the suns of England; his hands were nervous and sinewy.

His outlook on life too was just now extraordinarily inspiring. Val had learned, by merciless questioning, that he had played football for Rugby for two years before he left and during one year for Oxford. But what impressed him prodigiously was Tom's entire detachment from mere games. Obviously these things were, for Tom, just a recreation for boys; the real thing was climbing, for in climbing you were facing natural facts and not artificial situations. It stood, towards games, in the relation in which fencing stands to fighting.

On climbing, then, Tom was inexhaustible. In periods between conversations in the train he had indeed looked out with unconscious contempt now and again at wayside stations; he had emerged from silence to point out a stationmaster who was unusually fat; he had said that he believed that Sion had a cathedral; but he had detected the Weisshorn, and indicated it with a lean finger, when there was no more to be seen of it but a flash of white, seen between two hills and gone again. And all the rest of the time, till his mother fell asleep, he had discoursed almost endlessly on technical points. Val had even come into his bedroom late last night to hear some more, and Tom had sat up in bed to gratify him.

Well, even Val was too hot and breathless to ask anything more just now (they had come for fifty minutes without a break), and he too sat down and took out his handkerchief. Austin was already breathing rather emphatically, though even then with a certain reserve of self-respect, in the shade of a rock.

The view at which Val presently began to look
is, most certainly, one of the finest in the world.
They were just emerging out of the pines on to
the first slopes of the vast plateau on the top of
which stands the Riffelalp hotel. Beneath them lay
the valley from which they had come, sloping
abruptly down from the trees over which they
looked down to Zermatt itself, a village of toy-
houses, far away to the right. Then on the other
side rose up the great bastions of rock and pine and
scree, stripping themselves as they rose higher, up
into the giant fortifications that protect the mountains proper — first the spires and pinnacles of the
lower peaks, purple-shadowed here and there, lined
with delicate white; and then the enormous solem-
nities of the eternal snows. Over all lay the sky,
brilliantly blue, seeming to scorch the eyes with
its intensity; while the grave murmur of the fly-
haunted woods beneath, the ponderous far-off roar
of the streams, did little else but emphasise to the
subconscious attention the huge scale of the silence
and the space and the vastness in which all expressed
itself.

"By gad!" said Val presently.

Tom waved a hand.

"Ah! but that's the chap!" he said.

Val nodded.

For, hugely greater in its isolation than all else,

standing clear out, built as it seemed, as on a foundation, on the high line of which other peaks looked but a continuation, towered, out to the left, against the high sky, that enormous abrupt wedge of rock, so steep that the snow lies on it but in patches and drifts and lines — that wedge of rock known as the Matterhorn — a monster who has, all to himself, a little cemetery outside Zermatt where lie, as if ennobled by their fate, the "victims of Mont Cervin."

"And we're going to do him before we leave?"

Tom nodded. "We'll have a try," he said. And Val continued to stare.

Already even this peak bore to his mind a certain air of personality. For first he had read all about it; he had followed, almost breathlessly, Mr. Whymper's adventures on it, and had formed an opinion on the famous question as to whether the rope, whose parting had cost four lives, were snapped or deliberately cut; next he had heard Tom discourse upon the peak; and thirdly he now saw for himself what a self-sufficient giant it was, broad-based as if on great claws, with that famous sharp head, tilted ever so little as if to see who were the next adventurers who were going to attack. It was upon the Matterhorn, then, that his heart was chiefly set; it stood for him as a symbol of all he meant to do in life generally.

"They say there are a lot of chains on it now," he suddenly said.

"That's nonsense!" said Tom. "They're fused by lightning within a year or two. Besides, the climbing's just as difficult. Besides, you needn't use them."

"And we start on the Riffelhorn to-morrow?"

"This afternoon, if you're game."

"Tell us about it."

"Well, we must be getting on. I'll tell you as we go. . . . Look; isn't that them?"

He stood up, pointing down the slopes; and there, tiny as mechanical toys, there moved out of the shadow of the trees, five hundred feet below, the small and solemn procession of mules and porters with which the Meredith parents were ascending. Mr. Meredith had been perfectly explicit this morning. He would walk, he said, where it was absolutely impossible to be conveyed, provided it was reasonably flat going, and not too far. The boys might kill themselves as soon as they liked; but they must not ask him to accompany them.

"Yes; let's get on," said Val, getting to his feet once more.

It appeared that the Riffelhorn had been designed by an indulgent Providence as a kind of gymnasium for rock-climbers. It was a small peak of rock, jutting out from the Gorner Grat over the Gorner glacier; it possessed precipices quite deep enough to test the head (that on the glacier was a good thousand feet); it was constructed of excellent rock; and, best of all, there were no fewer than six ways to the top, namely, the ordinary way, the " sky-line," the ascent from the glacier, the ascent from the Gorner side, with two more on the side facing the Matterhorn — these latter both short, but exceeding steep. The ascent known as the Matterhorn chimney contained but two footholds in forty feet.

"Then how do you get up it?" panted Val; for they were swinging on again at a good pace.

"Shoulders and knees," said Tom tersely, " right across the chimney."

"Have you done it?"

"Lord, yes."

"And if you fall?"

"Oh! you'd go on to the glacier, I should think. But of course you have a rope."

(II)

A Riffelalp *table d'hôte* presents as remarkable contrasts as any *table d'hôte* in the world, since it comprises specimens of the most active and the most passive types of the human race. There are large, stately ladies there, suspiciously bright-eyed, in silk petticoats, with their lace-fringed parasols leaning in the corner; and there are lean, sun-dried athletes, who have ascended Monte Rosa yesterday and propose to start for the Weisshorn to-morrow. The complexions of the former are often perfectly preserved, since they have come up here in a litter, and have done no more than stroll for a quarter of a mile along the level path leading towards the Findelen glacier; the complexions of the latter are usually non-existent: at the best they are of a rich dry-leaf tint, at the worst they are olive, with a pink, peeled nose and puckered eyes set in the midst.

It was at the end of one of the two long tables, furnished with guests of these varieties, that the party of five sat down at about a quarter-past twelve. The parents had taken it easily, and appeared now, scarcely flushed — Mrs. Meredith a rather round-faced, happy-looking lady, in a blouse and twill skirt; Mr. Meredith a dry, thin man, looking to be exactly what he was — a lawyer — in a neat grey tailed suit, with a high forehead and humorous, sharp eyes. As a matter of fact, he was a K.C., sitting, so to speak, on the very edge of the bench.

" Now, Tom," he said, " tell us all about them. Who's here? I mean of your sort."

Tom took another careful survey of the faces and began. It was a big room, high-ceilinged and wide-windowed, looking straight out at the end by which the new party sat upon the Matterhorn end of the valley. There sat the monster, guarded by the little, black Hoinbi at his base, as a giant might sit with a small dog between his knees. And the whole view was sublime; it glimmered, from these windows, with the blue of a London riding-school. But it was not with this that Val was interested just now.

It was extraordinarily fascinating to Val, for there were at least two climbers at the table that day of whom he had actually read in printed books; and one of them James Armstrong, Secretary of the Alpine Club. (With infinite envy he saw Tom presently nod at him and receive a nod in return.) There were also, it appeared, staying in the hotel, though not present at this moment, a party of four men whom Tom had met and climbed with last year. They had gone for what was called a "training-walk" up to the top of the Breithorn, and would be back by evening. Tom had learned all those things from the hotel-porter upon his arrival.

"And what are you boys going to do this afternoon?"

"Riffelhorn, father."

His mother glanced at Val.

"You don't look very strong, Mr. Val," she said. "Are you sure ——"

"Oh! I'm all right, thanks."

He had determined to take a firm line at once. He was not going to be mothered.

"And you'll be back . . . ?"

"For *table d'hôte*, anyhow," said Tom.

"You three alone?"

"Oh! we'll go up the easy way, of course, unless Armstrong'll come. I'll ask him afterwards. Here he comes, by gad."

It was a very pleasant man, thought Val, and very admirable looking, who came and sat down by them on his way out. But he seemed very unsensational-looking for the Secretary of the Alpine Club, and indeed, with his short whiskers and bald forehead, rather resembled a Low Church clergyman. He was not even in knickerbockers, but in a grey flannel suit, and carried a white canvas hat. He actually had a gentian in his buttonhole. He moved slowly and easily, as if his limbs were loosely attached to his body.

"And what are you going to begin with, Tom?" he asked, when all the proper things had been said. "Monte Rosa between tea and dinner?"

"Riffelhorn," said Tom decisively. "We start in ten minutes from now. I wish you'd come."

The Secretary grinned.

"And you walked up from Zermatt this morning! And your friends?"

"They're coming too."

"Gentlemen," said the other gravely to the two

boys, " I solemnly warn you against Mr. Thomas Meredith. I hope you won't stand it for one moment. And wouldn't you much sooner sit quietly in the verandah for the rest of the day?"

Val dissented enthusiastically. (He thoroughly approved of this man.)

"Well, well; and so it's the Riffelhorn. Glacier side?"

Tom explained that his friends had never been in Switzerland before; he had proposed the easy way up, but if Mr. Armstrong would come they could take a rope and do the sky-line.

Mr. Armstrong sniffed.

"You'll be getting into mischief. I see that. Yes, I'll come if you'll give me half an hour for a cigar and won't walk too fast. . . . Yes, I should think we might manage the sky-line together."

He glanced at the three faces with an approving humour that made Val's heart leap with pleasure.

(III)

A marmot was feeding on the grass not a hundred yards from the foot of the Riffelhorn, and not fifty from the little lake in whose surface the Matterhorn lies reversed.

It was a day of extraordinary peace down here in the hollow. On all sides lay hummocky and broken ground, rocks, grass, wiry plants, rolling up and up towards the path far away that led to the Gorner Grat. Overhead lay the sky, an enormous hard-looking dome of intense blue deepening to black. It was an entire cosmos in itself, silent, self-sufficient, complete; for the iron crags of the Riffel-horn, black against the glaring sky, were as remote as the sun from the earth. Here was no sound, for the breeze had dropped, and not a thread of water moved; only the minute crunching and tearing of the marmot's teeth emphasised the stillness. Once he heard the shuffle of feet as his friend over the nearest slope moved to juicier pasture, and then silence fell again.

The isolation was so complete, the spaces so vast, that an interruption would seem to partake of the nature of the miraculous; for the world of consciousness within the marmot's tiny brain was as well rounded and secure as the hollow in which he browsed and the earth on which he lived. An eternity separated him from the warm morning into which he had come to take air and food and water; an eternity from the evening in which he would go back to his safe darkness and his lined nest. Only the sun moved overhead, a blazing pool of fire, like Destiny across the sky. He had his universe to which his instincts responded: there was that within him that had brought

him out a few hours ago, that would send him back
a few hours hence; there was that within him too
that would respond to the unexpected, should it
befall him, that would adapt him to his shattered
world. . . .

Well, the unexpected happened, as it always
does; and a phenomenon came into his life that of
course had come before with the advent of every
tourist, that, for all that, he continually forgot.

It began with a tremor of the earth, so subtle,
and originated at so great a distance, that it did no
more than cause him to lift his brown chin from
the grass. Presently it died away, and presently
began again.

He sat up abruptly. Still all was as it had been.
The vast blue vault was unmoved; the Matterhorn
remained unruffled in its perfect mirror; the Riffelhorn stood up abrupt and forbidding. No voice
or cry or shot broke the intense, hot silence. Yet
Destiny approached.

Five minutes later there was a shrill call and the
rush of scampering feet. His neighbour had gone
to ground. Down by the shore there rippled across
the grass yet another brown body, and vanished.
The marmots were going to earth.

Yet still he waited, his ears pricked, his nose moving gently. And then, as against the glaring hori-

zon twenty yards away, a white hat rose swinging,
he too whistled and went.

The cosmos was broken up. And beneath, in the
secure darkness, he began once more to adapt himself to his environment.

It was about two hours and a half after *table-
d'hôte* that Val suddenly found himself wishing he
had never been born. That moment comes sooner
or later to every living being who climbs a mountain.
It arises from a multitude of causes, and usually
passes away again with as startling a movement as
that with which it arrived. Val's moment was a
typical case.

They had started in less than half an hour after a
rather heavy meal, having preceded that meal with
an exceedingly hot walk up from the valley, and the
ascent to the base of the Riffelhorn seemed almost
endless to a mind accustomed only to English slopes
and distances. The sun shone straight down with
an astonishing force upon their backs as they ascended, and Val had almost despaired ever of reaching even the plateau of the lower Gorner Grat.
Then, when that was reached, there was a long
walk over tumbled ground, where Val had his first
sight of a marmot, and then, at the moment when
the first slopes of rock were reached and the Riffel-

horn itself, a towering white peak, stood straight overhead — at the moment when Val had expected to be allowed to throw himself flat on the ground to pant and to drink, Tom, with shining eyes, had exclaimed:

" Now we're going to begin."

Val looked desperately at Austin, and was enraged to see his calmness. Certainly that brother of his looked hotter than he had ever seen him before; he was flushed heavily, and his face was one thin sheet of wet that dripped off his chin and nose; but he did not seem at all distressingly exhausted, and made no protest. Very well then; Val would not either.

Then, without another word, Tom had set his hands upon the rock and risen some four feet. Austin came next, then Val, and last Mr. Armstrong, a little behind, since he had paused to arrange his handkerchief delicately under his hat and over the back of his neck. He was still in grey flannel trousers. . . .

The climbing did not seem impossibly difficult. Certainly it was unlike anything Val had ever done before, and it appeared to him strange that the rope was not put on, since after a quarter of an hour's climbing, there was a slope of rocks on their right that would certainly kill anyone who happened to fall over. But he made a strong act of faith in Tom

Meredith, and went on. On the whole he was pleased with his prowess. He was also pleased that the rope had not been mentioned again.

Then came the moment when he wished himself dead, suddenly and violently — or, rather, that he had never been born, since it seemed to him that death, abrupt and brutal, was his only possible prospect.

They had reached the foot of a little wall of rock about twelve feet in height, up which ran a deep crack, not deep enough to get inside. The wall appeared to Val absolutely insurmountable. Tom turned round.

"Look here," he said, "I think you'd better watch my feet, if you don't mind. This is absolutely the only bit of climbing on the thing at all. And if you start with the wrong foot, you'll find it hard."

Val regarded him with horror, but he said nothing.

For it seemed to him that not only had they been climbing, but that the climbing was quite tolerably hard. He looked down the side of rock up which they had scaled their way just now. The view ended abruptly some fifteen feet below him, and the next solid earth to be seen beyond was, perhaps, three hundred feet distant. And now they were to ascend on the top of all this, an apparently perpendicular wall. To fall on it would mean certain death. One would pitch first on the slope, roll three yards, fall again, bounce off, and then land — well — three hundred feet below. All this was entirely clear to him; and he marvelled. . . . He glanced at Mr. Armstrong.

That gentleman still held between his teeth a stalk of grass he had plucked at the foot of the little peak: he was twiddling it about with his tongue.

" This is your patent way up, isn't it, Tom? "

" Just a variation: we meet the regular way at the top of this."

" I thought so. Up you go, then."

Val leaned back and watched.

He looked first at Tom, who now resembled an enormous spider going up a wall, attached to it, it appeared, merely by some mysterious power of suction. His body seemed to have dwindled to nothing; there were just four limbs of unsuspected length, writhing their way upwards. Then he looked at Austin: Austin, silent and apparently unmoved, was watching closely where Tom put his hands and feet. Then he stared out desolately at the huge spaces about him, the gulf of air up which they had come; the enormous sky, hard and near-looking, just beyond those ruddy rocks. He considered that he was a fool; for the agony was not upon him yet — a fool, no more at present.

"Come on," said a voice; and there was Tom, grinning like a griffin on a gate-post, peering down from the summit of this wall that seemed now the end of all things. His face seemed sinister and dark against that tremendous blue sky — sinister even in its happy grin of physical delight.

But it was Austin's turn next; and with a kind of fascination, he watched his brother go up, aided by remarks — "Right foot *there;* . . . now your left hand here; . . . yes; let go with your right "— until with a heave, Austin wriggled over the top of the wall and instantly vanished.

And then he knew that he must go forward.

"Which foot first?" he stammered. . . .

The moment came when he was half-way up. Up to that point he had obeyed, simply and blindly, with a sense of fatality more weighty even than his own despair. He had found himself rising . . . rising, exactly as Tom told him; once even a flush of exultation thrilled through him, as he considered that he was doing very admirably for his first climb.

And immediately after the exultation came the horror. He put out his wrong hand, seeing, as he thought, a corner of rock which simply demanded it; he let go with his left hand, shifted his position, lost control; and for about five seconds hung, he thought, merely by one hand and one foot, and that

his foot was slipping. He was entirely unable to
speak. . . . No one spoke. . . .

In those instants came the full horror on him.
He saw, as in a vision, the rocks below him, the
gulf below the rocks. He was perfectly certain
that no power on earth could now save him; and
that interior act of which I have spoken, though
with a vehemence quite impossible to describe, ex-
ploded within him like gunpowder. Why had he
ever been born? His cosmos was unexpectedly
shattered. . . .

"Go on. I've got you," said a solemn and tran-
quil voice. "Yes, go on. Do as I tell you. Put
your left hand three inches higher."

He felt something firm grip his ankle. He did
what he was told. He felt his knees shaking violently; but the rest was easy; and he too wriggled
over the top, gripped by the shoulder as he did so,
and stood up on a broad platform, beside Austin.
Then the grave face of Mr. Armstrong, with the
grass-stalk still in his mouth, rose serene and beneficent over the beetling edge.

(IV)

The exultation that came on him as he swung his
way downwards at last, and dropped on to the
shingle an hour later, was proportionate to his bad
moment on the way up.

It seemed to him he had done extraordinarily well. Certainly he had had a horrible instant; but he had shown no signs of it, and that was exactly what courage meant. He had done, in fact, a good deal better than Austin, since Austin, through hearing what was said and doing it exactly, had had no real difficulty at all. Himself, on the other hand, had got into trouble, and had emerged from it triumphant.

There was a good deal of excuse for this exultation. The superb air in which he had climbed was like wine to his heart; his muscles had been exercised to the full. Besides, he had, actually, at his first attempt, succeeded in what really was rock-climbing, after all. Even Armstrong had implied that it was a good deal to do, after the morning walk from Zermatt.

"I thought you always put on the rope for the sky-line of the Riffelhorn," he said to Tom as they swung homewards.

" Most people do. I've done it without, though."

" I'm glad we didn't."

" Eh? "

" I'm glad we didn't," explained Val.

" That wasn't the sky-line we did."

" But ——"

" Good Lord, no; that's the ladies' way. All except the bit of wall where you were shoved."

"And that's the easiest way?" said Val, with sinking heart.

"Of course, my dear chap. Armstrong thought we'd better not try the sky-line till you'd seen what you could do."

"Oh!"

"There was a pause. Then Val put the question he had longed to put for the last hour.

"And did I . . . . we . . . . do pretty well?"

"Oh, yes," said Tom indifferently.

CHAPTER V

(1)

IT was rather distressing that the next day was Sunday, since convention at the Riffelalp (at least in those days) demanded that no big expedition should be undertaken, unless, indeed, a furtive start were made for one of the huts after dark had fallen. Besides, there was the difficulty of guides, since these insisted on hearing Mass sometime in the course of Sunday morning. Convention was enforced too by the almost incredible number of clergymen present in the hotel.

There was a small tin church standing somewhat to the rear of the hotel, where the English attended with a propriety which many of them, it is to be feared, did not show at home. The two young men in the big room had heard its bell rapidly summoning worshippers shortly before eight o'clock, and had made remarks. Then they had gone to sleep again. But three hours later, in the rear of the parents, they had obeyed its call, and presently found themselves inside in a temperature of not less than seventy-five degrees Fahrenheit. An

American organ, blown by its lady player in such
a manner that it always seemed out of breath, wel-
comed them to their seats.

Val as regarded his religion was exactly true to
type. He had been recently confirmed at Eton,
regarding it as a suitable ceremony of unknown but
vaguely spiritual import. He looked upon it as a
kind of religious coming of age. He had no kind
of doubt as to the existence of God, and he accepted
the Christian religion as he accepted the stars in
their courses and the British Constitution. And
that was about all.

He set himself to work therefore, as soon as he
had pulled his trousers up at the knee and resumed
his seat, to look carefully at everybody present in
church. He hoped to indentify the climbers, and
by the end of the Absolution, read by a Dean with
a brick-coloured face and a voice full of eloquent
expression, had detected half a dozen. (Tom had
said he would introduce him to some of them after
church.)

He was more enthusiastic than ever this morning,
since he felt he had taken his first step towards
experience on the previous afternoon. He had, of
course, dreamt of climbing nearly all night. Church
then, with the slight dreaminess induced by it, was
exactly the right *milieu* in which to think over future

conquests; and by the end of the Psalms, read in alternate verses by the eloquent Dean and the congregation, and each closed by the *Gloria Patri* to the accompaniment of the breathless instrument and the chant of Gadsby in C, was already half-way up the Matterhorn. Gertie too was with him by now, looking exceedingly graceful and slender in a short climbing skirt, a jacket, and gauntlets. There were no guides. They were just climbing together. . . . He was showing her where to put her hands and feet. . . .

For, beneath all the external interests, Gertie had been subconsciously present to him ever since he had left England. It gave him more than one ecstatic thrill, during an enormous first Lesson all about Ahab, to remember that she had pulled back her curtain to see him — or them — start. . . .

It was unhappily the Sunday for the Litany, and this religious exercise, coming on the top of the extreme heat of the church and the weariness resulting from the previous day, caught Val rather off his guard. For by the time that " the kindly fruits of the earth " were mentioned, he was once more cross-questioning himself severely as to whether or no there were in his own character a certain slight strain of weakness. It is very hard to lay interior ghosts quite satisfactorily. He thought he had laid this ghost once for all before he had left home, yet somehow it was looking at him again; and he even ventured to ask himself this morning whether that extreme agony of yesterday, when he had hung for five seconds over the gulf, were not a symptom of this weakness. It was not that he had the smallest doubt as to how he was going to behave in future. That had been entirely settled, partly on the way home from the Riffelhorn, chiefly after a couple of glasses of *Asti Spumante,* and finally and completely during the delicious moments immediately after getting between cool sheets and before going to sleep. In future nothing at all was to disturb him; he was to behave perfectly always. Only, in this drowsy atmosphere, lulled by the rhythm of the Litany, he thought it wise just to run over the past once more and make quite certain that his tremors had been no more than interior. Courage, he told himself, consisted in disregarding such tremors. . . .

(II)

It was really almost worth while to have gone to church, to come out into the delicious pine-scented air and the breeze, and to look upon the blue view. Mr. Meredith gave a long sigh of happiness.

"That's the fourth time, to my certain knowledge, that that man has preached on, Why hop ye so,

ye high hills? And it's a thing I've really never
seen them do."

Mr. Meredith presented an almost perfect picture
of the God-fearing English gentleman on a holiday.
He was in another grey tail-suit this morning of
a slightly more ample cut; he had on the top of
his clever head a neat Panama hat with a black
ribbon, and over his brown boots — presumably out
of respect for the day — a pair of white spats. He
had taken the bag round in church, too, with an
air of mingled humility and capability, and felt that
he had done his duty adequately and even generously,
till this time next week. . . . He did not very
often go to church at home.

But the Dean's sermon, which certainly had been
rather long for a hot Sunday morning, though as-
tonishingly fluent and verbose, seemed to have
rendered this listener of his a little peevish.

" I always feel like a Layman," he said, " of the
clerical sort, of course, whenever that man ——
Oh! how do you do, Mr. Dean? "

(He turned, all smiles, to greet his pastor, who
had saluted him in a virile voice.)

" I was just speaking of your excellent sermon,"
he continued. " What an eminently suitable text,
if I may say so."

" Oh! yes. You know," said the Dean (who
held evening services for men on Sundays in his

cathedral at home), " I always try to suit my matter to the occasion. . . . And those are your young people? . . . Good morning, Mrs. Meredith."

He patted Val briskly on the shoulder. He was always tactful and manly with males, and deferential to females.

Mr. Meredith explained.

" Ah! yes; just so. Of Medhurst, isn't it? I met your father only two years ago."

Val looked politely sullen, as boys of sixteen do.

" And I suppose you've come out to do great things," pursued the Dean, clapping him again on the shoulder.

Val's hatred rose to an acute point. But he grinned courteously and said nothing.

" Val," said a voice. And there was Tom, with two long-legged young men.

He detached himself courteously from the Dean.

" These are the two Mr. Ratcliffes," explained Tom rapidly and unceremoniously. . . . " Oh! this is Valentine Medd. I say, Val, they want us three for an expedition on Thursday."

Jack Ratcliffe explained.

It seemed that the other two of their party were leaving on Wednesday. There was a comparatively mild expedition that they wished to make; it began with the ascent of the Theodulhorn, continued with the ice *arête* running from that peak to the foot of

the Matterhorn. Then the lower slopes of the
Matterhorn itself were to be crossed, ending up below the Hoinbi. They would call for a meal at the
Schwarz-See hotel, and return to the Riffelalp during the afternoon.

"Look here," said Jack, " I can point it out from
just round the corner. Come this way."

They went round the angle of the hotel, on the
embattled terrace that looks out over the valley, and
Jack pointed it out. It looked a pretty long walk
even from here. It was an immense curved snow
wall, sharp and jagged against the sky.

"We'll have to start not later than four in the
morning. It's a perfectly gorgeous view — seventy
miles one way and a hundred the other. Are you
chaps in training?"

"We will be by Thursday."

"Well, you'll come? We need only take one
guide. I'll be leading guide. That settled?"

(He spoke in rapid, jerky sentences. He was
obviously a capable person.)

"Yes; we'll come. Rather. I've never done it.
You and Austin are game?"

Val nodded.

"Rather. . . . If you think we can do it,"
he added in a burst of modesty.

"Lord, yes! It's a ladies' climb; it's only rather
long."

The three toiled up the Gorner Grat that afternoon, for a "training walk." Civilised life in England permits to gather at certain points of the person deposits of a substance which is almost wholly useless for athletic purposes. It also allows to lapse by desuetude certain muscles, particularly in the thigh, which are essential to very prolonged walking. It was for the removal of the one and the development of the other that these three young men, in flannel trousers, heavy boots, and shirts, and carrying their jackets over their arms as soon as they got out of sight of the hotel, went almost wordlessly, so great was the pace, first up the zigzag ascent to the Riffelberg, then, leaving the vanquished Riffelhorn first on their right, up that enormous flat back which leads unsensationally to the summit of the Gorner.

The view from the top is superb. One is surrounded entirely by giant snow peaks, from Monte Rosa to the Matterhorn in one sweep; from the Matterhorn to the Weisshorn in another; and so round again, by the Dorn, back to Monte Rosa again. There they stand, that eternal ring of giants, one white blaze in the sunlight, backed by a sky darkening in the zenith almost to blackness, so rare is the air and so intense the blue. The vast glacier sleeps below, beneath the slopes of tumbled snow-fields from which the peaks begin — tumbled

as if monstrous children had been at play amongst
them. Yet, so vast are the distances that a large
party crossing the glacier at the nearer end would
look no more than a snippet of black thread against
the white.

"Fifty minutes since the last stop," panted Tom
as he touched the cairn. "We must do better than
that. Now, you chaps, we must do that downhill
in twenty. . . . I'll tell you the peaks in the
hotel this evening."

(III)

The conversation that night was tremendous.

The five sat out together on the terrace, with a
small table in the midst (the parents twenty yards
away talking to the Dean), and discussed climbing from every possible point of view. It is not
proposed to report their conversation. On the
table stood a tray with five glasses, a bottle, and
three siphons, and Jack Ratcliffe grew almost eloquent on the pernicious effects of spirits taken *en
route*, unless in the case of real exhaustion. In
the evening, it seemed, a glass or two would hurt
nobody; and Val, over the first whisky and soda
ever drunk by him, assented, shuddering furtively
meanwhile at the nauseous taste. Austin drank a
plain soda, and regarded his desperate young
brother with a face of discreet severity.

And meanwhile Val's enthusiasm grew higher every minute.

He relapsed into an intense silence at last, listening to the talk, watching Jack's face glow and darken again luridly as he drew on his cigarette, and meantime constructing and constructing day-dream after day-dream of Gertie and the mountains and the mountains and Gertie. He was in a pleasant glow after food and wine, a glow warmed up again by that exceedingly disagreeable drink he had had just now. His muscles were relaxed after the tense exercise of yesterday and to-day; and he was looking forward, with a zeal untouched now by even the faintest apprehensiveness, to the expedition up the Gorner glacier to-morrow.

("You chaps must have a bit of real ice-work before Thursday," Tom had panted parenthetically on the way down from the Gorner Grat this afternoon.)

Then, finally, as the terrace began to empty and Val to be aware of drowsiness, the subject was introduced which had been on his mind ever since yesterday morning, yet which he had not dared to mention again.

They had sat silent for a minute. Jim Ratcliffe, a stoutish young man of twenty-five, yet a " devil to go," as Tom had said this afternoon, had beaten out his pipe and stood up. The great silence of nightfall had descended; the murmur of streams released by the sun all day to pour in ten thousand channels down to the Zermatt valley, now lying in the darkness below, were chained up again by frost up there, four and five thousand feet above this hotel. To sight too the world had faded; or, rather, had closed in under cover of the night, so that the mountains far off across the valley now stood, it seemed, in shadowy lines scarcely a hundred yards away. Only there still stood out, dominant and tremendous, glimmering in starlight, itself blotting out the stars, as august and unattainable as ever, the huge wedge called the Matterhorn.

Then Tom spoke; and sentences followed with impressive and business-like rapidity.

" I say, Jack, these chaps want to do the Matterhorn before they go."

" Well, why shouldn't they? "

" Think it's all right? It's their first time, you know."

" Good Lord, that doesn't matter. They can do it all right. Who'll you get? "

" I thought of Ulrich Edersheim, if he isn't engaged; and Heinrich Almer."

" You'll be lucky if you get them."

" Think I could engage them now? "

" Armstrong's been climbing with Ulrich lately.

I'd speak to him if I were you; I rather think he's got first claim on him for the season."

" If you think there's any risk ——" began Austin's deliberate voice out of the darkness.

Val snorted uncontrollably. Sometimes he did it on purpose; but this time it was perfectly spontaneous.

" My dear chap," said Tom. " We've simply got to settle at once, if we're to get those guides. We've only a fortnight, you see."

" And do you think we're capable of doing it? " pursued Austin, with severe conscientiousness.

There was just the faintest pause of hesitation before the answer came. But when it came its heartiness made up for all.

" I'm perfectly certain you can — both of you. You climbed first-rate yesterday. Well, in the Matterhorn you've only got to go on doing it for eight hours, instead of half an hour."

"Of course we can do it, Austin," put in Val in a tone of indignant and contemptuous protest. " At least if we can't it'll be our own fault. We've plenty of time to learn the tricks."

" Exactly," said Tom briefly. " But you must work hard, you know. You must have a good go on ice."

" What's the matter with to-morrow? " said Jack,

who had spent the previous week in the company of Americans.

"That'll do very well," observed Tom. "We'll just have a good steady day on the Gorner. Start at ten."

"And we'll try to get Armstrong again."

(IV)

The parents Meredith stood at precisely the opposite standpoint, with regard to Switzerland, to that occupied by their young men. And, indeed, there is a great deal to be said for it.

For, to them, Switzerland was primarily a place of superb rest — of superb views, air, climate, and idleness. The hotel in which they stayed must be, as the advertisements here stated, replete with every modern convenience. It must be large, expensive, well served, provided with a lift; it must be surrounded by flat walks; it must contain a French chef; it must be filled with the right kind of people and not too many of the wrong; it must have bath-rooms, and, for Mrs. Meredith's sake at least, an English chapel and a chaplain, if possible, of a decent eminence in his own country.

All those things were, under the presidence of Herr Seiler, exactly suitable. One breakfasted, leisurely, about nine; one read the papers, smoked

a cigar or so, and looked at the view till lunch.
One slept gently for an hour or so; then, sometimes
with a tea-basket and sometimes without, walked
quite slowly a couple of miles through exquisite
pine forests, observed views once more, breathed
some quite first-rate air, and then strolled back
again in time to dress comfortably for dinner.
Food followed, and then an evening of gentle,
shrewd talk, some whisky and soda, three nice
cigars, and bed — altogether a blameless and re-
creating existence, almost perfectly calculated to
restore an extremely prosperous Counsel who
worked at a pressure and for periods that would
dismay those democratic philanthropists who were
beginning already to preach the gospel of Not Too
Much Work. And Mrs. Meredith supplied precisely
the right kind of temperament in which to lead such
a life.

There are few persons so delightful as first-rate
barristers on a holiday, and Mr. Meredith was a
first-rate specimen. He was emphatically a gentleman; he was shrewd, tolerant, humorous with a
touch of cynicism; scrupulously conventional in
manner and unconventional in mind. He looked
his part, too, to perfection; his face was keen and
kindly and clean shaven; he had an air of suppressed

and beneficent power. His old friends found him always the same, and new acquaintances rapidly considered themselves his friends. He was always in the most intelligent circle in the smoking-room and the verandahs; he told new stories exceedingly well; and he had the art of appearing subtly interested in anyone who spoke to him. Even the prize bore of the hotel thought him sympathetic.

He was gently but sincerely interested in the ardour of climbers; and he was discussing it over tea on this very Monday afternoon with a judge and the eloquent Dean. (Mrs. Meredith was sitting with the matrons in the drawing-room.)

"I am no climber," he was saying, "but I think I catch glimpses now and again of the divine secret of it. There's my boy Tom, for instance. I must confess I envy him sometimes."

The Judge nodded.

"I know what you mean," he said. "By the way, your boy Tom has promised to bring me a stone from the top of the Matterhorn."

"It's very good of you to ——"

"Not at all. I am perfectly genuine. I shall label it and put it in a cabinet with the date and circumstances."

"Well, that's almost an illustration of what I mean. Any stone would do, objectively, just as

well. And yet there's a subtle something . . .
By the way, a friend of mine promised to bring an
ivy-leaf from Wagner's grave, for an enthusiast in
England. He quite forgot it until he was half-
way back from Bayreuth, so he picked one in a
station in Germany instead."

"No doubt it did just as well," said the Dean,
smiling.

"You think so?" said the Judge, cocking an eye
at the ecclesiastic. "Well, to me that seems simply
an outrage. It makes no kind of difference that the
female enthusiast — (I take it that she was female?
. . . Just so . . .) — that the enthusiast
never knew. It was a grave moral crime in itself."

"Well," went on the lawyer, "climbing seems to
me an almost infinitely subtle thing. All sport is
subtle, of course. It is one of the innumerable
proofs that two and two make five quite as often as
they make four. Take shooting. Analyse it. It
consists of two elements and really no more — skill
and death-dealing. Now neither of these is sufficient in itself. No man in his senses would enjoy a
season in which he merely shot at elaborately concealed clay pigeons; and no man would enjoy killing pigs. Yet when you unite the two elements
you get sport."

"'Not a fourth ——, but a star,'" quoted

the Dean, who loved to think he could join in a lay conversation with intelligence.

" Exactly. Well, climbing ——"

" Yes," said the Judge, carefully brushing off the ash of his cigar on to the little stone wall beside him. (They were having tea on the terrace.) " Analyse climbing. I don't think I understand it."

" Well, first there's the skill. Call it gymnastics — elaborate and unexpected gymnastics. And then there's the danger."

" Do you think danger "——

" Certainly. No one would climb if there were nets everywhere. But combine skill and danger and you have the real thing — the sport. . . . Oh! I forgot the endurance. That certainly enters in. No one could be really keen on climbing rocks. It must be a sufficiently exhausting feat to expose the roots of the character, so to speak."

" You have left out the wonderful views that are surely a part of ——" began the Dean.

" Excuse me. I am quite confident that views do not enter in at all. I questioned my boy very carefully about that. He pretends that they do, of course; but it's obvious they don't. Why, only yesterday the three of them ran straight up to the top of the Gorner Grat and back again. They identified the names of the peaks that they ought to have seen, in a panoramic map, after dinner; but they didn't look at them at all."

"You think that climbing is a test of character then," asked the Judge.

"I think it one of the best I know; and it's an admirable trainer of character too. The fatigue of it soon rubs off all the merely showy qualities and leaves the real traits naked. And then the danger, which is there, more or less, the whole time, tests a man's fidelity to his ideals. A coward either funks at a critical moment, or he's foolhardy. And all the real climbers detest both equally. To hear Armstrong talk, you'd think that a man who refuses to wear a rope in bad places is as much of a poltroon as a man who refuses to follow the guide."

"By the way," put in the Judge, "are those two Medd boys you have with you the Medds of Medhurst?" Mr. Meredith nodded.

"A very finely bred family," he said. "They've avoided too much intermarrying too. It's extraordinary to me how anyone can deny heredity. And with regard to such qualities as pluck and honour, I'd trust either of those two boys absolutely — I don't say wisdom, or judgment; those come largely from experience; but for the real old chivalric virtues you simply cannot beat these old families. I'm a full-blooded plebeian myself; but I recognise descent when I see it."

"What about the chorus-girls, though, that most of them marry nowadays?"

"Well, I think a little of that blood doesn't do any harm. There's pluck there, you know, too. For sheer moral courage I think the courage of a chorus-girl, who dances on a lighted stage in an insufficient costume, before strangers on whose approval her whole future depends — well, it's hard to beat. But those Medds have done nothing of that sort. They and a few others like them are really the pride of our people. I wouldn't exchange them for ten thousand democracies."

"I think this is your party coming back, Mr. Meredith," observed the Dean, upon whose face a faintly grieved disapprobation was beginning to show itself. (He thought the subject of chorus-girls not wholly suitable to his friends' company.)

The lawyer lifted a slow eye over the terrace wall.

"Yes, there they are," he said. "Now look at that delightful roll they've all got, coming uphill. My boy explained it to me once. You must swing your feet round, not lift them. All the guides do it; it saves you enormous exertion in a long day. And what prudence! . . . And what perseverance to keep it up."

"Ah! they're in sight of the hotel now," observed the Judge cynically.

They looked strangely unsociable as they advanced, but exceedingly capable and business-like — muscular, spare figures in what is, after the days of ancient Greeks, perhaps the most picturesque costume known to the human race — well-made knickerbockers and jackets, caps, low gaiters, and great sensible boots moulded wonderfully to the foot. Each carried an axe whose head shone like silver in the low, level sunlight, and Tom, who led, carried a rope coiled over one shoulder and under the other arm; each was burnt by the glare of the sun on the ice all day to a fine manly bronze. And they came up, as the observer had pointed out, with that steady, strong swing that every climber who wishes to endure must set himself to acquire. Tom was leading, Austin followed, then after a space, walking by the side of the path, came Val, while the middle-aged man came last.

" Had a good day? " came a voice over the parapet as the party came beneath.

" Oh! it was all right," said Tom.

Mr. Meredith leant back again.

" Now what's up, I wonder," he said; " the boys have had a row. I know Tom's manner. I must examine Armstrong."

(v)

"I assure you it was nothing but inexperience," said the Secretary, as the two sat together in the gloom at the end of the long glass verandah, whither the lawyer had inveigled him after dinner. "Nothing but inexperience. He simply didn't know the danger."

The lawyer carefully squirted some soda-water into his long glass.

"The essence of the crime was insubordination, I gather? The recklessness was secondary?"

"I suppose you might say so. We had got to the foot of the *séracs* ——"

"Interpret, please."

"The *séracs* are the tumbled and broken part of the glacier — the actual fall of the river, so to speak. Well, I wouldn't dream of doing those *séracs* unroped, however experienced the climbers may be. To slip badly means death in nine cases out of ten. Of course you can't generally see the death; there's no great drop below you at any point down to the mean level. But there are first, the crevasses — some of which go down to the bed of the glacier — say eight hundred feet, and then there's the danger of an ice pinnacle falling."

"I see."

"Well, Master Val refused to put on the rope.

While I was getting the rope ready he went on, which he had no business to do, and got on the top of a ridge. I told him to come back, but he said he was all right, and he argued a bit while I was wrestling with a knot and talking in between. Then he went on again, and laughed out loud, and pretended it was a joke."

"You mean he flatly disobeyed."

"No, not flatly. Indirectly. I hardly liked to call him back outright. He was in quite a bad place, though it didn't look very bad. And I must say he climbed well. But you know that sort of thing really mustn't happen. I told him so plainly, and he did me the honour to sulk."

Mr. Meredith drank off the contents of his glass.

"Well, what am I to say to him? Shall I forbid him to climb again?"

"Good gad, no! It was simply ignorance of what he was doing. And he knows now. The elder boy gave him what for. You can always trust a brother to be brutal."

"And Tom?"

"Tom looked like Rhadamanthus. I don't think Master Val liked that. . . . No, just tell him quite gently and lightly (you know how) that no decent climber ever dreams of disobeying the leader of the party, and that you're perfectly certain he won't do it again.'

"He's got plenty of pluck, I suppose?"

"Oh, Lord! yes."

"Right. Well, I'll catch him before he goes to bed."

"Shall I send him to you? I saw him in the smoking-room just now."

"Do. Thanks very much. And you'll tell me if he ever behaves badly again. You're going with them on Monday, aren't you?"

"I think so. Oh! I'll tell you all right. But I don't think there'll be any need."

Val had a sprightly and genial air as presently he came along the corridor to where the lawyer waited for him. He made a handsome, smart figure with his white shirt-front and his browned, bright-eyed face, and he carried himself with a distinctly exaggerated ease.

"Want to see me, sir?"

"Yes, my boy. Sit down a minute. . . . It was about the expedition of this afternoon. . You know I'm bound to look after you a bit, aren't I?"

He glanced up with shrewd, kind eyes (Val was sitting absolutely motionless in an attitude of detached and frozen dignity). He didn't like doing it at all, but he did not propose to flinch.

"Well, I thought I'd better explain what perhaps

you didn't know: that on those climbing expeditions
one man must always take charge and be responsible.
I've been talking to Mr. Armstrong; he's a magnificent climber, you know, and by no means timid.
Well, he tells me you didn't seem to understand
about the rope, and thought you were safe without
it. I dare say you were — as certainly the event
proved — but for all that, the rest of the climbers
must always be very particular to observe dis-
cipline. . . ."

He paused, hoping to be reassured that the boy
was not still sulking. Val remained motionless and
silent.

"Well," said the older man a trifle more coldly,
"you must please to understand that what happened
this afternoon mustn't occur again. I don't ask you
to give me your word, because I'm certain that's
unnecessary. But it must not happen again. I am
responsible for you as long as you are with me; and
on climbing expeditions, when I'm not there, you
must please to regard the leader of the expedition,
whoever he may be, as your superior officer. When
you are head of any expedition yourself you will
have to demand the same thing from the rest."

Again there was a pause. It was obvious that
the boy was sulking badly. He remained perfectly
motionless, his eyelids slightly lowered in such a
way as to give him an air of extraordinary insolence.

A pang of real pity mingled with impatience touched the heart of the other. He knew exactly how the other felt — humiliated and enraged; and yet that his breeding forbade him to utter either emotion.

"Look here, my boy; I know it's disagreeable to be found fault with. But I should like to tell you, on the other side, that Mr. Armstrong said you climbed with real courage and skill. He particularly ——"

He stopped, astonished at the deep flush of pleasure in the boy's face. Val turned to him, his eyes swimming and his whole face a-smile.

"Thank you, sir. . . . And I beg your pardon. I have been behaving like a boor."

The elder man put out his hand, really touched by this self-humiliation and apology. Val took it.

"That's all right, old chap. That's all right."

He still sat on a minute or two after Val had left him for bed. (The boy said that the glare of the sunlit ice had made him by now almost blind with sleep.)

"Queer chap," he said to himself. "Bundle of nerves, I should say."

CHAPTER VI

(1)

"I DON'T see that it's anything to do with you," said Val coolly. "As a matter of fact——" He stopped abruptly as a waiter came, cleared away a little tray of glasses, and vanished once more.

The two brothers were talking to one another in the empty smoking-room, with that extraordinary frankness on which mere friends dare not venture lest the last ties of unity should be dissolved.

Austin had begun it, of course, by such a studiously tactful sentence that irritation on Val's part followed inevitably — a sentence accompanied by a careful adjustment of a little protruding tobacco at the end of his cigarette. And Austin had been provoked to it, he would have said, by Val's nonchalant air as he swaggered in. It was simply impossible for the elder brother to refrain from such criticisms sometimes, though he ought to have learned their futility long ago; for he was of those persons who are practically always in the right and have an amazing power of discerning when others are in the

106

wrong. If they themselves were wrong sometimes it would not matter nearly so much.

He had just observed for the second time that it was all very well talking, but the fact remained that Val had not observed the etiquette this afternoon. And he had added with a maddening humility:

" I've got to learn just as much as you have, my dear chap. I've got to do exactly what I'm told too."

When the waiter had gone again, yawning a little ostentatiously, for it was getting on for midnight, and he would have to be up and dressed by six, Val finished his sentence.

" As a matter of fact, I've talked it all out with old Meredith. I don't see there's any necessity for going into it again, particularly with you."

Austin half closed his eyes as if in resignation.

" And why not with me? "

" Because, as you've just said, you don't know anything about it."

This was precisely true. Austin had an impulse to say no more. But Val was sitting on the edge of a table and swinging his leg with such an air that it was impossible to be silent.

" I know enough about it to . . . to behave decently on the ice with a man like Armstrong. I was simply ashamed of you."

Val turned an insolent face on him.

"Awful good of you, old man. Hadn't you better keep your shame for the next time you want it yourself?"

Austin rose with dignity.

"I've no more to say after that," he said. "But you'll kindly remember that I am responsible for you to some extent at any rate; and I don't want to have to write home and say ——"

"Are you?" asked Val, with an air of bewildered innocence. "I thought Meredith was."

Austin went to the door. When he reached it he turned.

"Perhaps you aren't aware that you're keeping the whole hotel up? Everyone else has gone to bed."

"Well, you'd better look sharp, then," said Val, without turning round. "You mustn't lose your beauty sleep."

(II)

Five minutes later Val too walked along the corridors on his way to bed.

He had scored distinctly just now, in the little engagement. Usually it was he who lost his temper first and left the room. But in this instance, still vibrating from his encounter with "old Meredith," he had struck more sharply and shrewdly than usual, preserving his balance meanwhile.

Yet, by the time he had reached the room that the two brothers shared, his exultation was gone; and a rather hollow and sick feeling was beginning to reassert itself — the tide whose first bitter waves had broken on his conscience even while still on the glacier, so soon as he had recognised that recklessness was not thought admirable. It had seemed to him so fine at the time. . . . A spasm had seized him, and he had pushed on, knowing perfectly well that he ought not to have done so, yet impelled by a vague desire to prove himself as courageous as he had wished to be; he had gone up the edge of the *sérac* swiftly and cleverly, and had balanced himself on the top with a sense of triumph. And then, little by little, he had begun to realise he had behaved badly.

Austin was reading resolutely in bed, as the other came in. A dark head, a humped shoulder, and the pages of a Tauchnitz volume revealed him to be there and awake. Val began to whistle gently. The head moved irritably on the pillow. Val smiled deliberately to himself and stopped whistling.

" I beg your pardon," he said elaborately.

There was no answer.

By the time he was in bed a more generous mood was on him. He snuggled down into the sheets.

"I say, old man, will you put out the lights when you've done. I'm going to sleep."

"You can put them out now," said a cold voice. "I was only waiting for you."

"Sure? I can wait a few minutes if you want."

"No; it's all right."

Val sprang up in bed, switched off the lights, and sank down again.

"I say, Austin."

"Well?"

"I'm sorry I spoke like that just now," said Val, with an effort. "I was beastly; I'm sorry."

"That's all right," said the cold voice.

(It was one of the most emphatic rules of the brotherly warfare that an apology must be instantly accepted, and no further reference made to the crime by the injured party.)

But Val felt very generous just now.

"Yes, I really am," he said. "And I was entirely in the wrong this afternoon too."

Austin was still a little sore, and could not resist preaching.

"I'm glad you see that," came his voice from the darkness. "It's very important, you know, not to ——"

"I've said I'm sorry, haven't I? Do you want me to say it again?"

There was silence.

"I really thought it wasn't a bad place, you know," pursued Val. "But I quite see now that that makes no difference. Old Meredith gave me what for, all right. . . . I say, do you think Tom was sick?"

"Do you wish me to say? You found fault with me just now for saying anything after you'd said——"

"Good Lord!" snapped Val, breaking off this rather intricate sentence. "I asked you a question."

Austin sniffed. The sound was very distinct in the silent shadows.

"Well — yes, he was, if you want to know. He said——"

Austin broke off. He was simply an adept at provocative *aposiopeses;* and I am afraid they were frequently deliberate.

"What did he say?" asked Val all in one breath.

"He said it really wasn't safe to climb with people who wouldn't do what they were told."

"Did he?"

"I am saying that he did."

There followed a silence.

"Austin."

"Well?"

"I'd better apologise to him too, hadn't I?"

"I shouldn't think it would make much difference, your apologising. The thing to do is not to do it again."

There was an indignant rustle in the darkness.

"Good Lord, Austin. Can't you open your mouth without preaching? Haven't I said ——"

Then a solemn and judicial voice silenced him.

"I think you'd better go to sleep. You aren't in a frame of mind to talk about it to-night. Good night, Val."

An insolent snore answered him.

(III)

Tom Meredith came down to breakfast rather late next morning; and, as he passed through on to the verandah, whither he had bidden a passing waiter to bring his coffee and rolls, a knickerbockered figure in a white hat, sitting in the sun, rose and greeted him.

"Morning, Tom. Going to breakfast?"

Tom nodded.

"May I come and sit with you! I want to talk. Don't mind a cigarette, do you?"

When the waiter had gone again, Val began.

"I say, Tom; I wanted to say I was beastly sorry

about yesterday — about my not obeying, you know. Really I didn't know how important it was."

" That's all right, old chap," said Tom uncomfortably. (He privately wished people wouldn't talk like this.)

" No, really I didn't. I thought it wasn't a bad enough place," pursued Val eagerly. . . . " Yes, I know what you were going to say — that that doesn't make any difference. I know that too, now."

Tom miserably began to butter his roll. He couldn't conceive what all the fuss was about. Certainly Val had done what he shouldn't; but he had been told that, and naturally he wouldn't do it again.

Val drew three rapid breaths of cigarette-smoke.

" You won't mind my climbing with you again, will you? "

" Of course not, my good chap! What made you think ——"

" Didn't you say to Austin it wasn't safe to climb with people who didn't do what they were told? "

Poor Tom racked his memory. (Really this admiring youth was becoming something of a bore.)

" Er — I don't remember that I did."

" You didn't say it? "

" I don't think so."

Val rose impressively.

"Well, all that I can say is ——" he broke off.
"Well, I'm sorry, anyhow. And I thought I'd
better say so. And I promise not to do it again."

"That's all right," murmured Tom.

"See you later," said Val, vanishing.

"Austin," came a solemn voice five minutes afterwards in the smoking-room, "I want to speak to
you a moment. Do you mind coming out?"

Austin sighed elaborately, and followed him.

Val went, as one leading a criminal to execution,
out through the door, down the steps, and on to a
deserted corner of the sunlit terrace. And there he
turned.

"Didn't you tell me last night that Tom had said
he wouldn't climb again with anyone who disobeyed
during an expedition? Did you, or did you not?"

Austin sighed and sat down on the balustrade.

"I did not."

"You did!"

"I said that Tom said "— he clasped his head in
his hands in a gesture of resigned bewilderment —
"I said that Tom said that it wasn't safe to climb
with people who wouldn't do what they were told."

"It's exactly the same thing."

"There seems to me a difference," observed the
other wearily.

"Well, he didn't say it anyhow — or anything like it. I've just asked him."

"Then he's simply forgotten. I tell you he did say it to me — in the smoking-room directly after dinner."

"Was anyone else with you?"

"I think not at that moment."

Val sneered.

"Very convenient," he said. "Well, anyhow, Tom says he didn't. And he says he's simply delighted to go on climbing with me, just as before; and absolutely everything you said about him last night is rot. . . . I mean," explained Val, with offensive courtesy, "that you must have misunderstood him. . . . So there," he ended feebly.

"Is that what you brought me out here to tell me?"

"And enough too, I should think!"

"It seems to me singularly unimportant," remarked Austin, getting up again. "I told you exactly what Tom said to me — no more and no less. And you drag me out here and explain like . . . like a woman. . . . If you've quite done, I think I'll go indoors again."

And he moved back with a stately sauntering gait.

Now all this kind of thing was the worst of Val; for it was really characteristic of him. He had a nervous system strung on wires; a touch set all jangling. And then he would vibrate, and go on vibrating; and he would dive into his own being, and into little sentences that meant nothing, and torture himself and everyone else; and flick out particles of dust and disturb himself afresh. And then all would die into silence once more; and that same nervous system would inspire him to dreams and visions and dramatic situations and acute emotions that were never justified by the event.

And so, a couple of hours later, as the three boys set out for the Findelen glacier, ropes a-swing and axe heads marching in time, peace was returned to Val's soul, and Austin was beginning to recover his balance, and Tom was thinking that one really could have enough of a good thing — even of admiration for the Alps and for Alpine prowess.

CHAPTER VII

(1)

"NOW," said Armstrong, from the hind end of the party, "no talking until we're across. This is the one risky place, and talking might bring some ice down."

The expedition had gone excellently so far. They had started later than had been intended, and had been going now for some eight hours.

They had left the Riffel an hour or two before sunrise, led by the great Ulrich himself, a small-built man, so thin as to resemble a badly made dummy in loosely fitting clothes, wiry-bearded, burned to the colour of old oak, with narrow brighter slits for eyes, a snub nose, and a smiling mouth. He was in trousers, tied below the knee with string, and an ancient coat that had ascended every peak which its owner had climbed for the last five years. The first part of the walk, in the dark, had taken them across the lower slopes of the Gorner Grat and down on to the glacier — all simple and easy going — the rope was not even suggested. There they

had seen the sky grow from indigo to translucent
sapphire and the stars go out; the marvellous flush
of rose and gold crept down the peaks to meet them;
and by the time that they were on the summit of
the Theodulhorn — the outstanding tower, so to
speak, of the long ice-wall that ended far away on
the right in the Matterhorn itself — broad day was
come; and ten thousand water-tongues, loosened
by their lord the Sun, had swelled into that deep,
murmurous chorus that sings all day from fields of
ice and light.

From the Theodulhorn they had surveyed first
the great peaks about them — the Breithorn, the
twins beyond, and the enormous masses of Monte
Rosa herself on the one side, and the Matterhorn,
the Gabelhorn, the Weisshorn on the other. The
Riffelhorn looked like a little ruined house across
the glacier. Then they had examined their route.

This was the long *arête* leading from where they
stood up to the base of the Giant — a knife-edge,
serrated and jagged, it seemed, from where they
were, yet, as they presently found, easy going
enough if you omit the element of fatigue. For
the sun beat on them as from the open door of a
furnace; the ice was largely snow, into which now
and then an unwary traveller plunged to the knee;
there was a brisk wind blowing in their faces, cool-
ing indeed, but indescribably wearying from the

efforts they had to make against it. Twice they had stopped for food, and twice, therefore, Val for one had thought he would sooner die than go on again; and yet twice also he had not said an unnecessary word, but had set his face like a flint and plunged obediently forward in the steps of Ulrich, who led. A kind of fury, born of fatigue and monotony, seized him sometimes as he watched the unwearying legs move before him, each, it seemed, with incredible deliberation, yet somehow with a composite speed that almost broke the watcher's heart. It appeared to him as if the little trousered figure in front were lifted by the scruff of the neck, the legs would still move in the air like scissors driven by slow clockwork. . . . Behind Val came Tom Meredith, then the two Ratcliffes, then Austin, and last Armstrong. It was too big a party really for one rope, but the absence of all real danger excused the fact that they used no more.

It is exceedingly difficult to diagnose accurately the psychological effect of a very long expedition, the greater part of which takes place on the edge of gigantic slopes and precipices, even though on a perfectly safe path, with death, that is to say, regarding the traveller steadily and continuously, although from a decent and respectful distance, for about four hours. It is foolish to say that only three yards

separated these climbers from death, for a great
many other things separated them as well — the
rope for one thing, common prudence for another,
the experienced vigilance of a man at either end
of the rope for a third.   Yet to an imaginative mind
these things do not carry their proper weight, especially if that mind is possessed by an exceedingly
wearied boy of sixteen.   .   .   .

It would be quite untrue to say that Val had either
shown or even felt the slightest lack of nerve.   He
had not.   His first moment of tension had come at
the crossing of the *Bergschrund* in the ascent of the
Theodulhorn.   He had held his breath, as if for
buoyancy, and clenched his teeth on his lower lip,
as, staring in front yet perceiving the blue depths
beneath him on either side, he had stepped swiftly
over the irregular snow bridge that led across the
chasm.   But he had said not a word.   But now he
had looked down these even more terrifying gulfs
for over four hours; he had listened at the halting-
places to a dry description — all the more effective
because of its dryness — of the famous tragedy of
the Matterhorn in which four out of its seven first
conquerors had been killed on the way down, uttered
by Mr. Armstrong in response to urgent requests
from Austin and Val himself (the victims had " slid
on their backs," it seemed, " with outstretched
hands," and one by one had dropped over the in-

calculable edge like pebbles) ; and he had naturally rehearsed to himself not less than five or six times the probable details of a fall, should he slip out of the rope or should the rope break on either side of him. In most places he would first roll about three yards, then he would drop to an unknown depth, bounce once or twice, and finally disappear into another gulf of which the bottom was the Gorner glacier, now so far below them as to render a party walking upon it practically invisible, even against the white glare, or perhaps he would " slide with outstretched hands." . . .

He was appallingly tired too, as was but natural. That is to say (as the Judge had hinted on Monday night), all those external conventions and ideals which have not yet consolidated into character, were peeled off him, and there remained to carry him through just that bare naked self with which he had been born, hardly modified at all by his sixteen years of youth. . . .

And now they faced the Matterhorn, or rather they stood beneath it, tiny negligible specks of life in the midst of a white and glaring death. Above them, up to the zenith it seemed, towered this monster, inconceivably huge and grim, cutting off half the visible universe — gigantic slopes of rock, ribbed with snow where snow could lie; vast hollows, half a mile across; cruel and overshelving spikes; and there, beneath them, was the great cup-like slope down which they must go, curving across it up on to the rocks again above the Hornli, which, like a watch-dog with his back turned to them, gazed out over the blue valley, leagues away, where out of sight beneath bastions and forests, lay toy-like Zermatt, safe and secure and flat. More than once, as the boy had considered this, a passionate spasm of envy of the more prudent travellers had shaken him.

It was at the cup-like hollow immediately beneath that the boy now stared, suddenly conscious that this was going to be altogether different.

It is hard to say why it affected him so pro-foundly; possibly it was because there was no obvious path to follow, such as was suggested by the *arête* they had just traversed, possibly because Matterhorn towered so horribly over it — indeed it was the base of the Matterhorn itself that they were to cross. The dangers too were visible here. On the *arête* there was, at least, nothing threatening from above; here there were incalculable slopes and rocks and ice-fields rising far up into the sky, form-ing the ice-wall that was to be traversed. The end of any who fell was here full in view, unhidden by a merciful edge; for, beneath this tilted saucer across which they must go, tumbled masses of ice, pro-

truded, cracked and lined with streaks of blue that
marked vast openings into the bowels of the earth.
It was exceedingly easy to reconstruct here imaginatively the story of the tragedy. Should the whole
party fall, or should a single member become detached, the precise details would probably be re-
enacted; they would " slide with outstretched
hands," not fast at first, but quite irresistibly, increasing their pace, till . . .

It was at this moment that Armstrong observed
that there must be no talking, as the vibration might
loosen ice above them.

" And remember," said Tom dispassionately, " to
keep axes above, not below; and don't lean too hard
on them."

" Wait a minute," said Val. " What am I to do
if I slip? "

" You mustn't slip."

" But . . . but if I do? "

" You mustn't."

Val set his teeth in a kind of despair.

Ulrich turned round, smiling and nodding. He
wore heavy black glasses that gave him a grim, un-
winking, and enigmatical appearance. He seemed
to smile with his lips only. Then he lifted his axe,
and cut a single step beneath him.

" *Vorwarts!* " he exclaimed, and stepped over the
low edge.

(II)

It seemed to Austin, following patiently behind Jack Ratcliffe, that ice was not as difficult as he had been led to believe. . . .

Imagine, again, a saucer steeply tilted, with its lower edge set on the top of a heap of ice and pebbles, ten times the height of the saucer. On the top of the saucer imagine a conical, irregular hillock, perhaps three yards high, with snow and pebbles lying on its sides. Now make the saucer about three-quarters of a mile across, with the rest of the setting magnified to scale, and compose it of solid ice, with drifted snow lying here and there; set a party crossing it from the high left to the low right, and you have a tolerable picture of our friends' circumstances. Further, one has to remember that the saucer is extremely irregular, that rocks jut out in a few places, and that the ice itself protrudes here and there in small cliffs and angles.

It seemed to Austin, then, that the descent was not very difficult. It consisted, for him, in placing his feet carefully, one by one, in steps cut out by Ulrich in front. Each foot had to be set in the step very deliberately, since a bad slip would endanger the whole party; but there was plenty of time for this, as no one could move faster than Ulrich, who had to do the cutting. Austin, watching Jack in front, imitated him scrupulously in the holding of his axe; he grasped it very tightly with both hands, its head uppermost and on the left; he drove this in slightly, in advance of himself, before making a stride, and preserved his balance by leaning on it during the actual movement.

It seemed to him not difficult, compared, let us say, with gymnastics. Yet, for all that, he was conscious of a certain strain as the minutes went by. The taking of each step was, in itself, quite a simple matter, like catching a ball; but the catching of a ball five hundred times is considerably more than the mere total of five hundred risks taken separately. (As the lawyer had remarked three days before, two and two by no means always make four.) There was this, then, first: the consciousness that he must make no mistake in a simple operation repeated five hundred times.

And there were other considerations as well. First, no two steps were exactly the same; and the stride between each was about two inches longer than he liked. They had been rather late in starting for their expedition, the sun had been a long while now upon this cradle of avalanches and Ulrich obviously thought it prudent not to take longer over step-cutting than was really necessary. In a few places where the snow was deep he cut no steps at all. Next, the contemplation of the steps above and below undoubtedly had a certain psychological effect. They looked so extremely steep, the distances were so enormous, and the catastrophe of a fall so very obvious. It was like being constantly threatened by a blow which never fell. . . . And then the intellect chimed in and remarked insistently: " Kindly remember that all this while you are on ice — *ice*. And ice is notoriously slippery. . . ." When all these considerations surged up in line to take the nerves by storm, and all in the dead silence that had been commanded, Austin thought it prudent to think about other things.

Certainly there were many things to think about.

He forced himself to notice the effect of sun on chipped ice — the indescribably luscious appearance of the crumbled diamonds, and he thought of long drinks in tall, clinking tumblers. He would have given five pounds for one. He had melted some snow into brandy and water at their last halt; but it had burned his palate more than it had refreshed it. An extremely vivid image of the smoking-room at Medhurst, of the tray of syphons and ice and lemonade, floated before him. . . .

He noticed the texture of Jack Ratcliffe's stocking. It emerged, curved over a massive muscle, between a slightly crumpled yellow gaiter and the wet folds of a homespun knickerbocker. He thought, somehow, that that kind of stocking came from Scotland; or was it Paisley? No, shawls came from Paisley.

Then once or twice he considered Val, and wondered how he was getting on, there in front. He caught a glimpse of his cap now and then, with a salmon-fly sticking up at the top. (He had mocked at the wearing of a salmon-fly in Switzerland.) Val seemed to be getting on all right. . . . He had certainly been subdued by the row on Monday. He had talked very little to-day, and had been scrupulously obedient. . . .

Then he had to take a longer step than usual. He hesitated a moment, then he drove his axe in with all his force, and jumped. (There was, at any rate, one perceptible instant in which neither foot rested on the ice.) He landed safely, and stood poised, conscious of a faint prickling on his upper lip and forehead. He found himself wondering how Val had done it. He also discovered in himself an extraordinary desire to be on the rocks again, over there, half a mile across and down.

They were now about a third of the way across the slope, and the tilt was more marked as well as the surface more broken. They had altered their course a little and were going more directly downwards. At first he did not see why; but in the pauses, while the others moved and he stood still, anchored by his axe, he presently noticed that the line was steering so as to pass beneath a mass of ice clustered about a rock that jutted out some way ahead.

Then, as they drew nearer, step by step, he saw and understood.

Right in the middle of their old course this mass of stuff projected, resembling a broken cliff some fifteen or twenty feet high, as if suddenly arrested in a downward movement. Above it lay piled snow and stones so high as to blot out, to the eyes of those who stood beneath it, all but the very topmost peak of the Matterhorn itself. It looked, to unskilled eyes, as if it were the crest of an avalanche suddenly pulled up sharp in full career. Beneath it, in a long precipitous curve, lay a deep channel of ice, smooth as glass, sloping down at a far more acute angle than that which they were traversing, losing itself perhaps three hundred feet below in the general slopes of the ice-wall.

Austin had a minute or two to regard all this closely and carefully, as the procession in front had halted; and even he, little as he knew, understood that this was by far the most difficult passage that he had yet encountered; and, not only the most difficult, but the most dangerous; and not only the most dangerous, but the most terrifying.

Let me explain again exactly why.

Beneath the avalanche head (if it may be called so) there was a deep channel, like a gutter-pipe, at least fifteen feet deep and a good twenty yards across, and the whole of this, with the exception of the edges, was smooth and glassy ice. There were two possible ways to get across it. Either the channel itself must be negotiated, down across and up again, or the jutting cliff must be traversed. In the one case an ice-wall of extreme abruptness must be crossed; in the other, that same ice-wall, or rather channel, would be immediately beneath. And in both, a fall would be as serious as possible. . . .

He wondered why they were waiting. Jack Ratcliffe in front stood like a pillar, both feet in the step, anchored to the slope above him by his axe; beyond him Jim, also motionless. Beyond he could make out Tom Meredith's head and left shoulder. All were motionless. He could hear Armstrong whispering to himself and fidgeting behind. Obviously Ulrich was reconnoitring as to which of the two courses were the safer. Austin could hear the chipping of an axe in front.

Then a decision was apparently arrived at, and Austin drew a breath of relief. (Anything was better than this waiting.) For he suddenly saw the bearded face of the guide in profile turn to the left and his broad shoulders follow it. They were going to cross the cliff.

The slope was so acute that he could see no more of Ulrich than down to the knees; but all that he could see was active and alert. He stood facing the edge of the cliff, hacking at it in vast strokes; and between the strokes the clear tinkle and clash of the fragments of ice sounded in the channel below. Then, suddenly, his whole figure appeared, swift as a spider as he rose on to the wide step he had made; and again came the clash of the axe as he attacked the next point. . . .

Austin began to observe more closely the probable course that would be taken.

First there was the big hummock of ice on which Ulrich was now standing. It would take perhaps four steps to cross this. Then, from where he was now standing, all that he could see was a tall edge of rock, leaning forward over the channel beneath; and it was either under or over this rock that they would have to go. He had seen, however, just before that there was ice again beyond this, before the ordinary slopes could be reached. . . .

He watched Ulrich in a kind of dream, as the guide slowly mounted the hummock; and he saw, too, Val presently pass up to the left to allow more rope-room for the leader. The boy stood quite motionless, his head down, visible as the guide had been just before, from his knees upwards. The rest of the party remained in their steps.

Then Ulrich turned round and beckoned, leaning his axe against the rock, and gathering up the rope in both hands. He made a vivid little picture as he stood there, his legs wide apart, his eager bird-like face bent down, and his whole outline standing out sharp and distinct against the blazing slopes behind.

Then Val mounted, driving his axe above him; and, simultaneously, Tom Meredith followed to the vacated place, and Austin prepared to go forward. He heard Mr. Armstrong shifting his axe behind.

When Austin himself at last arrived at the foot of the hummock, and was turning to look down at the treacherous channel that sloped away to the right, he heard a sharp whisper in German from Mr. Armstrong, who had followed him step by step, and saw Ulrich's face peering over the shoulders of the three who were now mounted on the hummock.

There was a short dialogue, all in whispers between the two. Ulrich nodded once or twice, and then disappeared again.

"Look here, you fellows," whispered Armstrong from below. "We've got to jump. Val, you're

the first. Watch Ulrich closely. Put your feet
where he does, and jump when he tells you. The
rest hold on tight. We mustn't have any mistake
here. . . . Wait a second. And let no one
move till the word's given."

He waved Austin aside, and came past him with
extraordinary agility in so heavy a man. He in-
sinuated himself right against the side of the jutting
cliff, chipped out a couple of heel-holes, and then
braced himself in his place, holding the rope in both
hands. Austin understood that this was done in
case the party fell. But it still seemed incredible to
the young man that such a jump could be
made. . . .

"Now then," the other whispered sharply.
"Brace yourself tight. . . . Go on, Jack."

From where Austin crouched, beneath the hummock, holding on firmly with his axe, with both
heels together in a crack of ice, he could hear the
preparations being made overhead, and a whisper
or two.

The situation was pretty plain.

Beyond the jutting rock wall were (as he remembered having seen from further up the slope)
hummocks of ice corresponding to these on this side.
Now the rock was at least perpendicular, and so
worn with ice and snow as to afford no foot or
handhold; and it ran down, moreover, sheer on to

the ice channel beneath. Of course two other ways
over were conceivable. Either the channel itself
might have been traversed, or a way, perhaps, found
somewhere far overhead. But it was the middle
course that had been chosen, and this involved,
apparently, a jump. This jump must, obviously, be
formidable. It would mean leaping from the ice
hummock on this side, past the rock, and alighting
on the ice on the other side. And there would be
the cheering view of glassy ice channel, seen at a
very acute angle beneath. . . . Well, he supposed it was all right. . . . He found a certain
difficulty in swallowing, and he tried to moisten his
lips. . . . How lovely the valley looked right
down there beneath him, beyond the snow. . . .

Then Ulrich jumped.

There was a stir in the figures above him as each
gripped himself into his place in case of a slip;
but the sound of the alighting feet came sharp and
clear without the hint even of a scramble.

Austin could see nothing of the proceedings at
all. He was observing with great attention Jack
Ratcliffe's boots, that were planted on the ice not a
foot away from his own head.

"Wait a second, Val," came a sharp whisper,
which Austin recognised as Tom's. "Ulrich's not
ready. . . . Now then. . . ."

There was a pause.

"Axe-head to the left. . . . Both feet together. . . . Good Lord? . . ."

Austin waited.

"Go on . . . go on . . ." whispered Mr. Armstrong's voice, as if to himself.

Austin waited. What an enormous time Val seemed to be. . . .

Then, without warning, the man beside him sprang upright, and without a word of apology, pushed abruptly by him and scrambled on to the first step of the hummock.

"Will you ——" he began in a fierce whisper.

But there came an interruption.

Suddenly, without the faintest warning, without even an attempt at a whisper, there rose up a wailing, miserable cry which, for the first moment, Austin could not believe was the voice of Val.

"I can't! I can't," wailed the voice. "It's no good. I can't. It's too far. I can't. . . . Oh ——"

"Val! Jump at once! Don't be an ass!" came the sharp order, from immediately over Austin's head.

"My good chap ——" began a remonstrative whisper from Tom.

"Leave him to me, sir," came the sharp, impera-

tive voice again. "Stand up, Val. I'm ashamed
of you. . . . Now will you jump? I shall tell
Ulrich to pull you if you don't."

"I can't. . . . I can't. . . . No! No,
don't."

It seemed to Austin as an incredible dream.
Nothing seemed real, except the biting snow into
which his fingers were clenched, and the gaitered
legs of the man who stood now in Tom's place
. . . the tiny details within the immediate
reach of his senses. . . .

Then the gaitered legs scrambled fiercely and
violently. There was a movement overhead as the
others shifted to let him come by, and then again
the ruthless voice began.

"Do you want to be kicked over it, sir? . . .
I swear I'll kick you over it if you don't jump.
. . . Stand up, I tell you. . . . Don't
crouch there. . . . Now jump. . . ."

Again there was silence.

It seemed to Austin afterwards as if at least half
an hour had passed before the party came back, first
Mr. Armstrong, white and furious, swinging himself down from the hummock as if wholly reckless;
then the three friends, with faces at once quiet and
excited; and finally Val . . . Val looking like

someone else. A trail of rope came after him; it caught somewhere as he climbed, shaking all over, down on to the slope. Austin, without a word, jerked it clear.

But it could not have been more than ten minutes.

Ulrich had joined in once or twice, his German sounding more impossibly unintelligible than usual from beyond the rock behind which he stood; and the miserable talk had become at last a dialogue between the Secretary and the guide. Then there had been movements and shiftings overhead. Then, it seemed, Ulrich had unroped, as it was impossible for him to get back to the rest.

Austin laid a hand on Tom's arm, as he went past him.

" What are we going to do? " he whispered.

Tom jerked his head upwards. There were many emotions in his eyes. . . .

" Armstrong's going to take us over the top," he said.

(III)

" Some people are just made that way," said Armstrong genially. " I don't know that you can blame them. It's just nervous weakness."

It was a depressing little council of three that

was gathered the same night in the Merediths' sitting-room — the two Meredith parents and the Secretary.

The climbing party had got back just in time for *table d'hôte;* they had been delayed contrary to expectation by the unfortunate little incident; but the rest of the expedition had gone well. They had been obliged to return on their track a certain distance, and to strike higher up over the top of the obstacle which had proved too much for Val's nerves; and here Ulrich, climbing back alone, had met them and reunited himself to the rope. From that point onwards the party had gone with speed and security, had struck the path above Hornli, and the rest had been simple.

"But it was just funk — the Philistine would say," observed the lawyer with the cool, detached voice known so well to the clients of the other side. "And I gather you told him so."

"Certainly I told him so when it might have been of use. Sometimes a sense of acute shame will overcome the nervous fear. I've known that happen."

The other looked up, flicking the ash from his cigar.

"Oh! you've known it happen before?"

"I've seen it four times altogether. In two in-

stances the man overcame it almost at once — when
. . . when it was put to him plainly. The
third case was a woman who went into hysterics,
and had to be dragged up a bad bit like a sack of
coals. And the fourth case failed."

"What happened?"

"Well, it got as far as kicking him. There was
real danger, you understand, to the whole party;
and there was no other way round."

"But it failed, you say?"

"It did. We spent the night on the rocks, and
came down at our leisure."

"Why didn't you kick Val?"

The Secretary paused.

"I couldn't," he said briefly; "though I very
nearly did. But he looked at me so wretch-
edly. . . . Besides, there was another way
round, you see."

There was a pause, and Mrs. Meredith resumed
her knitting.

It had been an exceedingly unpleasant business,
breaking it to those two. Armstrong only thanked
his stars that they were not the boys' parents; but
it was quite bad enough.

It had been obvious at dinner that something had
gone very wrong indeed. Austin had appeared,
silent and morose, ten minutes after the rest. Tom

had refused to say anything at all except that they had to retrace their steps at one point; and Val had not appeared at all until dinner was ending. It seemed that he had been having a hot bath and that he hadn't been able to get any hot water for a long time.

The Secretary, viewing this scene from across the room, had determined on solving the intolerable situation as soon as possible, and, with infinite guile, had caused a note to be placed in Mr. Meredith's hands as he left the table. And so, here they were.

"I gather that you talked to the boy on the way back?"

"Yes; he had fallen behind the rest, after the Hornli; so I broke a bootlace and caught him."

"Well?"

"Perhaps I was weak," said the other meditatively, getting out his pouch. "Of course I made it perfectly clear that there must be no more big expeditions, but, for the rest, I let him down as easily as I could. Besides, I really believed what I said."

"What did you say?"

"I told him not to blame himself. I said that there were some people who simply had not the head for climbing. There was a V.C. I knew who turned green in the face when he looked down a precipice. And I said that I was very sorry for his disappointment, but that he must reckon himself one of those."

" Well?"

" He seemed enormously cheered," said the other rather drily, after a good blow down his pipe. ("By the way, may I smoke a pipe down here?) Enormously cheered. He's an emotional chap . . . and I'm very sorry for him," he added emphatically.

" Do you believe one word you've been saying?" asked the lawyer delicately.

The other laughed outright.

" Well, I do, you know. At least, I believe it's perfectly true of a great many people. It's the people on the border-line I'm doubtful about — the people, I mean, who honestly haven't got very good heads, and with whom it's just touch and go whether their will is master or not."

" And Val's one of them?"

" I've got no right to assume that. Remember, he was actually rash the last time he went out. It may very well have been that the bit to-day really was too much for his head, and that no amount of resolution could have got him over."

" And was it a really dangerous bit?"

" It was what I should call a nasty bit. Perfectly safe, you know, *if* you did the right thing;

and entirely within the power of every one of the party."

"Describe it."

"Well," went on the Secretary, drawing at his pipe, "it was a ten-foot jump, and downwards. There was a good take off, and a good landing. The only nasty thing was the rock. It looked as if one might hit against it. On the other hand, there was the rope. I shouldn't blame a man for missing his foothold; but then, you see, we were all roped. At the worst one would have got a bang or two."

"It was, honestly, within the boy's power?"

The other looked up for a sharp instant.

"I shouldn't have asked him to jump if it hadn't been," he said quietly. "It certainly was within his physical power. But it seems not to have been within his moral power."

The lawyer got up and went to the table.

"Well," he said, taking the stopper out of the decanter, "say when."

(IV)

Austin went up to bed that night with a queer mixture of feelings, in which vicarious shame, a sort of compassion, and a faint element of triumph were discernible in turns. It was his Meddity, so to say, that was responsible for the first, and his

humanity for the second, and he would scarcely
have been an earthly elder brother if the third element had been wholly wanting.

He had had ample time to arrange his attitude
by now; for he had not exchanged five words with
Val since the catastrophe. The walk back had
been as Mr. Armstrong had described it; and as
soon as they got upstairs Val had whisked in,
snatched a bath-towel, and vanished again till the
end of dinner. And, ever since, Austin had sat
with Tom and the Ratcliffes in august conclave on
the terrace to discuss the Matterhorn, and the question as to how Val had best be told that he mustn't
come with them. Once Austin had seen his brother
pass across a lighted window, and later he had
heard his voice from another group at the other end
of the terrace.

The attitude he had determined on is best described as falling under the " Poor-old-chap "
category. He proposed to be extremely magnanimous, to assign Val's deplorable exhibition to
merely physical causes, and so to lead up to the
delicate conclusion with regard to the Matterhorn.
For this, on the whole, had been the attitude of
the Ratcliffes. They too had described, as out
of the experience of years, parallel cases to Val's;
they too had advanced the very same instance of
the V.C. who could not look over a precipice.

Tom had been more silent; he had smoked a great deal and said very little. Once, when Austin appealed to him, he had assented politely and shortly to the effect that the " physical-nerve thing " was by far the most probable. In short, it had been an exceedingly charitable, if slightly superior conversation; and it was this precise blend of charity and superiority, warmed up by a bottle of fizzy wine, that Austin carried him into the large, white, bare room, lit by electricity, where he and his brother slept.

Val was already in bed, deep in a Tauchnitz volume, as Austin had been a few nights before, lying on his back with the book held above him. He gave a brotherly murmur of greeting and continued to read. Then, as Austin finished his prayers and stood up to disrobe, Val shut the book sharply enough to attract attention, made somewhat of a commotion as he snuggled down into the bedclothes, and took up his parable in a loud and cheerful voice.

" I say, Austin, what an ass I made of myself to-day ! "

" Oh! well ——" began the other, taken by surprise. But there was no need to make any comment. Val proceeded, with almost a suspicious rapidity, to lay the case open.

"Yes, a real ass of myself. I'm jolly ashamed. And I've had a good talk to Armstrong; and he quite agrees I mustn't try the Matterhorn, after all. He tells me he's known other people just the same. There was a V.C. who couldn't look over a precipice without turning green. . . . I'm beastly sorry, old chap, for having made such an ass of myself. I oughtn't to have tried it at all. But, you know, I couldn't tell without trying as to whether my head would stand it or not. And it seems it won't. So there's an end of it."

Austin was conscious of a sudden and violent wave of irritation. This was precisely what he had intended to say himself; yet it seemed as if his compassion left him wholly as soon as Val said it. He folded his dress-jacket carefully on the chair and laid his waistcoat on the top.

"I shall envy you frightfully, old chap, when you do the Matterhorn. But Armstrong quite agrees with me that I mustn't even attempt it."

"So did we this evening downstairs," said Austin cruelly.

"We? Who?"

"Tom and the Ratcliffes and myself."

He heard Val swallow in his throat. But the boy went on gallantly.

"Ah! I thought you must be talking about that," he said. "Of course, it's the only possible thing

to do. I'm frightfully sick at the thought of it
. . . after coming out here on purpose. But
you do agree, don't you, that I'd better not try?"

Austin slipped off his trousers and turned for
his pyjamas.

"Yes," he said. "It's a pity you didn't find
out before to-day."

Again there was that slight pause, and again the
boy kept up his pose magnificently.

"I know," he said. "But I couldn't tell before
trying a really bad place; and ——"

"Tom says it wasn't really bad at all. There
was no danger, you know."

Val laughed; and even unperceptive Austin recognised that the laughter came from the throat,
not the heart.

"Well, it was bad enough for me, anyhow. It
looked bad; and that's the thing, Armstrong says,
that matters if you haven't got the climbing head."

Austin got into bed and drew the clothes to his
chin.

"Yes, I suppose so. . . . Do you mind putting the light out? I want to go to sleep."

The switch was beside Val's bed, and the light
went out with astounding promptness.

"I say, Austin; do you want to go to sleep at
once?"

"Yes."

"I wish you'd talk——" began the voice, with ever so slight a quaver, out of the darkness.

"My good chap, there'll be plenty of time to talk to-morrow. . . . Good night."

There was silence.

"Good night," said Austin again, seized with compunction.

Again there was silence.

"Sulky brute," said Austin to himself beneath the bedclothes. He felt he wanted a little re-assurance.

Once in the night he woke, wide awake in an instant, from a savagely vivid dream of enormous white toppling peaks and cavernous green ice, and turned over in bed. Then he listened for Val's breathing. There was none; and he knew with an intuition, of which there was no questioning, that the boy was lying awake too, in an agony of self-contempt and misery. He knew, in those few minutes in which he was too proud and self-righteous to speak, that he had known all along that Val's pose was no more than a pose — a pose snatched at and gripped, since self-respect stood or fell with it. Yet he did not speak. He told him-self that it was good for his younger brother to be humiliated for once; perhaps he wouldn't be so complacent after this. So he said nothing, and presently was asleep again.

When he awoke again, not only was it broad day, but Val was gone.

When he was dressed he went to the window; and there, in the sunlight on the terrace, was Val, talking eagerly, and, it seemed, even eloquently, to Tom and the two Ratcliffes. And at that sight his heart hardened again.

As he went past Val's bed to get to the door, something about the smoothness of the pillow attracted his attention. Obviously Val had turned it over for some reason. So Austin turned it back, and the pillow was moist on the lower side. He looked at it a minute or two. Then he turned it carefully back and went down to breakfast.

CHAPTER VIII

(1)

"YOU see I just hadn't the head for it," explained Val for the tenth time — this time to his mother — with an air of mingled ease and humility that increased on every occasion. "Armstrong said"— (and there followed *da capo* the Tale of the Green-faced Officer.)

Home-coming had not been the triumph that Val had expected; and what triumph there was rested wholly upon Austin, who had, actually, climbed the Matterhorn and acquitted himself with credit. The brothers had not talked much one to the other on the way: Val had read Tauchnitz volumes a great deal with a studiously interested air; and Austin had spent most of his time in low-voiced conversation with Tom. At Dover they had parted from the Merediths, and thenceforward the silence between the two had been even more marked. And now they were at home again, eating a late supper. Their mother and May sat with them in the dining-room, listening to the tale of adventure; the General and Miss Deverell, it was understood, were play-

148

ing backgammon in the hall. Gertie, Val had learned within ten minutes of his arrival, without mentioning her name, had gone home a week earlier, after all.

" Poor boy!" said Lady Beatrice.

" Hard lines," said May.

" Tell us about the Matterhorn," said Lady Beatrice, turning to Austin.

It was really rather trying for Val to have to sit through the next twenty minutes. Austin became unusually excited — he had eaten and drunk well — and before long was piling a salt-cellar on to a silver mug and a pepper-pot on to the salt-cellar in order to make absolutely clear the nature of the performance he had achieved. It was up this slope that the work had been hardest; it was round this corner that the wind had suddenly met them; it was from the angle of the salt-cellar nearest to May that they had seen the clouds clear and Zermatt show itself like a group of pebbles on a billiard-table. Then, as the party approached the final summit, Austin demonstrated too vividly, and the entire Matterhorn fell on to the tablecloth, pouring salt in one direction and pepper in the other. Val emitted a single syllable of bitter merriment and Austin glanced up at him, frowning.

"I see perfectly," cried Lady Beatrice, with an excellent enthusiasm. "No; don't bother to put them up again: that's one of the Queen Anne salts, you know."

"Well, you see, don't you?" said Austin. "It was round that curve I was just touching that the last slope lies. Then you only have a couple of hundred yards, and you're at the top."

"Oh, how gorgeous!" sighed May, who had sat propping her chin on her hands and staring fascinated. "Oh, Val; if only you'd been there too!"

Val put his last piece of pudding into his mouth and said nothing.

"What's that, Austin?" cried May again, as the elder boy, after fumbling in his breast pocket, brought out two flat, grey pebbles and laid them solemnly on the cloth.

"These are the two stones I've got left from the top of the Matterhorn," he said impressively. "May, would you like one? or would you have it, mother?"

"Let May have it," said his mother, smiling.

"Oh, Austin! Really?"

Austin with a tremendous air pushed over the larger of the two stones toward his sister.

"Take it, May," he said.

Val felt his heart growing, apparently, more and
more contracted during all this. It was far more
trying even than he had anticipated, to assist at
these grave ceremonies and descriptions. He had,
with eager prudence, established first his own im-
peccability: and he had made it so clear to everyone else that nothing except an unfortunate physical
defect had stood between him and the summit of the
Matterhorn, that he was really almost beginning to
believe it himself. But this hero-worship seemed
to him intolerable. He was absolutely certain that
Austin had not really the same climbing powers and
general fortitude as himself — there was the *sérac*
incident to prove it; and it appeared to him that
he was very deeply misunderstood. . . .

"I say, Austin; do you remember the time I got
into such a row on the glacier?"

"What was that?" asked May eagerly.

Val emptied his glass.

"Oh! nothing much. We were out on the
glacier; and while the others were putting on the
rope I went on ahead. My word! Old Armstrong did let me have it!"

"Was it dangerous?"

"It didn't seem to me so. Armstrong seemed to
think it was. . . . Yes: I suppose it was,
rather. It was the top of an ice-peak, you

know,— on the glacier; with crevasses all round."

Austin laughed sardonically. Val went on superbly:

"Of course I oughtn't to have done it. I was awfully ashamed of myself afterwards. But I didn't know it was dangerous at the time, I suppose." '

"Oh, Val!" cried May.

"Well, if you boys have finished, let's go and tell your father all about it," said Lady Beatrice, reaching for her stick. "He'll want to hear."

Val sat apart a little, while the entire story was told again, edited for fathers. Names of peaks, for example, had to be mentioned with some particularity; and the kindness of Mr. and Mrs. Meredith had to be referred to once or twice. (It is quite extraordinarily instructive to hear the same story recounted to a father and a mother respectively.) But Val felt more content, at least superficially. He had drawn general attention to himself just now in the dining-room, and had established a reputation for individual daring, to compensate for his physical weakness.

The General leaned back from his backgammon board to listen. Both boys had to talk, but Austin presently held the field, and the ascent of the Matterhorn was once more exhaustively described, from the start made at the Schwarz-See to the return to the Riffelhorn the following evening. Austin rolled out with great fluency the names of the principal peaks that could be viewed from the summit. . . .

"And you, Val," said the old gentleman presently. "I don't understand why you didn't go too."

Val licked his lips for another effort.

"I found I had a bad head, father," he said. "I couldn't be sure of myself. Mr. Armstrong advised me not to go; he said he knew a man once, who had the V.C., who ——"

"Pooh! That's nothing. You could have got over it."

"Well, I thought it better to do what Armstrong ——"

"Yes, yes," said his father, with a touch of impatience.

"Val wanted to go very much," said Austin generously, "but we all — I mean the Merediths and Armstrong and the Ratcliffes all thought it would be better not."

The General was silent.

"Well, you've had a good time, boys, haven't you? That's right," he said suddenly. "Miss Deverell, I think we must leave the game for to-night. It's getting late."

(11)

Val preceded Austin upstairs, once more trembling with resentment and shame. His father had taken so exactly the wrong line and thrown him again on guard. If only the boy could have produced the conviction in everyone else that he had behaved on the whole with a right prudence and with no lack of courage, it would have been so infinitely easier to have established that conviction in himself too. Yet his anger partly reassured him as well; it was so necessary to ward off external attacks that at present he had no energy to turn inwards and learn what he really himself believed.

As he came into his room, an old figure in cap and apron straightened itself from over the fire.

" Eh-h! " she cried, with upraised hands.

Val kissed the old nurse mechanically.

" I've been warming your pyjamas," proceeded Benty, " and to-morrow morning I'm coming in to know what you'll take with you to Eton."

" Oh! I can't be bothered," snapped Val.

" But you go on Friday afternoon! " exclaimed Benty in dismay.

" Pack what you like. I don't care. I must go to bed. I'm tired."

Benty regarded him a moment in deep disappointment. She had expected him to be so pleased to see her; and she had rehearsed to herself with such expectancy the solemn consultation that would take place next morning, as to whether the *old* yellow socks were to go in his portmanteau as well as the *new* blue ones, and as to whether Master Val wouldn't let her order him a dozen new shirts — the cuffs of the old ones were beginning to fray. She had looked them all over in her room this afternoon.

"Then I must speak to your mamma," she said at last, with a distinct and unusual lack of tact.

"Don't bother me, Benty," said Val, sitting heavily down on his bed and beginning to untie his shoes. "Can't you see I'm dog-tired?"

Then her dignity melted.

"Eh! then; go to bed, like a good boy."

"Good night, Benty."

He lifted his face to kiss her.

Just before he got into bed he remembered he hadn't got a book to read, so he put on his slippers and went out into the sitting-room. As he knelt by the low bookcase Austin came in.

"Hullo!" said Austin.

"Hullo!" said Val.

Austin pottered about for a few minutes, setting a couple of guide-books to Switzerland in his own private shelf, opening a couple of letters that were lying on his table, warming his hands at the fire, and finally placing with an exaggerated care (as Val, pretending to look for a book, noticed perfectly well), his grey stone from the top of the Matterhorn under a glasscase that already sheltered a fives cup.

" I say, Val."

" Well."

" I've put my stone here. Don't move it, will you? I'm going to label it to-morrow."

" I don't want to move it," snapped Val.

Austin preserved an offensive silence. Presently he took off his shoes, sat down in an easy chair, and prepared to read.

" Good night," he said, as Val went to the door at last with a suitable book. (It dealt neither with riding nor climbing.)

" 'Night," grunted Val, shutting the door upon the word.

" Sulky brute," murmured Austin to himself aloud for his own satisfaction.

Austin was marvellously well pleased with himself to-night. He had come back, after a really notable achievement, considering his few years and his short experience, and had found himself entirely appreciated. His mother had been attentive and admirative; May had been ecstatic; his father had been attentive and even respectful. Above all, Val had been obliged definitely to take second place. Of course it was only right that he should do so, but Val did not appear usually over-ready to recognise the obligation. But now there was no doubt at all about it. Austin had climbed the Matterhorn; Val had not. And Austin understood perfectly the desperate wriggle Val had made to get back into the middle of the stage by his reference to the *sérac* incident, and that he knew, and that Austin himself knew, and that Val knew that Austin knew that it had not been really successful. Everyone knew the name of the Matterhorn; the *sérac* had none to be known. Besides, obviously, Val's treasury of self-respect must have run pretty low if he was forced to draw upon a discreditable incident to restore his credit.

No, the thing was settled now. He had scored one; he had acted like a real elder brother; he had done what the younger could not; and he had actually been so evidently in advance as to be able to afford a generous remark just now, down in the hall.

So Austin sat and read, till his toes tingled and his head swam with sleep. Then he proceeded to his bedroom with the air of Tired Warrior, and went solemnly to bed.

(iii)

Twenty minutes later the door of Val's room opened cautiously. Nothing else happened at all for a full twenty seconds. Then, without a sound, Val himself, in blue pyjamas and with bare feet, with a candle in his hand, appeared rigid as a ghost, listening. No sound at all met his ears. Then he advanced down the passage, stopping to listen at Austin's door and to peer for any sign of light. Then once more he advanced, pushed open the door of the sitting-room, and went in, still with a noiseless and rigid carriage. He had come to look again at the grey stone under the glass dome: nothing else.

The moment he had seen it downstairs in the dining-room, he had perceived that it would become for him a symbol for ever. It was an outward and visible sign of an inward and spiritual disgrace. He hated with an extraordinary intensity of feeling, even while he adored it. It had actually lain on the summit of the Matterhorn and had been borne thence by human hands; but the hatefulness of it lay in the fact that it had been his brother's hands, when it might have been his own. If anyone else had brought it down he would have asked for a splinter from it. Since it was Austin he would have wished to annihilate it. An added touch of bitterness lay in Austin's not confiding in him before that there was such a stone in existence. They had talked together of many things since the ascent; yet Austin had for the first time produced it at the dramatic moment in the dining-room when the Family incense was going up in fragrance about the hero. . . . It was intolerable. Yet he must look at it again.

There, then, it lay, leaning on the blue velvet and just touching the silver cup. It was a split-looking fragment that had scaled off from its parent rock: it was grey in colour, with sparkling points in it, as of mica or quartz. It must have lain there on the stormy top from the earliest dawn of time — rent, perhaps, centuries ago, from the mass of which it had once formed a part, by the stroke of lightning.

He stared at it, fascinated. . . .

Ah! if it had been his own; and it might have been. Already, since he had seen it an hour ago, he had made his supposititious plans. He would have mounted it on a wooden pedestal, with a small brass plate let into it, protected by a glass dome, and . . . and presented the whole affair to Gertie, with a few properly self-depreciatory remarks. He moved the candle this way and that, and the sparkling surface rippled with points of light as the flame moved.

Then he thought he must touch and hold the hateful, admirable thing.

Very carefully he set the bell-glass on one side, putting his candle in a safe place, and took up the stone. He felt its texture, its sharp edges, its angles. It weighed perhaps three or four ounces, no more.

Then he began to dream again. The dying fire was pleasant to his legs; the woolly matter to his bare feet. And he began to picture again exactly the sort of mounting he would have had made for it — just an unpolished block of old oak, appropriate to the age and rugged history of the stone; a light blue velvet socket and fringe to the stand; and a small brass plate, inscribed " V. M. to G. M."— no more. G. M. would have had it on her writing-table, always; it would have been a reminder to her of the prowess and gallantry of V. M.

Ah! and it was not hers, and never could be. It was the property of Austin — his property by every claim, the pledge of his courage and fortitude; and Austin lay snoring next door, to awake again to-morrow to his inalienable rights over it.

Val's eyes wandered round the room. Those

cups on the mantelpiece were Austin's; those hare-pads and masks on the brown shields were his; this copy of Pop Rules in light blue ribbon was his. And now this eloquent piece of stone was his. And Val? . . . Well, that single cup was his on the corner of the group by Hills and Saunders, and the small silver egg-cup under glass on the top of the bureau was his — he had won it as junior partner in house-fives two years ago. And that was absolutely all, of everything that mattered.

He stared down at the scrap of stone again, miserable and depressed. Why should Austin have everything, and he nothing? — everything, down even to this final symbol of the elder brother's fortitude and the younger's weakness? *And it might have been his . . . it might have been his.*

Then with a sudden spasm of rage he dashed the stone into the sofa-cushions, and stood trembling.

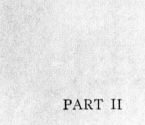

PART II

CHAPTER I

(1)

"MY dear girl," said Val tranquilly, and with an air of extraordinary experience, " apart from exceptional cases and circumstances, men are infinitely braver than women. There's nothing to be ashamed of, I assure you. Women aren't meant to be brave. They've . . . they've got other advantages instead," he ended vaguely.

Val and Gertrude Marjoribanks, in the old schoolroom upstairs after tea, were discussing women's rights; and it was rapidly becoming an enumeration of masculine and feminine virtues, with a complete dissatisfaction to both sides.

" What advantages? " asked Gertrude, slightly flushed with argument. And Val, compelled to be precise, began to explain.

Val had grown up with great rapidity during the past three years, and had entirely fulfilled his rather hobbledehoyish promise. He had become, in fact, an exceedingly pleasant-looking young man — though with the Medd nose and chin always in evidence. These redeemed his face, however, from the ordinariness of young men of nineteen, and with his clean-shaven lips, his brown eyes, his wholesome pallor, he was distinctly of a romantic appearance.

Gertrude too had improved enormously. She had been rather markedly *jeune fille,* rather too slender and delicate and, simultaneously, rather abrupt and disturbing. But she had settled down by now into a poise of self-restrained youthfulness and even dignity, and her slight jerkiness had transformed itself into magnetism. She had made her curtsey at Court under Lady Beatrice's protection last summer; her portrait had appeared in a good many newspapers, and her name in lists of house-parties, especially where there were theatricals. She was taking herself rather seriously just now, as she was perfectly aware of her success; but it certainly did not detract from her charm. She was on a round of visits just now, and was spending Christmas with her old friends the Medds.

And now these two had drifted upstairs after tea, and were discussing women's rights with extreme vivacity. Val had reached the point of explaining that the great charm of women lay in their dependence and their sympathy. He even condescended to remark that a man's character was not complete without a woman's; that a man's natural courage was too hard a quality until lined, so to speak, with a woman's tenderness, and his recklessness softened by her prudence. And Gertie listened to him with intense eagerness, contradicted him warmly, and when she was not looking at his face, watched his shoe impatiently beating in the firelight. It may be added that she was dressed in a very charming tea-gown, which she had put on immediately after a hasty cup of tea in the hall, drank by her while her riding-habit still reeked and steamed with wet; and that she made great play with a fan with which she was protecting her face from the roaring glare of the wood fire.

"When are you leaving here?" asked Val abruptly; suddenly tired, it seemed, of women's rights. (After all, had not that question been settled, a hundred times, in as many undergraduates' rooms in Cambridge?)

"My aunt's coming to take me on to the Northamptons on Tuesday. I'm in some theatricals there, you know."

"Oh! Tuesday," said Val reflectively. "What are you acting in?"

He watched her as she described her part. . . . It seemed that Royalty was to be present, too.

Now of course Val was sentimental. Let that be
said at once. And it must further be remarked
that no young man of his age and temperament
could possibly be anything else. He thought a
great deal, that is to say, about negligible ex-
ternals — about the texture of this girl's hair; the
gleam on her stocking: he liked to think of her
when he had got into bed and turned the light off,
to make small plans for next day, to rehearse the
incidents of the past day; even to design a vague
but delicious future when Gertie and he should
have a moderately sized house in the country and
a little flat in town, and be perfectly reasonable
and sympathetic one to another without growing
any older, for ever and ever. All this, of course,
was perfectly suitable and inevitable; and the only
significant point, distinguishing Val's love-career
from that of the perfectly ordinary boy, was that
it had lasted three years, with more or less con-
tinuity, ever since the day when, to the sound of
music in the hall, he had first perceived that she
was charming and lovable. Other girls had, of
course, flitted across his vision; but they had never
stayed. Gertrude Marjoribanks had been the un-
derlying type and model of them. He had seen
her fairly frequently. She had been up to Cambridge with May to see him row; he had shot with
her people; and she came to Medhurst at least

twice a year for a tolerably long stay. It was
a clean, honest adoration; and he was beginning
to feel, at last, that it was getting a little too much
for him and that something must be done. After
all, he would be far from penniless in a few years'
time; and she too would be moderately well off.
They could manage the flat in town, anyhow; and
perhaps Medhurst would serve for the present as
their country house.

In other respects the three years that had elapsed
since the Switzerland affair had developed the
situation on orderly and conventional lines. Austin
had grown a moustache at Cambridge, and had cut
it off again when he began to eat his dinners in
the Temple; and was now a perfectly respectable
barrister and something of a prig. He was to stand
for Parliament when a suitable occasion arose. He
and Val saw very little of one another, and got on
as well as such brothers usually do; that is to say,
they were quite reasonably polite to one another,
and occasionally, with a pregnant word or two,
began and ended small decorous quarrels. Val
thought Austin a prig, and Austin thought Val immature and rather conceited; and they were both
quite right. May had also become three years
older, and had began to be what is called "a good
daughter"; that is to say, she used to help her

mother to write invitations, and to tell her father, playfully, not to sit up too late. The General's confusion when this happened for the first time, and his acquiescence in it when he understood that it was only playful, and quite suitable, was really edifying. He too was three years older, rather grey about the ears, and rather bald on the top of his head; and his wife too had developed along parallel feminine lines; that is to say that she walked less, and rather slower, and was more tolerant of the High-Church pranks of her vicar.

All things, therefore, were as they should be, after three years. People came and went as usual; they shot, they danced, they spent peaceful if rather un-eventful week-ends at Medhurst. Everybody went up to London at the end of May and came away again at the end of July. And the great house sat still and unchanged; it buzzed with subdued life below in the servants' quarters, and beat tranquilly with stateliness and beauty above. The pheasants clucked over their young during the spring in the deep woods, and flew cackling over the guns in the winter. The horses came round as usual, the bell rang from the stable-turret, and the gong sounded within. There was still the annual flower-show, and the harvest festival, and all the other proper things. And the Medd pride lay over all like a benediction, and burned within like a steady flame of fire.

(II)

"I quite agree with you," said Gertie suddenly, "that men must be brave. If they aren't that they aren't men. But, as a matter of fact, women are just as brave, and often a good deal braver."

"I used to think I was a coward," said Val, smiling reminiscently. "Do you remember my being thrown off Quentin three years ago? Well, you know, I was awfully nervous next day. I couldn't ride anyhow, as I had strained myself. But, you know, I was awfully glad I couldn't."

She looked up.

"Yes?"

"Well, it was all nonsense, of course. Of course I should have ridden if I had been able. And the feeling frightened one couldn't help. I remember reading in a book on riding that that often happened when one fell slowly."

She nodded.

"Yes, I see. So long as one does ride, the feeling doesn't matter."

"Well, when I came back from Switzerland, of course I rode just as usual. Oh! and the same thing happened in Switzerland — the time I found out I hadn't any head for climbing. I was horribly ashamed at first, until a man out there — the Secretary of the Alpine Club — told me he had known just the same thing happen to a V.C. He just couldn't look over a precipice. I was frightfully sick at the time. I'd have given anything to have climbed the Matterhorn with the rest; but it simply wasn't fair on the others that I should try, with a head like mine."

" Yes, I see. And I should think not climbing the Matterhorn was really braver than climbing it."

Val shifted comfortably in his chair. The firelight fell on his face, and she noticed his eyes sparkle.

" Well, I know it seemed much harder, anyhow. To have to stop at home and grin — to see them off to the Schwarz-See, and then to go back to dinner with all the old women, when one knew perfectly well that if it wasn't for one's beastly head one could climb it perfectly —— ? "

He stopped dramatically.

Gertie was in that warm and genial mood that follows an afternoon's hard exercise, closed by tea and a hot bath, and a complete change into very charming and comfortable clothes; and it seemed to her that this boy was really a very fine creature. He seemed to her so modest and so subtly courageous. Most young men would have shirked such a story. He faced it. She felt a real and rather subtle admiration for him.

"Look here, Gertie," said Val suddenly. "If you're going on Tuesday, I wish you'd come a really long ride with me one day first. You said you'd never seen Penshurst. Why shouldn't we go over?"

She began to smile, and then stopped.

"Oh! do you think we could?" she said.

"Why not? On Monday. We'd take lunch and go easily."

"There's the dance in the evening."

"We'd be back before dark."

She was silent.

Gertie was no more calculating or ambitious than the average girl. Her people were reasonably well to do, and she was the only daughter. There certainly had been moments this previous year when various prospects of rather a glittering nature had passed before her eyes; it had occurred to her, for instance, that it would be extremely pleasant to be a Viscountess, and not altogether inconceivable. . . . But somehow these things faded rather at Medhurst, and it was a fact that the Viscount in question had shown no signs of his existence since August, though she believed she was to meet him at the Northamptons'. Meanwhile here was Med-

hurst; and here was Val — Val, whom she had
known for three years, with whom she had danced,
played, ridden, skated; who was always pleasant to
her, and courteous and natural. Of course, he was
only a Cambridge undergraduate at present; but he
would not be that for more than two years more.
. . . And . . . and he obviously liked her
very much.

So, suddenly in the firelight (they had not troubled to turn on the electricity) it seemed to her that
prudence was a very ignoble thing — the prudence,
that is, which sets a Viscount before a Medd. Anyhow, this was a very splendid place, and had a great
tradition, even though the physical possession of it
would never be Val's. (He was to "be an en-
gineer," she believed, when he left Cambridge;
which would mean that he played at work for a few
years, and then began to work at playing instead,
on a very competent income.) Yes, prudence and
calculation were detestable and cold-blooded things;
and Val looked very gallant and sweet in the firelight.

"Well, I'll come," she said, "if you'll arrange it
all."

(III)

Austin, meanwhile, was holding forth to his
mother in her morning-room on the very same

subject. He was standing on the hearth-rug, his legs rather wide apart, looking almost too mature and dignified for twenty-two. He was in his dinner-jacket and trousers, for he too had changed on coming in; and he held his dark, well-shaped head rather high.

Now Austin had been perfectly loyal to his younger brother over the Swiss business. He had repeated, though coldly, Val's voluble and warm-blooded explanations upon their return. For, indeed, it was impossible to do anything else. But he had remembered the facts; and, if the truth must be confessed, was not sorry to have a definite peg on which to hang that very natural and almost universal elder brother's contempt for a younger. But he was prig enough to be unaware of all this; he only told himself now and then, when a safety-valve was needed, that poor Val must not be blamed too much: somehow or another an unfortunate strain had got into his blood. This was very convenient and soothing when Val made himself a nuisance, as it preserved his own dignity and made him feel magnanimous.

The fact that Val was, officially, a " man," made things harder. You can treat a boy as a boy; you cannot treat an undergraduate as a child. Val smoked now openly, and drank whisky unrebuked; he had a dressing-case with silver fittings; he shaved every day — he did, in fact, all those things that had separated him and Austin three years before. And now he was making love too, in an offhand way, and it was not actually ridiculous; at least it needed to be called ridiculous before it was so.

This was what Austin was doing.

"I feel rather foolish," he said, looking very wise and mature, "in speaking about it at all, mother. Of course I haven't said a word to Val; he wouldn't stand it. But do you think it's quite wise to let those two — Val and Gertie, I mean — go about alone together so much?"

His mother was just a shade respectful to him now. Sir James Meredith, K.C., had been very complimentary about the application and solid conscientiousness of this son of hers, though he had not used the word "brilliance." And he was the son and heir, and had a great deal of dignity.

"Are they so much alone together? And ——"

"Why, they rode together all to-day, away from the rest of us. I don't think father liked it."

"But they've known one another a long time, Austin ——"

"And I'm sure Val's got some plan in his head for Monday. Gertie goes on Tuesday, doesn't she?" (Austin was not quite so much detached

as he wished to think himself. To be perfectly
frank, he had attempted a few solemn courtesies
to Gertie himself, and he had gathered that they
were met with irony — almost with amusement.
But he honestly did not know that this was affec-
ting him in his very conscientious remarks this evening.)

He proceeded to explain that Val was only nineteen and Gertie eighteen; that Val had to apply
himself very steadily if he was to pass his engineer-
ing examinations; and that while it was not for one
single instant his business to interfere, if Val chose
to engage himself at this absurd age to a girl
who was not in the least suited to him, yet he
. . . well, he considered it his duty to do so.
It was all said with a tremendous air of responsibility, and his mother was conscious more than
once of a desire to laugh. But that would never
do.

"Well, my son," she said, "I'm glad you've
told me. I don't think I'd better interfere, though.
Gertie's going on Tuesday, anyhow. And even if
you're right, and it's more than a mere boy and girl
affair, I'm not quite so sure as you are that it would
be such a bad thing. She's a very good girl, you
know, and Val will have nearly a thousand a year of
his own when he leaves Cambridge."

Austin thrust his chin a shade higher.

" Oh! that's all right," he said; " so long as you
know.   But I thought I'd better tell you."

" Thank you, Austin," she said quite gravely.

Austin's very slightly ruffled feelings were not
smoothed by his reception in the schoolroom.   This
was one of those delightful nondescript rooms
which girls have in big houses, as much theirs as
the smoking-room is the men's, or, in this case, as the
sitting-room at the end of the north wing was the
boys'.   Here small, inconvenient tables occupied
the spaces in front of the low mullioned windows;
pieces of embroidery were pinned upon the walls;
low white chairs were gathered round the open fire-
place; china was grouped in corners and on the
mantelshelf.   It was a room entirely white and
green, suggestive of innocence and cleanliness.
The boys only came here on invitation expressed or
understood; and there was no room to do anything
anywhere, as every vacant space on table and floor
was occupied with partly finished works in paint or
pokerwork or needlework — with easels, and work-
boxes, and a large spinning-wheel completely out
of repair.

Austin came in here with stately step, and was
confounded by the darkness and the sound of a faint
movement.

"That you, Austin?" came from a boy's figure outlined against the glowing chimney.

Austin switched on the light.

"Yes," he said, "I came to see if — er — May ——"

"May's playing pool with Tom Meredith and Miss Deverell. She was here a little while ago." (To be perfectly accurate, May had looked in to find a ball which she had taken upstairs to amuse the kitten with, at a quarter to six. It was now ten minutes past seven.)

"Oh!" said Austin.

"Anything else I can do for you?" enquired Val politely.

Gertie stood up, looking at a watch on her bracelet.

"Good gracious!" she said. "It's after seven. I must fly."

She flew. Austin held the door politely open and closed it after her.

Then he advanced a step.

"Val," he said.

"Yes?"

"Rather odd your sitting all alone here with Gertie so long."

"I beg your pardon?"

Now Austin ought to have detected from a

peculiar tone in the other's voice that this was, emphatically, not the time to advance criticisms. Val still had within him the warm, tingling effect of an hour and a half alone with a very charming and magnetic girl, and his mood was one that can only be called dangerous.

Besides, it was an entire surprise to him (as it always is in such cases) that anyone else had noticed the faintest possible relationship, beyond the most ordinary between himself and Gertie. He thought that no one was aware of it except himself.

Well, Austin in his rectitude knew nothing of this. He thought it merely a good opportunity of acting in a superior and elder-brotherly manner.

"I say," he repeated firmly, "that it's rather odd your sitting all alone with Gertie here, ever since tea — in the dark," he added as a clincher.

There was a moment's silence. Then he saw Val lick his lips, and perceived that he looked odd; and simultaneously realised that in his passion for decorum he had gone a shade too far. He recoiled, interiorly.

"I've never heard such vile insolence in my life. How dare you speak to me like that!"

"My dear chap ——"

"You'd better get out of this room," went on Val, still icily, though his voice quavered ever so slightly. "I don't want to hit you in the face."

Austin perceived that Val, with his hand still on the chair-back which he had gripped on rising, swayed a shade nearer him.

He wheeled sharply on his heel, so resolutely as to silence any question of his courage. At the door he turned again.

"It's disgraceful you should speak to me like that," he said quietly. "I simply came to ———"

"You'd better not say any more. Get out of my sight."

Val took a step nearer his brother. He regretted this afterwards, for Austin instantly sat down on a little white sofa and put one knee over the other. This was a distinct challenge; and Austin, to his satisfaction, saw that Val hesitated.

"I shall not go," said the elder, "at your bidding. . . . Val; sit down a minute. You must hear what I have to say, in justice to myself."

Val sat down, slowly, as if his righteous anger were just, and only just, curbed by his keen sense of justice. Austin perceived his own advantage, but resolved to be magnanimous.

"Look here," he said, "I'm tired of these perpetual rows. I came in here ———"

"And say something offensive," spat Val, shaken by a spasm of indignation.

"I came in here," repeated Austin, "simply to warn you that you're making . . . that you'll

be making an exhibition of yourself with Gertie
if you don't look out. I should have thought ——"

"You're very good," said Val bitterly. "It's
extraordinarily kind of you to. And may I ask
what business it is of yours?"

Austin felt the battle was won. There had certainly been a moment when he had been slightly
frightened himself; but he saw he was on top now.
He stood up and put his hand on the door again.

"My good chap. If you think it's not my business, there's no more to be said. Personally, I
should have been grateful under the same circumstances; but I see you're not. Very good. I won't
bother you again."

"I suppose you mean to imply that I'm .   .   .
I'm in love with Gertie?"

"I ——"

"Will you be good enough to answer my question?"

Austin dropped the handle again.

"I meant nothing more than that it looked like
it," he said.

"Well then, it looked wrong," said Val, deliberately and consciously lying. "It's simply
scandalous that I can't be friends with a girl who's
been in and out of this house for three years, without people poking and prying and suspecting I'm in
love. I like Gertie; and I'm going to do exactly

and precisely as I like. I'm going a long ride with her on Monday, if that's any satisfaction to you. And I'll thank you to keep your remarks to yourself, and to mind your own business."

Austin smiled gently. He even bowed a little.

" Then I think," he remarked, " there's no more to be said."

His knees shook a little as he went down the passage, humming just loud enough for Val to hear.

" Poor chap!" he said to himself. " He funked me badly then."

Val remained standing. He heard Austin humming. He smiled by a muscular effort.

" I frightened him rather badly that time, I think," he said out loud.

CHAPTER II

(1)

THERE is no period of the year in which a long ride can be more delightful than in winter, if circumstances are propitious. For both heat and flies, those supreme enemies to comfort, are absent; the horses are vivacious; and if the sky is clear, though without frost (for that tingles the toes), and windless, and if there is not too much mud, both body and mind are happy.

They had had an exceedingly pleasant visit to Penshurst; there were no other visitors, and the old caretaker, on recognising they had come from Medhurst, was deferential and intelligent. They ate their sandwiches in the garden, and by two o'clock were well on their way homewards.

Their conversation is not worth recording. It was startlingly unimportant, and the only valuable element in the experience was the degree of intimacy that grew upon them both with every mile they traversed. They rode by by-ways and fields. Val opened gates; pheasants ran and scurried in the undergrowth; pigeons sailed over them, shying

suddenly like a boat caught in a gust as the riders
became visible; the pleasant wintry air, clear and
fresh, bearing just the faintest whiff of frost as the
sun declined, breathed round them; and the sky
gradually began to marshal its colours for a fine
sunset effect. Once Gertie dropped her whip; Val
was off and up again in an instant; their eyes met
as he handed it back to her.

Of course they had arranged about the evening
an hour after they had left home. Gertie was to
dance with Val at such-and-such times; they were
to go to supper together. A certain corner of the
music-gallery was to be a kind of trysting-place if
either should feel bored. They laughed and their
eyes sparkled as they arranged this.

They both really played the game very well.
Each was perfectly aware that the stage of intimacy
towards which they were advancing was a delicate
one and easily upset.

An over-intimate remark, a touch of disproportionate sentimentality, a single unwarranted
assumption — any of these things would have disturbed the balance and set it swinging. Both were
inexperienced, yet both had a certain sensitiveness
of intuition that guided them surely and safely.
It might have seemed a little immature to experts
in flirtation; Gertie's management of her eyes, for
instance, was a degree over-emphatic once or twice;

Val's silences had occasionally a touch of *gaucherie;* but it suited these two very well. They were *gour- mands* in sensation, rather than *gourmets.* They did not enjoy the infinite subtleties of young men of forty and young women of thirty; but they would not have understood them either. They were just boy and girl; but they were well-bred boy and girl.

As the sky reached the climax of its evening glory, they came side by side along a field-path up to rising ground where pines stood. It was a kind of vantage-ground over the country round them, and they drew rein at the further edge of the trees to look about them. Behind lay Kent; before them Sussex; and Ashdown Forest stretched away, dark and golden, in front, beneath the wide, glowing sky.

Gertie looked wonderful, thought Val, as he glanced at her sideways, with that splendid sunlight straight in her face. Her dark eyes gleamed in the midst of her face, and her face shone like warm ivory. She was ever so slightly flushed with the exercise. Her dark green habit fitted her young outline like a glove; she sat on her white mare like Diana. . . .

And he too, though she never seemed to look at him, appeared a Sir Percival. He was in grey. His face was grave and serious; his hair caught the sunshine and was turned to sombre gold. He seemed to her young and virile and quiet and romantic. . . .

So they sat silent for an instant or two — boy and girl — looking out upon the sea of sunlit air, the golden cloud-islands of the west, the carpet of tree-tops; and each saw what each looked upon only as a framework and a setting for the thought of the other. For each the other was sovereign, and all else a world fit to lie only beneath the other's feet. . . .

(II)

" Let's canter down here," said Gertie, without looking at him. " It's getting late." She lifted her reins and leaned forward, and the white mare was off.

It was a long, straight ride that lay before them, and both knew it well; for they were not an hour's distance from Medhurst.

" Remember the quarry at the end," cried Val, and she nodded sideways at him over her shoulder.

Now there was a cock pheasant who had had a very agitating experience on the previous day. No less than twice had he been aroused by talking persons with sticks and compelled to fly over the tree-tops; and no less than twice had there been a sudden nerve-shattering din beneath him as he flew, protesting, and a horribly suggestive screaming sound in the air immediately behind him. He had arrived in safety again at last a mile from home, with one resolution firmly embedded among his instincts, inherited and acquired, to the effect that it was better to lie still beneath bracken than to run, and better to run than to fly.

He was out walking out this evening in the sunshine, picking at such beech-nuts and small grubs as attracted his attention, not a yard away from the ride down which a girl on a white mare happened to be cantering. First he lifted his head, with one foot upraised, as he heard the quick thudding noise grow nearer. Then he put down his head and began to run with extraordinary swiftness and silence, parallel to the ride, since a disagreeable low wire-fence prevented his escape to the right. Yet the thudding noise gained on him. His wings were out behind, hanging wide and loose, and he helped his speed now and again by a flap. Yet the thudding noise gained on him, and now he was aware out of one flaming eye that a disconcerting group was descending straight upon him, as it seemed — first a white and black monster, then a black and grey.

Then, as he lifted himself indeed to fly, and drew

that final breath before uttering the cry that was at
once his appeal and his defiance, he perceived that
the fence on his right wheeled suddenly inwards
and barred his way. There was no help for it; he
rose with a noise like a rocket, twisted his flight
simultaneously, and burst out of his thicket sideways, scarcely a foot in front of the white mare's
head. . . . Higher and higher he rose, far into
the sunlight above the pine tops, still crowing with
agitated triumph till far away across the woods he
saw his goal; then, like a boat coming into harbour
at last, he spread his wings, stiff and resolute, and
down the long slide of air, descended by a magnificent *vol plané* down among the tree-tops, down
between their stems; landed, ran, walked, and
couched, silent again, listening for the sounds of
pursuit.

And meanwhile the white mare had swerved,
tossed her head, snorted, and bolted, mad with
fright, straight down the ride at the end of which
lay the quarry-edge, not five hundred yards away.

The moment the first wild scurry was over Gertie
settled down to her task. She had torn at the reins
in the hope of breaking the rush short before it had
settled down into the bolt proper. Then she jerked
the snaffle-reins loose and put her whole strength
into the curb, sawing first on this side, then on that;

yet she dared not saw too hard, lest the jerk should carry her more into the trees on either side.

It is impossible to say that she was frightened. She saw the facts before her — the possibility that the mare might fall on the slope, the probability that both would go over the quarry-edge together, and the calamity of death if they did. But these facts were remote as a horizon; the immediate thing was that the mare must be stopped. She leaned back, she tugged, she tossed her whip aside, she jerked; then she leaned back again . . . and *da capo*.

Little scenes and ideas flitted before her with the speed of intense thought. She seemed to herself to be two persons — the one remote and detached, regarding a fallen log, the amber sky, the flattened ears of the mare, the flying mane; the other at first passionately attentive to the need of stopping this flight, then furious, then miserable. For it seems in such instants as if the two " selves " of modern psychology — the subjective and the objective — are wrenched apart in such critical moments as these; as if each exists on its own lines, follows its own course, and makes its own observations. . . .

Then, at a turn in the ride where the space broadened, she saw straight in front, perhaps a hundred and fifty yards ahead, the low belt of underwood that fringed the edge of the quarry into

which she had peered with Val and Austin a week
or two before, and beyond it the opposite cliff,
crowned with pines, black against the glowing sky.
And, simultaneously, two things happened; she
began to sob — at least one part of her began to sob
— and she saw on the right side Quentin's head
move up, first to the girths of her own mare, then
level with the mare's head, and Val's hand shot out
to clutch her reins.

Val was shouting, she remembered afterwards,
but neither then nor afterwards did she know what
he shouted. For she was overwhelmed by a sense
of relief; she leaned back on the dancing saddle,
half closing her eyes; the sickening sense of loneliness was gone; a male was beside her .   .   .   Val,
dear Val. She did not exactly consider whether or
no the two would go over the edge together, for she
did not really care.   .   .   .

Then came the reaction.   .   .   .   Val had seized
her reins by now, and the two beasts tore together,
jostling and impeding one another. She understood, and once more her spirit returned; she sat
up again, vivid and keen; once more she tugged at
the reins, throwing her strength chiefly to the
left.   .   .   .   The mare threw up her head; the
pace grew suddenly short and tempestuous.   .   .   .

And then her mare had stopped, shaking and

sweating, and Val, still holding the rein, was in front of her, leaning right forward over his horse's neck, staring at her, his face set and resolute, while Quentin capered gently. The underwood that fringed the edge of the quarry was still forty yards away.

"Thanks very much," said Gertie. . . . "Oh! Val. . . ."

The ride home was very tremulous. They rode at a foot's pace, and Val's belt was clasped round the mare's curb-chain. He had the other end in his left hand. They talked and retalked, over and over the same ground, as to the unexpectedness of the pheasant, the excuses that must be made for the mare, the rival advantages of long, steady pulls with pauses and of the sawing of the curb. Val supported the former, Gertie the latter.

Val himself was radiant. His manhood stood out from him like an aura. He glanced at her as he talked, and even in the deepening gloom of the woods she could see that his eyes shone and that his mouth alternately was stern and smiled. But they were both tremulous; their voices quavered now and then, and there were long silences.

Val told her that never had Quentin seemed so slow. He could not get him into a gallop. Quentin had slipped a little, it seemed, at the corner. Then he had got him into a gallop without difficulty.

He told her that his one fear was that Quentin would bolt too and get out of hand, and patting him, had praised him in extravagant language for keeping his head and being so sensible. He described it all admirably — his terror that the mare would fall and roll over; that he would not be in time; his vision of a rabbit that must have run out, it seemed to him, actually between Quentin's feet.

But he did not tell her — in fact, he was practically unconscious of it so long as he talked — that a vow had registered itself within him like an explosion, that if he missed her rein in that wild dash for it, sixty yards from the edge, he would pull up . . . for . . . for fear that he might do more harm than good. . . .

(III)

They sat together in the little entry to the south door, and the sound of the band came to them like celestial music. They had sat there now for a full five minutes without speaking.

They were perfectly retired here from the world, for Val had slipped a tall screen over the entrance. (She had pretended not to notice.)

Over there beyond the passages moved ordinary human beings — phantom personages of a world that had lost all interest. Austin was there somewhere, no doubt, priggish and prosaic, in his solemn suit of evening clothes. His mother still sat there, no doubt, with her stick beside her, talking to Professor Macintosh, in his brown velvet coat and his ridiculous frilled shirt with pearl buttons. The master of the house was there, John Medd of Medhurst, tall and unadorned, dancing for the third time, probably, with the flimsy and black-silk Miss Deverell; and the Merediths were there; and the Vicar and his wife, and old Lady Debenham, and the parties that had driven over from every house in the neighborhood, and the little doctor, and the rest of the crowd of guests that supposed themselves to be real and human. . . . Val had seen them all just now, had moved through them, smiling and speaking — he even condescended to that — until he had seen Her in Her blue dress, Her slender brown arms ending in long white gloves, Her bright dark eyes that had met his . . . talking to a fat, red Captain who had driven over with the Fergussons.

Then he had come up and led her away. Neither had spoken; they had danced together; then, as if by some strange sympathy, they had hesitated together as they came near the door. The rhythm of the feet had ceased; and they walked together, her hand in his arm, through the two parlours, set out with chrysanthemums, with their furniture pushed against the wall, into the passage by the billiard-room, round to the right, and so into the

south porch.   There he had drawn the screen across
the entrance.   .   .   .   They had not yet spoken.
The world was gone; only, now and again, the gusts
of music swept out from the hall.

He suddenly put out his hand and took hers.   It
lay in his passively, and he closed his other upon
it.   .   .   .
    " Gertie   .   .   ." he whispered.

Every pulse and fibre of his being seemed alive as
never before.   His imagination was drunk with joy
and courage.   He had saved her life to-day; his
mother had kissed him; his father had said three
words, looking at him kindly; Austin had eyed him
oddly.   And she herself, it had seemed to him, had
said little or nothing, had refused to meet his eyes,
yet had been conscious of him with a power that
thrilled his very life.   She seemed even now to be
trembling a little.
    His hand stole upon her arm and fumbled at the
buttons beneath her smooth elbow.   She withdrew
her arm suddenly, drawing a swift breath.
    " No   .   .   .   no; take it off," he whispered.
" I   .   .   .   I want to kiss your hand."
    Oh! it was clumsy love-making, I know that; but
it did very well for these two.   Gertie could have
taught him far more of the art than he knew, yet

she loved him for the very artlessness; it was in keeping with his courage, his virile honour, his simplicity, his clean boyishness; and it was with these that she was in love just now. He was her Man, not her Troubadour. He had ridden with her to-day; he had pulled up her mare, protected her and saved her. It had been the crown and climax of that intimacy that had deepened all to-day, that had begun — to her knowledge at least — on that summer morning when she had heard the sound of wheels and stolen to the window to look out at the boy who was to do such great things in Switzerland. She felt older than him now and again; she had smiled to herself when he sulked with Austin; she had laughed tenderly over him with his sister; and even now she was aware that that strange motherly instinct was mixed with her admiration. Yet just now she felt as young as he. She trembled to feel him so near to her. She pictured him strong, virile, courageous — her Man, I say, not a Troubadour.

And for him, this was the very ecstasy of all. This wonderful girl was, for these moments, in his possession. It was incredible, yet inevitable. How could it not be that a love like his should win? She was near him — nearer in this darkness than in the blaze of light in the hall, nearer than when he had her there, before the eyes of all.

So, presently, he had kissed her hand; and then,

in an instant, had his arms about her and his face
against her cheek.

(IV)

.   .   .   "Then that's settled," whispered Val ten
minutes later.   "We're absolutely engaged.   And
neither of us must say a word to anyone."

She began to whisper back rapidly and confusedly.

"My darling, it's no good," went on Val.   "We
can't have half-and-half things.   If we tell a
soul we shan't be allowed to see one another any
more.   And you're going to-morrow.   .   .   .   Oh,
Gertie!"

Absolute blankness seemed to open before him as
he contemplated this.   She was explicitly and objectively a part of his life, now that he had spoken.
Life was unthinkable without her.   .   .   .   And
after the desolation of Medhurst would come the
wilderness of Cambridge.   .   .   .

"You must come again at Easter," he said.

"Val dear, what's the good?   We   .   .   .   we
shan't be allowed ——"

His will rose up in resolution.

"I tell you we shall.   And if we're not we'll do
it without.   Tell me, Gertie, would you run away
with me if that was our only chance?"

There was no answer.   He could hear her breathing in the darkness; he could feel beneath his arm

her pulses beating; he could see a glimmer of her pale face beneath her heavy hair, itself darkness.

He burst out into whispered entreaties, drawing her closer, flinging his other arm about her too and clasping his hands. She seemed to him a child in his arms, so slender and unresisting was she, so determined and nerve-contracted was he.

"Oh! Gertie . . . say you would . . . say you would. I love you more than all the world. . . . I'd . . . I'd die for you . . . We shan't have to . . . it'll be all right. But tell me you would; tell me you would. . . ."

He slipped down on to his knees, still holding her, drawing her down to himself. Her face was very near his; he could perceive the faint perfume of her hair; her bare arm lay clenched across his hands. She struggled a little, almost gasping. . . . Then she grew passive.

And then the response came.

For an instant she tore herself free. Then he felt himself seized, and kissed, kissed, kissed, on mouth and eyes and forehead.

"Yes, I would, my darling; I would," she stammered. "I'd do anything for you, Val . . . anything. . . . Oh! my Val, I do love you . . . I'd die for you . . . you're . . . you're so strong, and so brave. . . ."

(v)

Professor Macintosh was describing to Miss Deverell at supper, now that Lady Beatrice was talking to her partner on the other side, the proper way to manage a runaway horse. It seemed that one had but to keep one's head, and to pull quite steadily and unagitatedly, talking, if possible, all the while in a soothing and reassuring manner. .Jerking was fatal. So was fright; as it was communicated so easily to the horse.

He looked up and saw a pair advancing from the door.

" Why, here come the hero and the heroine ! "

He rose from the table and began to wave his hands as if conducting a band.

" See the conquering hero comes! " he sang in a large resonant voice.

" There's a seat over there, my son," said Lady Beatrice. " Two. How late you are ! "

Val took Gertie to the chair, and then went to the sideboard for cold chicken and a jug of champagne-cup.

CHAPTER III

(1)

THE emotion called "calf-love" is not only beautiful, it is often singularly constant; and Val carried back with him to Cambridge a photograph in a tiny locket with a concealed catch, two much creased letters, and a very potent Ideal.

Her handwriting — rather large and bold — was dearer to him even than the photograph; the one was a mere reproduction, the other an emanation. Her hand had actually rested on the paper, the emphatic little dashes here and there were the direct outcome of her actual feeling; so he made a little parcel of the locket and the letters, had them sewn into oil-silk with an outer covering of embroidery, and carried the whole on a thin chain inside his shirt, like a scapular. It was kissed night and morning; and it rested between his fingers as he knelt by his bedside, having rediscovered since Christmas the exquisite luxury that can be obtained from prayers.

Such was one manifestation of the new Ideal; but it worked in a hundred other directions as well, some of which would have been strangely bewilder-

ing to Gertie herself, had she known of them. It
became a matter of common knowledge presently
that Val Medd did not appreciate certain kinds of
conversation, that he would not play poker for
more than halfpenny points, and that he was in
real danger of becoming a Sap. So mightily and
sweetly did this Ideal order all things, that even
Punctuality at Lectures came beneath its sway.
Certain pictures disappeared from Medd's walls and
were found by interested friends carefully packed
in a pile on the top of his bedroom wardrobe. He
still gave dinners in Jesus Lane, but they were
peaceful and orderly affairs. He frequented the
Pitt Club much as usual, but he straddled less across
the fire in the smoking-room, and read more maga-
zines in the reading-room. (Remonstrances were
useless.)

Interiorly, therefore, the Ideal triumphed even
more completely; and certain things henceforward
became impossible for him; and among these, his
old fear of Fear. It seemed to him sometimes, as
he reflected during those long intervals which a boy
in love will contrive to get for himself, merely
incredible that cowardice had ever had any relations
with him whatever. And even more than this;
for he came presently to recognise for the first time,
and without any emotion but that of a detached
astonishment, that he had not always behaved with

that fortitude which he would have wished. Of
course his repeated explanations and acts of faith in
himself had obscured his self-knowledge; and he
still believed that it was a proper prudence only
that had restrained him from attempting the ascent
of the Matterhorn; yet he did now begin to understand that it was not a purely physical and
irresistible force, independent of his own will, that
had caused him to cry out, "I can't . . . I
can't . . ." on the lower slope of the mountain.
So complete, however, was the sweep which his
Ideal had made of his imagination, that he could
face this memory without shame. It was simply
another Valentine Medd altogether who had done
this thing, not the lover of Gertie Marjoribanks.
Old things had passed away; all things were made
new.

Meanwhile a very pretty little plot engaged his
diplomatic powers, and he took his part in it with
considerable skill.

He began by writing two letters, one in each of
the first two weeks of the Lent term, to his sister
May, explaining in the first that he was sorry he had
given up doing his duty in this way since he had
left Eton. This first letter, too, was honestly unpre-
meditated; he was only conscious of a vague impulse
to be in closer touch, not with his sister, but with
Gertie's friend. The second letter was deliberately

guileful, and he ended it with a P. S.: " Why hasn't mother ever let you go abroad? I'd come with you like a shot any time you liked."

This produced, of course, a wail from May, saying how unfair it was that boys always had the best of everything, and inviting suggestions. And then Val unmasked one of his guns, said that he believed that Rome at Easter was perfectly charming, and why shouldn't he and May go there for a fortnight in the vacation? Would May see how the land lay? And then Val drew his breath hard, so to speak, and prayed and willed and rehearsed.

There followed a silence, and every day that passed at once deferred and rekindled hope. But his intuitions had been perfectly right and his trains of powder admirably laid. It was quite obvious that two girls would be better than one; that Gertie Marjoribanks, who knew French and Italian really well and was May's adored friend, was the proper person to be asked; so exactly ten days after Val's adroit remarks had left the Pitt Club letter-box, he sat smiling one morning, silent and preoccupied, over breakfast, to the indignation of Jim Waterbury, with whom he " kept," conscious that, tucked in between the kippers and the toast, was an incoherent torrent of delight from May announcing that consent had been given, and that on the Monday before Easter she and Gertie Marjoribanks and Val were to be permitted to start for Rome. One single trail of cloud dimmed the perfection of the sky, and that was the possibility, added in a postscript, that Austin might also be coming with them.

This, however, was comparatively of little importance. Even Austin could not destroy the delight of a fortnight's travel with Gertie. And she was coming to Medhurst again in the summer, and again at Christmas; and he was to shoot at a house where she was to be staying in September.

The necessary secrecy of the whole affair, too, added poignancy. It was delicious in a certain sense that Gertie could not be written to; for the two had resolved with excellent prudence not to write to one another more than once in six weeks. And, instead, there was the sense of a joy shared in silence, of two hearts exulting together without hint or sign to the one from the other. . . .

(II)

It is harder to describe Gertie's own attitude, since in her more complex emotions were at work. In the case of Val there was but one supreme white-hot fact — the fact of the ten times refined love of a young male to his mate — refined by romance, by heredity, and permitted to burn the more purely from the rather simple nature of the fuel. But the girl, younger in years, was not only more complex, but infinitely more experienced. Music and acting had been her outlet up to now, and these had increased her imaginative range as well as developing her powers of sensation. The two hearts were, one to the other, as a bow to a violin. It is the violin that actually holds the music, from the shrill cry of the treble to the languorous murmur of the bass; and if the bow shivers with the ecstasy of the touch, it is a single ecstasy and not a thousand. It is true that just now the music was being called out by the bow; that Gertie answered Val; that the boy was dominant; but it is no less true that the music was in the violin, not in the bow; and, though she played his tune just now with all her heart, that she was capable of other melodies as well. If the bow were to be broken another could be made; if the violin were broken its exact fellow could not be found.

Very well, then; it was one aspect of Val that for the present held her vision, and to that she bowed down her whole being, genuinely and even profoundly. She had got accustomed to him in the intimacy of Medhurst, and having worked through those superficial awkwardnesses and unfamiliarities that otherwise might have hindered her knowledge of him, had arrived at a stratum of his character — his romantic faculties and imaginations — which she thought were so well illustrated by his external appearance. He had a knightly sort of face, grim and pure, a down-bent nose, thin, compressed lips, a projecting chin, and crisp hair; he was long-limbed and sinewy. . . . And he had ridden after her at a gallop and saved her life. He stood to her, therefore, as a kind of gallant; he had made love ardently and simply; and so at last her rather rich nature had fastened upon him as a kind of Sir Percival, had decked him out in virtues such as those of courage and strength, and crowned him king.

She was behaving, then, as such girls will. At first she had carried the little ring he had sent her, set with one large turquoise, where he carried her locket, and it had risen and fallen with her breathing. Then, greatly daring, she had put it on, where she had worn it ever since. She too remembered him continually, when she woke and before she slept; she too locked her door sometimes, put out the light, and dreamed before the fire. All this was perfectly genuine; she loved to think of herself with him, obeying him, yielding to him, leaning upon him; she was magnificently aloof with the middle-aged Viscount, and wondered whether she showed signs of a secret sorrow; she acted and played with real passion. . . . She was more often silent; and she wrote to May every single day, laying it upon herself not to mention Val's name more than once a fortnight.

Now all this was perfectly simple and genuine; it was schoolgirl love, no doubt, but it was none the worse for that; it was perfectly sweet and fresh; it was the strongest emotion she had ever felt. There was no coquetry in it; to have given him pain would have given her agony; it was her deliberate and sincere resolve to carry through the engagement to its conclusion; she saw herself as his wife; as the mother of his children. She proposed to grow aged and silver-haired in his love service, and exactly to resemble Lady Beatrice Medd thirty years hence. And so forth.

But her complexity vented itself in her consciousness of herself as performing those duties, and in an idea that she had a wider range than Val. In him, all other emotions had vanished in his love; in her, other emotions ministered to love, but preserved their own identity. For example, she wondered whether, as has been said, she showed signs of a secret sorrow; and Val never wondered at all — he would have been miserable and ashamed at the thought that such a thing could possibly happen to himself. Two months ago he might have so wondered; now his complexity was gone. Or, again, she formed little pictures of herself as " managing " him; Val thought of nothing but of loving her. In

fact, she flattered herself, as feminine minds will, by
dwelling upon his dear simplicity, while Val thought
nothing of her qualities and all of her. Lastly, she
measured her love to him by the sacrifices that she
was so gladly making for him (the Viscount, for
instance). She wondered whether it was conceivable that Providence might arrange for Val's inherit-
ing of Medhurst, whereas Val forgot to think of
sacrifices at all.

Here, then, the two were; eighty miles apart as
we measure space, utterly together as both sincerely
believed. Again and again Val, brooding happily
over the fire after a lonely dinner, watched her in
imagination as she lay down to sleep. . . .
Again and again Gertie, lying down to sleep,
watched Val in imagination brooding over the fire.
. . . They were boy and girl indeed. But they
were none the worse for that.

So much for Psychology.

CHAPTER IV

(1)

"THEN to-morrow," said May, with an air of great decision, "we'll see the sunset from the Pincian for the last time. And on Wednesday everyone'll dawdle and pack."

They had done all the proper things in the proper way — St. Peter's twice, the Catacombs, the Forum, a public audience, tea in the Piazza Spagna, St. Mary Major, the models and the almond blossom on the steps of the Trinità, St. John Lateran. They had made the proper remarks about unshaven priests, about the scarlet German seminarians; they had gravely attended Sung Matins in the little Gothic church of All Saints in the Via Babnino on their two Sundays, at eleven, in best clothes; having previously talked out loud during high mass at St. Peter's, sitting on camp-stools; they had cheered the little king as he sat on a high seat in a dog-cart beside his tall wife; they had agreed with an English clergyman that Cardinal Merry del Val was an unscrupulous and incompetent diplomatist. They

had conducted themselves, in fact, harmlessly and
decorously, and vaguely felt that their horizons were
enlarged.

And of real Rome, of course, they had seen nothing at all. Figures had moved before them — the
insolent light-blue cloaks of soldiers who resembled
French tram-conductors; seedy-looking priests who
went hurriedly and softly with downcast eyes; coun-
trymen — real ones, not the sham ones of Trinità —
asleep in little canopied carts that roared over the
cobblestones; endless companies of handsomely
bearded bourgeois clerks and tradesmen, pacing
slowly up and down the Corso and eyeing brutally
every female figure in range. They had seen crumbling ruins against the sky; little churches, rather
dingy, looking squeezed and asleep, between new
white houses with balconies and uncountable windows; and they had understood absolutely less than
nothing (since they had misconceived the whole)
of all that their eyes and ears had taken in. They
had believed themselves, for example, to be by nature on the side of the Government and the new
hotels and the trams and the clean white squares;
they had not understood that that which they dismissed as ecclesiasticism and *intransigeance* was the
only element with which they had anything in common, and that this, and this only, had developed
their aristocracy in the past as well as being its only

hope for the future. They had not understood that all this, in terms of Italy, was a translation of their own instincts and circumstances at home.

The two lovers had behaved with marvellous discretion. Austin, for instance, saw plainly that something was up, and was not furnished with the faintest handle for rebuke. He found himself allowed to escort Gertie, to hand her into the little cabs, and to give her useful and accurate information, to his heart's content; and scarcely once had Val been otherwise than reasonable and friendly — he seemed quite content to pair off with May and was hardly ever irritable and fractious.

For the bliss that the boy went through was occupation enough for him. The days went by in a delicious dream; since, with the understanding that was now so perfectly established, it contented him quite tolerably to know that Gertie was next door to him, sat opposite to him at table, and, now and then, caught his eyes. Of course they had interviews and exchanged sentences — in dark churches, on terraces; again and again the two were separated from the rest, yet always naturally and sometimes almost unnoticeably; and for one delicious hour they had sat together on the balconies of their respective bedrooms after dark, one low railing only between them, looking out on to the garden as the full moon rose. . . . But it was all done with an intense and strenuous natural air, which, if it would not have deceived elders, was quite enough for Austin and May.

It was their last evening but two, however; and the strain of living up to the Ideal, coupled with the fact that the sands were running out, was beginning to have its effect on Val. He was a little silent this evening — silent with a touch of feverishness.

They had been playing bridge since dinner, at a little table in the corner of the big hall where smoking was permitted, when May, putting up the cards again into their leather case, had announced the Pincian for the next evening. (The Vatican galleries were to be inspected in the morning and the Palatine in the afternoon.)

"I've got to see a man at the Embassy," announced Austin; "I think I'd better go in the afternoon." Austin was a little too much pleased with "the man at the Embassy," and had mentioned him several times. He had just begun to be aware that importance in the world was as valuable as at Eton. Val sat back in silence and took out his cigarette-case. May stood up.

"Well, I'm off to bed. . . . All right. We'll settle other things in the morning. . . . Coming, Gertie?"

Gertie rose obediently, and Val indulged himself with a good look at her.

She really was startlingly pretty; and the hum of talk at the next table died away as she stood up. May was extremely ordinary beside her.

For Gertie's southern blood seemed less exotic here in Rome. She was in the very height of health; and this tearing about in the Easter sun of Italy had deepened the wholesome pallor of her face. She was in white this evening, with a blue flower in her hair, and suggestions of embroidery here and there upon her dress; she carried on her white shoulders a scarf, as the evenings were chilly; and her dark eyes blazed with tiredness and pleasure. She wore Val's turquoise on her finger. She looked upright and bright and keen — as she nodded to the boys, and moved off behind May with that admirable arrogance that a certain kind of breeding and life seems to confer. .   .   .

" Play you montana," said Val suddenly.

Austin sank down again, with just a touch of indulgence that Val sometimes found trying.

" Well, one game, if you like," he said.

Montana is perhaps the most trying game invented by man — to temperaments, at any rate, that are in the least degree nervous. It is a kind of

double patience; but the excitement lies in the fact
that the packs which are gradually built up are common to both sides, with result that the virtue of patience is perhaps the last one required. One needs
quick sight, unerring judgment, immense decision of
character, ruthlessness, and, above all, a kind of
intoxicated yet clear-headed dash such as a cavalry-
leader might need. There come moments when the
losing player, fascinated and paralysed, has all that
he can do not to cry out that his opponent must be
cheating, as he sees cards, fired with the speed of
Maxim bullets, flying to their several places. There
come moments when the winning player, after such
a run, when his cards have shifted and melted like
magic, has all that he can do not to laugh and triumph aloud. It is practically impossible to smoke,
so swift and violent is the game; it is sometimes
difficult even to breathe aright. . . .

Twenty minutes later Val, a little flushed, swept
up his cards and began to reshuffle.

"That's nine points to you," he said. "It was
that knave I dropped, you know."

"I said only one game," said Austin. "I'm——"

"Oh! that's rot. It was a wretched game. . . .
That knave did me. We must have one more."

Austin lifted his eyebrows with a deliberate
weariness. He took up his cards.

"Well, a short one. Up to twenty."

Val said nothing, but began to deal out his preliminary seven heaps.

Contempt was never very far away from Austin's view of Val. It was, as has been hinted before, the main sort of self-protection that he allowed himself. Certainly he was superior to Val in practically everything. He rode better, shot better, had been more successful in work, had been in " Pop " at Eton, and on the Committee of the Pitt Club at Cambridge. But Val was never very far behind him, and occasionally shot up with a kind of fitful brilliance, as, for instance, when he had stopped Gertie's runaway horse. He had too a kind of interior intensity which Austin lacked — a fervour and a positiveness that might be dangerous some day. For Austin's peace of mind, then, an arranged attitude towards Val was necessary; he must be self-controlled and modest, where Val tended to be spasmodic and boastful; and together with these ingredients there was added, as has been said, a touch of contempt.

Take card-games, for example. At purely intellectual games Austin was undoubtedly the superior; at games which required dash and speed Val won at least as often as he lost. But Val, Austin reflected, showed too much keenness for absolutely good form; he was apt to sparkle too much when he won and to be too silent when he lost. Montana was a kind of symbol between them. Val won perhaps three times out of four; and it was necessary therefore to allow him to play this sometimes when he had been unfortunate at bridge. This restored serenity to the atmosphere and gave Austin a sense of generous rectitude.

They played in silence for a few minutes; and indeed, with the exception of sudden cries and exclamations, it is difficult to play montana except in silence. Val began well; his cards fell right; and he called for a truce to order something to drink. Austin regarded him coldly, and determined to win.

"I think *mine*," said Val firmly, producing a crumpled nine of hearts from beneath Austin's; the two had dashed upon the uncovered eight almost exactly at the same moment.

Obviously it was Val's. Austin registered one more resolution, and drew his chair an inch nearer. Ten minutes later one of those developments appeared which occasionally do assert themselves inexplicably. Every card of Austin's fell right; every card of Val's wrong. Twice Val flew into a breach a fraction of a second late. . . . There was a whirling of hands and cards. . . . Austin's heaps vanished like snow in sunshine. Val fumbled badly; dropped a card; and when he had it again Austin's heaps had gone.

" That was a pretty good run," remarked Austin, flushed with victory, beginning to push back his chair. (It was plain that the " twenty " was more than reached.)

Now Val was in that indescribably irritated state that games do seem sometimes to produce in their players. He was the more annoyed as he considered himself Austin's superior in montana.

" We generally use only one hand," he said in a head-voice, beginning to rake his widespread cards together.

" That's what I thought," said Austin, perceiving that war was declared.

" I thought I saw you use two," pursued Val, with the same air of deadly detachment. " When I was picking up the card I had dropped."

" You thought wrong then," said Austin. " I did nothing of the sort."

Val smiled deliberately and carefully with one side of his mouth.

Anger rose within Austin like a torrent. He looked quickly from side to side, and saw that the room was nearly empty. Then he stood up, leaning forward with his hands upon the table.

" You shouldn't play games if you can't keep your temper," he said in a sharp undertone. " To accuse me of cheating is simply ridiculous; and you know it."

Then he wheeled away without a word, seeing Val's pale face flush suddenly into fury.

(II)

When a storm breaks after a prolonged drought, it is usually rather a severe one; since weather averages must be preserved at all costs; and the quarrel of the two brothers took the same course. They had not openly quarrelled or insulted one another for at least three months. Val had been at Cambridge and Austin in London nearly all that time, and there simply had been no opportunity at all until the journey; as has been remarked, Val's Ideal had kept him pacific ever since they had left Victoria Station.

The girls, of course, noticed nothing next morning, except that the two were alternately polite to one another and unconscious of one another's presence; but for all that the fires burned deeply. Austin kept on telling himself that Val was an ill-mannered cub who could not keep his temper, and Val kept on telling himself that Austin had cheated (though he knew perfectly well he had not), and that he was simply impossible. . . .

They inspected the Vatican galleries in the morning, with their sense of duty more apparent than that of beauty, and got home in unusually good time for lunch. But they set out in two cabs — Austin and Gertie together in the one, Val and May in the other — resolutely enough, at half-past two.

They were more polite than ever to one another on the Palatine — polite with irony as visible as a dagger-blade among flowers. Val offered Austin his Baedeker, and begged him to read aloud the information, as he read so well; and Austin returned with many apologies a small tin match-box which he noticed fall out of Val's pocket as he pulled out his handkerchief. Gertie eyed the two sharply once or twice, and then was more affectionate than ever to May.

To tell the truth, all four were becoming a little worn out with sight-seeing. It is not easy in the Italian climate to take an intelligent interest in antiquities and churches, every day for a fortnight, from ten to twelve and two to five, without showing signs of weariness or irritation; and an atmosphere of relief became very visible as they emerged again at last by the Arch of Titus.

"I say, it isn't four yet," said Austin. . . .

May sighed.

"I can't help it," she said. "And I'm just dying for tea. Let's go home and have it, and then walk up the Pincian afterwards before sunset. I'm nearly dead."

"Our cabs are waiting over there," said Val, nodding towards the Coliseum.

Something of regret, however — in fact, a real and inexplicable depression — came on him as he drove back with Gertie. (They had changed partners this time.) It seemed to him as if the evening and the morrow that still remained to them, the journey home together, and the three or four days that Gertie would spend at Medhurst, were little better than mockeries. . . . He said so, sitting carefully apart in his corner in the little victoria, lest the others should turn and see them.

"Gertie," he said, "I feel beastly. Only one more day here, and then that vile Cambridge." (It was sweet to them both to talk in this way — as husband and wife might talk, without endearments. They had discovered its peculiarly exquisite aroma during the journey out.) She assumed the maternal pose.

"My dear boy, don't be ridiculous. We've had a heavenly time; and there's . . . there's nearly a week more altogether."

Val sighed again, looking rather cross.

"Is anything the matter between you and Austin?"

"Oh, yes!" said Val wearily. "He can't behave himself at cards. And I told him so."

A bubble of laughter broke from the girl.

"Oh! you boys," she said.

"Austin really won't do at all, you know," went on Val, with the air of forty-five finding fault with seventeen. "He cannot keep his temper."

"Tell me what happened."

"I asked him whether he hadn't used two hands by mistake at montana. Lots of people do, you know. And he flew into a violent temper and became offensive."

"And you?"

"I said nothing whatever."

"Oh! you boys," said Gertie again. "Really, you're old enough to have got over that sort of thing."

"I can't help it if Austin behaves like a cad," pursued Val, intent on his wrongs, and really not conscious that he had misrepresented anything. Had he not told the literal truth?

"I think you're rather annoying sometimes to him, you know, Val," went on Gertie, seriously. (She happened to remember at this moment how great a woman's influence ought to be for good.)

Val shrugged his shoulders slightly and spread his hands in a little Italian gesture.

"Oh! I must put up with him, I know. But he's the kind of person you can't ask favours from, you know. I asked him to play last night, and this is the result."

"But you won't quarrel any more with him?"

"Oh! I shall be polite to him all right. But, as I say, no more favours from him."

CHAPTER V

(1)

"YES," pronounced Austin, after a prolonged and judicial look, " it's very wonderful."

" That's settled then," murmured Val under his breath.

The four were standing together on the top terrace of the Pincian at sunset.

They had been told by the English chaplain that this was one of the things to be seen; and May, at least, who really wished to take an intelligent interest in everything, had gathered that an appreciation of it was one of the marks of the initiate; that while ordinary Philistines just charged about St. Peter's and the Catacombs, the truly understanding soul came and looked at Rome from the Pincian at sunset; so she had insisted on a second visit here.

What they saw from that place was certainly remarkable and beautiful, indeed " very wonderful," as Austin had most correctly observed. They stood on the very edge of a terraced precipice, their hands

223

resting on a balustrade, looking out over the whole
of medieval Rome bathed in a dusty glory of blue
and gold; the roofs, broken here and there by domes
and spires, stretched completely round the half-
circle to right and left, in a kind of flat amphitheatre
of which the arena, crawling with cabs and pedes-
trians, was the Piazza del Popolo, where Luther
walked after saying mass in the church on the right.
All this was lovely enough — the smoke went up
straight, delicate as lawn against the glorious evening sky; cypresses rose, tall and sombre, beneath
them, and barred the sky far away like blots of
black against an open furnace-door; and sounds
came up here, mellow and gentle — the crack of
whips, bells, cries, the roll of wheels, across the
cobbles of the Piazza. But that to which both eye
and thought returned again and again was the vast
bed of purple shadow, lit with rose, that dominated
the whole, straight in front, and is called the dome
of St. Peter's. It rested there, like a flower descending from heaven, and at this very instant
the sun, hidden behind it, shone through the windows, clean through from side to side, making it
as unsubstantial as a shell of foam. It hung there,
itself the symbol of a benediction, as if held by an
invisible thread from the very throne of God, supported from below, it seemed, by earthly buildings
that had sprung up to meet it, and now pushed and

jostled that they might rest beneath its shadow.
Beyond, again, fine as lacework, trees stood up,
minute and delicate and distant, like black feathers
seen against firelight. Only, this firelight, deepening to rose and crimson as they looked, filled the
whole sky with flame, satisfying the eye as water a
thirsty throat.

This then was what they saw. They would be
able to describe all this later, and even, after consulting Baedeker, to name the domes and towers
that helped to make up the whole — the white dome
of the Jewish synagogue, for instance, that mocked
and caricatured the gentle giant beyond, like a
street-boy imitating a king. They would be able
to wave their hands, for lack of description. . . .
They would be able to rave vaguely about Italy and
its colours. Austin would be able to draw striking
contrasts between modern Rome and ancient Athens
(which he had conscientiously visited in the company of Eton masters two years ago). And they
both would be able to show that they belonged to
the elect company of the initiates, in that they would
say that what impressed them far more than St.
Peter's or St. John Lateran was the view of Rome
at sunset from the Pincian.

Now of course there is a great deal more to see
from the Pincian at sunset than what has been set

down here. It is the history of the human race, and
the love of God, and the story of how One " came
to His own and His own received Him not," and
the significance of the City of the World, and the
conjunction of small human affairs with Eternity,
and their reconciliation with it through the airy
shell of foam which, as a matter of realistic fact,
consists of uncountable tons of masonry — in fact,
the reconciliation of all paradoxes, and the solution
of all doubts, and the incarnation of all mysteries,
and the final complete satisfaction of the Creator
with the creature and of the creature with the Creator — all these things, with their correlatives, find
voice and shape and colour in the view of Rome
from the Pincian at sunset. For here, where the
watchers stand, is modern Italy, gross, fleshly, complacent, and blind. There are white marble busts
here, of bearded men and decadent poets, and wholly
unimportant celebrities, standing in rows beneath
the ilexes like self-conscious philosophers; and chat-
tering crowds surge to and fro; and men eye women,
and women, with their noses in the air, lean back in
rather shabby carriages and pretend not to see the
men; and the seminarians go by, swift processions
of boys, walking rapidly, as troops on alien ground,
with the sleeves of their sopranos flying behind
them, intent on getting back to their seminaries
before *Ave Maria* rings; and belated children scream

and laugh — thin-legged, frilled children, with peevish eyes, who call one another Ercole and Louise
and Tito and Elena; and bourgeois families in silk
and broadcloth, with the eyes of Augustus and
Poppæa and the souls of dirty shrimps, pace
solemnly about, arm in arm, and believe themselves
fashionable and enlightened and modern. All these
things and persons are here, and it is from this
world and from this standpoint that one looks back
and forward through the centuries — back to the
roots that crept along the Catacombs, that pushed
up stems in the little old churches with white
marble choirs, and that blossomed at last into that
astounding, full-orbed flower that hangs there, full
of gold and blue and orange and sunlight; and on,
from that flower to the seed it is shedding in every
land, and to the Forest of the Future. . . .

(II)

It is probable that Val was the only one of the
four who perceived that there was more than he
actually saw (if we except Austin, who was already
drawing mental comparisons between this view and
that of the Acropolis at Athens, to the advantage,
of course, of the latter; for this one had reached
precisely that stage of mental development in which
it appears truly broad-minded to prefer Paganism
to Christianity under all possible circumstances).

Yet Val could put nothing of it into words, even to himself. But he was strung up by various emotions — by his proximity to Gertie, whose hand was almost touching his upon the balustrade; by his knowledge that the day after to-morrow they would have to leave for England by the eight o'clock train in the morning; by the quarrel with Austin, which still gently vibrated his heart-strings — by all these emotions acting upon a highly strung and imaginative nature.

Gertie was feeling nothing particular, except a general sense of being surrounded by extreme beauty, and a sensation, half of pleasure, half of angry and resentful disgust, towards a young man with a moustache who was staring straight at her from an abutment of the terrace not a dozen yards away. She recognized him also as having stared at her before, when she went to post a letter at S. Silvestro after lunch. . . .

But Val really did feel something vague and tumultuous as he stared out at the view, quite unconscious of the young man. He felt that emotions and sensations were all about him — suggestions which he could not hear and glimpses which he could not see. He felt that all this meant more than it said; that there were innuendoes and hints which were too subtle, prophecies and predictions shouted too largely to be articulate. . . .

He turned away at last with a jerk, annoyed that he could not understand.

"Let's have a look from the terrace below," he said to Gertie; "on the way down."

The view from the terrace below is good, but it is not so good, although there is a charm in the flatter angle from which the city is seen. It was empty when they reached it, and Val stood a moment staring with Gertie beside him. Then he remembered the other two, and wondered if they were following. It was difficult to make out their heads in the frieze of faces that fringed the parapet above, and he went a dozen steps to one side, in the direction from which they themselves had come down, to see if they were following; and as he glanced up Austin and May appeared at the head of the steps.

"Oh! there you are," cried May, waving to him.

Val nodded; and as he turned back to go to Gertie, he saw a young man come towards her from the opposite side, raising his hat, and smiling so that he showed an even row of white teeth. He was holding a flower in his fingers which he had evidently just taken from his buttonhole. Then he kissed this flower and held it out, saying something.

Val stared a moment, wondering whether the girl had by any chance suddenly come across a friend; then, as he went forward, Gertie took a swift step

towards him, and in her white face he saw terror
and anger.

" He . . . he spoke to me . . . he insulted me," she said in a harsh, frightened whisper.

Val stared at her, not wholly taking in the situation.

" Who? . . . I don't understand."

" That man," she said. " He's been following me
. . . since this morning. He . . . he insulted me."

Val's heart beat suddenly and furiously at the
base of his throat, and a mist seemed to pass between his eyes and the brilliant air. An enormous
emotion seized him, which he thought was anger.

He took a couple of steps forward. . . .

" How . . . how dare you, sir? " he stammered roughly, in English.

The young man stood, apparently unperturbed,
still smiling, and holding his rejected flower delicately between his thin brown fingers. He was
smartly, but not extravagantly dressed; he was
obviously not of the shopkeeper class. Val noticed
even then that he seemed to be a gentleman.

The young man made a little gesture with his
cane, still smiling, as if to wave Val out of the way,
and again extended slightly his flower. . . .

A gasp broke from Gertie behind; and Val,
impelled partly by a sudden anger that burst upwards

at the contemptuous slight he had received, and
partly by a sense that something violent was expected
of him, with a quick breath stepped forward and
slapped the brown smiling face with all his force,
across the cheek nearest to him. . . .

It was amazing how swiftly there was a group
about them.

The Italian had changed in an instant from a
smiling gallant into a tiger-cat. He had sprung
back at the blow, and had seemed to hesitate, with
clenched fists and blazing eyes — (he had dropped
his malacca cane at the onslaught) — to hesitate
whether to fly at Val, all teeth and claws, or to assault him more reputably. The flower lay on the
middle step between them, like a spot of blood.

Val stood waiting, prepared to repel attack, and
beginning to wonder, as his anger, relieved by the
blow, sank swiftly, whether or no he had done
the right thing. He was conscious, the instant after
the blow, while he yet waited for the riposte, that a
babble of voices and cries had broken out from the
frieze of heads that looked down from the upper
terrace. But he stood there, a fine figure of gallantry, upright, white-faced and determined.

Then, almost before the Italian had recovered his
balance, steps tore down the stairs on either side,
and a crying, babbling group surrounded the three;

for Austin had turned the corner as the blow was
given and had dashed forward to his brother's side.

It was difficult for Austin to remember afterwards
the exact course which events took. He had been
just in time to see Val's hand whirl out and to hear
the sound of the slap; and then, telling May to go
straight home with Gertie, was at Val's side in a
moment. There was no time to ask explanations,
and indeed, these were not necessary. Three or four
men were by the Italian's side an instant later, having run down the steps from above; and one Austin
noticed particularly — a small, soldierly-looking
man, with fierce grey moustaches, who seized the
young man by the arm, though with a certain air of
deference all through, and began both to soothe and
question in torrential Italian. Behind them the
group increased rapidly.

Then the young man seemed to recover himself.
He pushed the old soldier aside, and, his face red-
dened on the left cheek by Val's blow, came a step
forward.

"You are an Englishman, sir?" he asked, with a
strong accent; ". . . a gentleman?"

Val nodded.

The Italian, who was recovering his self-com-
mand with extraordinary swiftness, stooped and
took up his cane. Then he lifted it.

"Is this necessary, sir?"

Val recoiled half a step at the suggested threat.

"What's all this?" cried Austin sharply.

Val turned a white face on him.

"The . . . the beast insulted Gertie . . . he offered her a flower."

The Italian lowered his stick, and said something rapidly to the soldier. Then he took off his hat politely, and slipped away into the group behind, who made way for him to pass. The soldier stepped forward.

"Your . . . your carta, sir," he said.

"He wants your card," said Austin. "Summons for assault. Make haste, Val. . . . We don't want another scene."

Val fumbled in his pockets — the soldier waiting politely, stroking his moustache and eyeing the two Englishmen carefully — and drew out his cigarette-case. He gave his card to Austin.

"The card, sir," said Austin in tolerable Italian, holding it out. "And we are staying at the Hotel des Etrangers."

The soldier took it, glanced at it, and put it in his pocket. Then he drew out his own case, and took out his own card and offered it. It was inscribed with the name of General Antonio Villanuova, and was surmounted by a small coronet. Austin took it, trying to assume the same competent and assured air as the other. Then the two lifted their hats; while the soldier's heels clicked together as he bowed; and the next moment Austin had Val by the arm, and was hurrying him away through the crowd and down the steps towards their hotel.

(III)

"Now tell me the whole thing," he said, as soon as they had got clear of the people and were striding down the steep slope.

Val related it, his voice shaking and quavering still with excitement.

"So I slapped his dirty face for him," he added.

"It's a confounded nuisance," said Austin. "Now there'll be a summons and the devil to pay. And Lord knows when we shall get away."

(He was faintly conscious that this language lacked repose; but he couldn't bother to pick his words just now. There was annoyance also in his mind at the fact that it was Val who was the occasion of the trouble.)

"I don't care a damn!" exclaimed Val. "I'd do it again twenty times over . . . the dirty blackguard!"

He seemed all a-shake again with excitement now that the crisis was past.

"Well, if we can slip away the day after to-morrow before they can take any steps —— Why, there are the girls waiting for us!"

Something of Val's old dreams seemed to come true as he walked back to the hotel in silence with Gertie and the others. He said nothing, nor did she; they walked together without speaking, while Austin summed up the situation in terse sentences, and speculated hopefully on the slowness of Italian justice.

"There wasn't a blessed *gendarme* in sight," he said. "Why, in England we'd have half a dozen policemen in two minutes, all taking notes."

"I think it's scandalous," said May energetically. . . . "Oh, Val! . . . If you'd been stabbed."

There was no doubt as to the sentiments of the company, and Val found it all wonderfully sweet. For once, at any rate, he had behaved with decision and courage, and all for the sake of and in the presence of the Beloved. Stopping the runaway horse was nothing to this. . . . He walked in a dream of delight across the cobbled square, rather shaky still, but conscious of his manhood. His pulses tingled to his finger-tips and beat in his head a joyous rhythm. The suggestion that he might have been stabbed added to his delight: he had faced that too, then, unflinching: everyone knew that

Italians produced stilettos on the smallest provo-
cation.

He strode on then, confident and exultant, welcoming rather than otherwise the thought of police-
court proceedings: it would underline and emphasise
what he had done.   He eyed a cabman who shouted
at him to get out of the way, proudly and disdain-
fully: he went past the hall-porter, standing laced
cap in hand, as if unconscious of his presence.

There was one delicious moment at the top of the
stairs.   May and Austin were in front, still talking;
and Gertie turned round full and looked at him.
Her eyes were bright as if with tears, and her parted
lips moved: she gave him her hand, and he kissed it
with quite an Italian air.

(IV)

Dinner was a joyous affair that night.   The band
was playing out of sight in the winter garden; and
the four had a round table to themselves, placed
where in the pauses of conversation the music
sounded clear and inspiriting, like an undercurrent
of gallant thought.   They talked briskly and excitedly, conscious of adventure; and they rallied Val
cheerfully on the probability of an escort appearing
before the ice-pudding, armed cap-à-pie with revol-
vers, swords, and breastplates, to conduct him to a
dungeon.

"The guests will rise," cried Gertie, "like a stage crowd; the band will cease and the lights go down. Then I shall shriek and faint in red limelight which will change slowly to blue. Gongs will then begin to sound, and ——"

"And I shall fling myself upon Val," remarked May, "and say that they shall only reach him over his sister's dead body."

"Don't talk so loud," said Austin vehemently. "There's a clergyman over there ——"

"He's an Archdeacon," said Gertie. "He puts on his gaiters for dinner. He shall advance with upraised hand to denounce the tyranny of a priest-ridden monarchy."

Val listened with growing delight. It seemed to him that this manner of treating an arrest that seemed really quite possible was entirely worthy of Englishmen in Italy. This potty little country, it appeared to him, could really not be taken seriously. And, at any rate, it was good to play the fool. He would play the fool, he determined, even if the comic-opera *gendarme* did arrive.

But ice-pudding came and was eaten undisturbed; and then cheese-straws, and finally some excellent fruit; and then Austin leaned back and ordered Chartreuse for four.

"To drink Val's health," said May.

This was solemnly done. May made a short speech, without rising, proposing the health of the preserver of all female sufferers, " coupled with the health of our fellow-countryman, Mr. Valentine Medd, who on this auspicious occasion " and then May laughed.

But Val, glancing round the eyes of the three, caught and held an instant those of Gertie.

" Don't be long," said Austin, as they got up from the table. " We'll keep a table till you come down."

" We've just five things to pack which we bought to-day," said May. " There's some lace, and . . ."

" Oh! go on, and make haste," said Val. " And Gertie's my partner to-night."

Their table was vacant, and Val plunged into a deep chair beyond it in the corner, whence he could watch for Gertie's coming. He loved to think of the moment when she would come rustling across the hall, and the heads turned to look at her. . . . He lit a cigarette.

" Seriously," said Austin, " if there is a row I'll go straight to my man at the Embassy. He's half Italian himself, you know, and he'll know their little ways."

" Oh! that's bosh," said Val. " It'll be just a fine to-morrow, if there is anything. But they won't dare to do it. The blackguard'll funk the story coming out. He looked like a gentleman, too."

" Well, but —— Hullo! here's the porter coming. I wonder if it's us he wants."

Val was conscious of a faint quickening of his heart as the great man, carrying his gold-laced cap, threaded his way between the tables. In his other hand he carried a salver.

" By George, it is! ——" he said.

The man came up to them and extended the salver, disclosing with his thumb a card printed with a name and a small coronet. He held it impartially between the two brothers.

" Which of us is it for?"

" For Mr. Valentine Medd," said the man.

Val took it, read it, and passed it to Austin.

" It's the General," he said. (His lips were gone dry and he licked them.)

" Look here," said Austin, getting up; " I'd better go instead. I know more Italian. They've probably come to apologise; and one must be decently polite if they have. Where is the gentleman?"

" There are two gentlemen, sir. They're in the little *sallone* next the hall-door."

" Very good," said Austin.

He nodded to Val and went.

(v)

Val roused himself and sat up five minutes later, as the two girls came threading their way, exactly as he had pictured, between the tables. The heads did turn to look at Gertie, but she seemed wholly unconscious. Her face was radiant and smiling.

" At last," she said. . . . " Where's Austin? "

" The beggars have come to apologise," growled Val. " He's interviewing them."

" My gracious! . . . Well, we'll soon hear. Let's play jacoby till he comes."

Val had had a very bad five minutes. Certain vague suspicions that he had resolutely silenced before recurred to him with great intensity. He refused, even now, to consider them seriously; but they were there. He had reflected that Italians were a queer people, with queer ideas. . . . One never knew quite what view they would take of things. . . .

But with the coming of the two girls things looked better. They brought naturalness and familiarity with them, and the home atmosphere; and Val dealt for jacoby with considerable verve, commenting once or twice on Austin's probable adventures.

But the game was doomed never to be played,

for as Gertie selected her card, once more the hall-porter came threading his way among the tables.

"Eh?" said Val, as the man suddenly stood opposite him.

"Mr. Medd. . . . he wishes to see you, sir."

Val stood up, commanding himself with an effort.

"Well, I suppose I must go and receive it in person," he said. "Don't look at my hand, anybody, while I'm away."

The man led him, not to the *sallone* next the hall-door, but to a second smaller one which opened out of it by glass doors. He pushed the door open and Val went in. Austin was standing there, looking strangely pale and agitated.

"Look here," he said sharply, glancing to see that the two doors were closed, "we're in a mess. Don't talk loud; they're in the next room."

"Who are?"

"That blasted General and another chap. . . . It seems the chap whose face you slapped is a Prince, or next door to one. . . ."

He indicated a card lying on the table. Val took it up; it was inscribed with the name of Don Adriano Valentini-Mezzia, and was topped by a crown and a crowd of flourishes. Very small, down in the corner, ran the words " Palazzo Valentini-Mezzia, Roma."

"He's a younger brother of the Prince," said Austin.

"Well?"

"Well, there's the devil of a row. I told them plainly what I thought — that if brothers of Princes go about insulting English ladies they must expect to have their faces slapped. They shrugged their shoulders at that, and said something. Good Lord! I wish I was better at Italian."

"But what the devil do they want?" said Val vindictively. "Haven't they come to apologise?"

"No, they haven't," Austin almost shouted suddenly. "They've come to bring his challenge to you — a duel. And if you don't fight they swear he'll horsewhip you publicly. It's perfectly outrageous."

Val sat down. Then he took out his cigarette-case. He had still enough sense to notice that his hands were shaking too violently for him to take out a cigarette, and he remained still, balancing the case in his hands.

"Are you serious?"

"Serious! . . . Why. . . . Good Lord! They know all about us, I tell you. They even know we're going by the eight o'clock train on Thursday; so, to suit our convenience, they say, they've arranged a meeting for to-morrow morning at five. They've got some beastly garden somewhere, where they say we shall be undisturbed. And they have the cheek to ask whether the arrangements are satisfactory."

"What did you say?"

"I told them to go to hell. I said that Englishmen didn't fight duels. I said they fought with their fists or not at all. I said I'd go to the Ambassador."

"And what did they say?"

"They laughed. They said that that was not usual in Italy, and that if English gentlemen chose to honour Italy with their presence, they must further honour her by conforming to her customs. They put it all so infernally well and politely too."

Austin was completely bewildered. He knew nothing whatever of Italian ways, and knew that he knew nothing. All the Englishman in him told him to flatly refuse such ridiculous suggestions, but the Medd in him equally strongly asserted that one must behave like a gentleman. He had thought of telephoning to his friend at the Embassy, but then again he was wondering as to whether this was a decent thing to do or not. . . .

"What do you think?" asked Val in a dry voice that sounded oddly in his own ears.

"I don't know what to think. . . ."
(Austin began to bite his nails — a thing he was

always most particular not to do.) . . . "I don't know what to think. It seems to me all a lot of tommy-rot, of course, but one doesn't know. . . . He's the brother of a Prince, you know, and he ought to know."

Val lifted his head as if to speak, but Austin's next words silenced him.

"And one doesn't like to ask anybody. It looks like sneaking and trying to get off. . . . Look here; will you come and see them yourself?"

Val swallowed in his throat.

"Wait," he said. "Did they say anything about weapons?"

"Yes, rapiers."

"Wait," said Val again. "Yes . . . I'll see them. And I'll fight."

"Eh?"

Val stood up. His face was like ashes and his eyes like coals, but he carried his head high and tried to clench his shaking lips together.

"I'll fight," he said. "I won't funk. Come on, Austin; we'll tell them."

CHAPTER VI

(1)

R OME is silent for one short half-hour each
night during the tourist season — that and
no more. Until three o'clock cabs still remain on
the stand, their drivers talk and quarrel, and their
horses stamp. At about the same time the last
restaurant emits its last revellers, and the post-
office officials go home, and all to the sound of singing. You hear an air of an opera begin out of the
distance like a thread of sound. It waxes and it
wanes; it grows suddenly louder; it peals out below
your window, sung often so exceedingly well that
you begin to wonder whether the man is a professional; then again it dies away by degrees, and is
drowned at last in some new and nearer noise.
There follows silence; the old city sighs once and
falls asleep, to be awakened at half-past three o'clock
by the country carts coming in from the Campagna,
laden with the old necessaries of man — food and
wine and oil — that Rome for twenty-three and a
half hours more may cook and eat and drink. It
seems as though the city which has lived so long
and known so much, which is in her heart so con-

templative and so quiet and so brooding, in that
heart of hers that the tourist never sees, in her old,
disused churches and her hidden courts, needs but
little sleep, for she has much to ponder in her
heart. . . .

At half-past two Val sprang up again with a sudden movement from his bed; and barefooted, in his
pyjamas began to walk up and down, up and down,
as half a dozen times already he had walked this
night. In the dim light that came from the shaded
electric lamp which burnt by his bed he looked alert
and even keen; his eyes were bright and wide; his
lips were open as if he were running; again and
again he murmured little soundless sentences. For
perhaps ten minutes he so walked up and down; then
he threw himself suddenly face downward on the
bed, threw out his hands to clasp his pillow, and so
remained, all a-sprawl across the bed.

It seemed now as if days had passed — or rather
an eternity of consciousness, since dinner-time the
night before. And yet the chime of one clock
seemed scarcely silent before another sounded, so
swiftly did the quarters of each hour flit by. It
was in some remote period, such as that of child-
hood, that his health had been drunk in Chartreuse. . . .

He had not been able to face the girls. Austin

had told him not to; he said that Val's manner
would tell them that something was wrong; and
it was most important that they should suspect nothing. It was Austin himself who went and told
them that Val was not well, and that he had gone
straight to bed; he had also told them that the two
Italians had come and talked a great deal and very
fast, and that he thought there would be no more
trouble. Then Austin had come to Val's room to
see if he was comfortable and to talk over the situation.

They had been together till half-past eleven —
Austin moody and doubtful; Val alternately violently talkative and silent. More than once Austin
had been on the very point of going down to the
telephone, and it was not Val who had dissuaded
him. Val had said that he would leave himself in
Austin's hands.

Then they had fenced a little with walking-sticks;
Austin had gone over a few strokes with him, and
made him practise a certain feint in *seconde* that he
seemed to think a good deal of. He said it was new.
. . . And it had been Val who had tossed his
stick suddenly on the bed and said that it would
be much better for him to have a bit of sleep.
Austin agreed; and as he went to the door, promising to wake Val at four, the boy had called him
back.

"One minute, Austin."

The other paused.

"You'll give all messages if . . . if it's necessary?"

"Nonsense. . . . You'll get him in the sword arm in three minutes," said Austin harshly.

Val jerked his head. Then he was motionless.

"Don't forget, old chap . . . if it's necessary. Mother and father and May, and — and Gertie. Tell her ——" He stopped.

"I'm very fond of Gertie," he said lamentably.

Austin nodded sharply. Sentiment was not very far under the surface; and he felt it had better stop there. Then he thought himself a shade untender.

"Don't bother your head, old boy. It'll be all perfectly right. . . . Good night."

"Good night. . . . I say, Austin."

"Well?"

"I've been a beast to you — always. I'm sorry. That's all. Good night."

"Good night."

Then Austin had softly closed the door and gone to his own room.

(II)

Indeed, Val seemed to him very admirable, as he too turned from side to side, and listened to the clocks and the stamp of horses and the unintelligible conversations beneath his window. He had behaved like a gentleman this afternoon, as of course a Medd always must. Nothing could have been more proper and respectable, even though a trifle hasty and indiscreet, than the slapping of the young man's face. Austin doubted whether he himself would have had the nerve to act so decisively and vigorously at a moment's notice; but Val always had had a nervous sort of courage. There was the affair of Gertie's horse, for instance. He, Austin, would probably have fumbled, and wondered whether it was wise to gallop after a bolting horse; it might easily have done more harm than good. But Val had galloped; and had succeeded.

Then the affair of the Matterhorn slope recurred to his mind; and he acknowledged that this affair in Rome, first the slapping, and then the cool determination to fight, completely altered his former interpretation of the climbing incident. Poor old Val must have, as he had said, simply lost his physical head; it had been a task simply beyond him. For now that the boy was faced by a far greater peril, and one, too, that advanced steadily as each minute went by through hour after hour, he showed no sign of faltering at all. He had been unjust in dreaming even of real cowardice.

Austin went through, then, during the hours of that night, a very considerable fit of repentance.

He acknowledged to himself frankly that he had misjudged Val; he resolved if — (no, not if, but *when* . . .) — when this affair was over he would be more cordial — more cordial and appreciative.

Until about one o'clock those thoughts came and went, interspersed, however, with others far more agonising that concerned his own part in the affair.

It must be remembered, in justice to Austin, that he was still quite young: he had not left Cambridge more than two or three years; and although he possessed to the full the Englishman's instinctive hatred and contempt of the duel, together with a very superior attitude towards foreign ways, yet it was a considerable bewilderment to him as to the course to be pursued, when he found himself faced by the brother of a Prince, a general and a lieutenant of the Italian army, all of whom blandly assumed that an English gentleman in Italy must behave like an Italian gentleman, or forfeit his own right to the name altogether. And he thought himself debarred by this very consideration from consulting anyone else. Probably, however, even then he would have done so in the long run, if Val had not interposed so sharply. But, at the very instant in which he was swaying this way and that, the boy had started up and said he would fight; and a feather, when the balance is delicate, will weigh down one side.

But all this did not save Austin from a very disagreeable hour and a half, until about one o'clock he fell asleep. He knew perfectly well that he would be held responsible at home; that he had been sent out because Val was not thought old enough or steady enough to take charge of the party; and he simply did not dare to contemplate what in the world would be said to him if . . . well, if Val did not come home again — and, in fact, anyhow. Well, that was not his affair now; the thing had been settled; the challenge had been accepted. It must be seen through.

He slept miserably. Once, about two, he got up, and stole out down the thick-carpeted passage to Val's door, but there was dead silence within. Through the passage window, at the end, he heard a sudden stamp of a horse, drawn up in his place on the cabstand outside. He must not disturb Val. He went back to bed, looking once more at his alarum-clock, set at ten minutes before four.

An hour later he woke again, and heard the three silver chimes from the tall clock downstairs, and then, in the breathless silence that had fallen, he heard even the solemn tick. He counted a dozen, and it seemed to him suddenly horrible. These seconds were, literally, ticking out Val's life, or, at

least, its grave peril. He pulled the sheet over his
ears, and presently fell asleep once more, to dream,
as he had dreamt during the last two hours, of
swords and Val's face, and moustached opponents
larger than human, and a pleasant old garden, such
as he had seen last week, backed by a crumbling
palace. . . .

He awoke suddenly, terrified, and shocked; for
there was a bright light in his eyes, which for an
instant he thought the light of broad day; and he
sprang up to a sitting position, bewildered and con-
fused. Then he saw Val's face close to his own;
the boy was half sitting on the bed, and shaking
him by the shoulder.

"Eh? What? Is it time?" . . .

Then he saw Val's face more plainly, and for an
instant thought himself dreaming again. For it
seemed, since he had left him three or four hours
ago, as if that face had thinned down into the looks
of an old man, or of one struck by mortal sickness.
The hair was tumbled, the lips were pale and parted,
and the eyes seemed drawn down as by strange lines
that faded into dark patches above the cheek-bone.

"Good Lord!" he said. "What's the matter?
Are you ill?"

He jumped out of bed and stood looking at him.
The white face nodded at him.

"Yes," said the white lips, "I'm ill . . . I'm ill . . . I can't go."

"Can't go! . . . My dear chap, you simply must. Good God! Whatever would——?"

The eyes looking into his own wavered.

"I can't go," repeated the pale mouth. "I can't go. I'm ill."

"But——"

Then the boy gave way. He cast himself down across the bed, and that miserable quavering cry which once before Austin had heard, as the two faced together a visible peril, rose lamentably up, half stifled by the bedclothes on which his face lay.

"I can't . . . I can't . . . I simply can't. . . . I'm not fit. I . . . I can't fence. You know it. You're ever so much better. . . . Oh! I can't . . . I can't."

"Sit up, Val. . . . Look here——"

Then the alarum clock burst into clamour, strident and metallic. It seemed that it must wake the house and the city to this appalling shame. Austin seized it, wrenched at the handles, desperate and furious, yet it clattered on. He turned hopelessly, still holding it. Then he dashed it into the seat of the deep chair that stood by his bed-foot, and it was silent — silent even to its tick. A splinter of glass tinkled down on to the polished floor.

Austin turned again, and there was a new ring of severity in his voice.

"Val . . . tell me. You mean to say you're not going? — that you're afraid?"

There was silence. The writhed figure on the bed lay still.

Austin came a step nearer and tapped the extended bare foot sharply, twice.

"Come," he said. "Tell me at once. Don't tell me you're a cur after all."

(For here swelled up in the elder boy at this instant all the old bitterness and contempt, multiplied a thousand-fold.

He saw here before him one of his blood that was a craven and a weakling; one who disgraced the name that he himself bore.)

The face on the pillow turned a little.

"I can't" . . . moaned the broken voice.

Austin did not speak. For one tense instant he stood motionless. Then his fingers went to his throat and ripped down the buttons of the pyjama jacket, then he slipped it off, and tossed it on to the bed, careless whether it fell on his brother or not; pulled at the tassel of his trousers so that they fell to the ground, stepped free; and then a slim, boyish figure went across to where his clothes lay folded for the morning. He first poured out cold water and submerged his head; then he splashed water up his arms to the elbows, ran a rough towel over himself, and shook the drops from his hair. Then he took up his clothes and began to dress.

As he sat at last on his chair, lacing his shoes, he spoke, without looking up.

"You'll be good enough to explain matters to May, if it is necessary. I don't care what lies you tell. But you're responsible."

There was no answer. He glanced up, and saw that Val was sitting upright again, looking at him. He turned away his own eyes.

"You're responsible," he said again.

He had to pass to the further side of the bed to get his watch, and to lift down his light covert-coat that hung on the pegs beyond. When he turned again Val was standing by the door, as if to bar the way. He had not heard the sound of the bare feet on the thick carpet. The first country cart was rattling past outside.

"What are you going to do?" asked a voice that was all but soundless.

Austin paid no attention. He slipped on his coat and turned up the collar, as the morning seemed chilly. Then he put on his hat and took his stick. (It was one Val had given him the week before — a dome-palm. But he did not remember this just then.) Then he came towards the door.

"What are you going to do?" asked the boy again.

"Get out of my way," snarled the elder brother so suddenly and fiercely that Val recoiled. Austin pushed by him and went out, leaving the door open.

As he reached the hall he glanced back, scarcely knowing why, at a little gallery that hung out from the passage where the four had their rooms. There was a figure standing there, in pyjamas, relieved against the glimmer of light that came from the open door beyond; and this figure seemed to be looking at him.

Then he went on.

The night-porter in his little glazed shelter woke from his doze with a start. A young man in a covert-coat and a bowler hat was standing over him. This young man jerked his head toward the great entrance without speaking. When the door was unlocked the young man went out, still in silence. The porter looked after him, at the pale, empty square, colourless as a dead man's face. Overhead the sky was streaked with rose. Then the porter went back to doze again.

CHAPTER VII

(1)

IT was very still in the room where the boy,
crouched in a chair, listened for every sound
that might bring him news; but it was a stillness
of intensity and thought rather than of realistic fact,
since outside, as the minutes went by, Rome awoke
more and more to her new day. The conversations beneath the windows did not die out into
silence, as earlier in the night; one was succeeded
by another, until voices became general; now the
call of a cabman, now the cry of a trader, now
the talking of friends. So too with the sound of
wheels; there was not a crescendo, a roar, and a
long diminuendo down into stillness again; but roar
succeeded roar, and the beat of hoofs the beat of
hoofs.

Within the great hotel, too, life came back.
Doors opened and closed; there was the noise of
water dashed against steps at back and front; footsteps went over paved places; soft vibrations made
themselves perceived as men and maids passed overhead and beneath along the thick-carpeted passages.

257

Once there was a bustle; sounds of the moving of heavy weights shook the air; voices and steps sounded about; doors banged: and the boy started up, wide-eyed and white, his whole conscious thought concentrated into the sense of hearing. But the noises passed; wheels rolled over the stones; and he, peeping between the curtains, saw an open cab drive away with travellers and luggage. And once he sprang to the door and listened, for a slow footstep had gone by and paused, it seemed, at Austin's door. He listened in an agony, the heavy beating in his throat drowning all sounds. Then he peeped out, and a maid was looking at him, curiously, he thought, from his brother's half-open door.

In a tremendous climax of anxiety there is no consecutiveness of thought, and very little orderly consideration at all. Visions, rather, come and go; little scenes present themselves. It was so with this boy. He saw a hundred vignettes, and some of them over and over again, scarcely modified even in detail. Austin wounded or dead; a group in a garden; Austin pale and victorious, with blood on his rapier-blade; Austin threatening him; Italian faces mocking and sardonic; Italian faces terrified and distraught. He saw his father too, either quiet and ordinary, or transfigured with passion and contempt; his mother swooning; his mother hard and brutal; his mother gracious and stately and unknowing. And, again and again, Gertie, in every pose and in every mood — forgiving, compassionate, furious, overwhelmed, sneering, and then compassionate once more. . . .

There were just three or four lines of thought that presented themselves; but each broke off and tangled itself inextricably with the rest, or snapped at some external sound from the square without or the hotel within, or led up to a white wall of despair which there was no scaling.

First there was the part he himself had played. Now he was contrite and humiliated, now overwhelmed with misery, now resentful and self-acquitting, snatching in a passion of self-preservation at any excuse: he was honestly ill . . . it was cruel that such a strain should be put on him; Austin was at once the elder brother and the better fencer: Austin should have insisted at once on taking his place. And then misery and self-contempt all over again. Once or twice he considered the possibility of throwing himself on the floor and feigning unconsciousness, to prove his own physical collapse; but he was unable even to do this.

Next there was the consideration as to what was happening. He knew nothing except that Austin had gone to keep the appointment, whether to dep-

recate, to apologise, to make excuses, to make another appointment, or to fight — he had not an
idea. Now he felt that Austin must surely manage
to explain things away, to tide matters over; now
that he must surely fight in his younger brother's
place. . . . What were elder brothers for if not
to take responsibilities as well as privileges?

Thirdly — and this so repeatedly that it drove him
nearly mad — he rehearsed explanations and argu-
ments by which he could put himself right with
Gertie and May. He would have presently to go
downstairs and meet them at breakfast. . . .
Why did not Austin come back? . . . In God's
name, *why did not Austin come back?* . . .
What could he say? He knew nothing. . . .
Perhaps Austin was back: perhaps he had not gone
after all; perhaps he was already at breakfast with
the rest, discussing him. . . .

A clock chimed. He listened in an agony. There
were two chimes, and the space between seemed an
eternity. Silence followed. Was that two in the
afternoon, or half-past eight? He sprang up and
ran to his bedside. The hands of his watch pointed
to half-past six. He shook his watch; held it to
his ear and listened; then he stared at the moving
hand that marked the seconds. Was it truly only
half-past six?

Then he laid it down, softly, as if for fear of waking a child; for a footstep came past his door. It went on, and ceased; and he heard a door close. Then, through the wall, with his ear laid against it, he heard someone moving in the next room.

At his own door he paused, his mouth hanging open; his mind revolved like a pack of wheels. . . . Then he opened his door, and without looking behind him went swiftly up the passage to Austin's door. It was closed. He tapped once, but there was no answer. He opened it and went in. Austin, with his coat and waistcoat off, was bending over the basin, and there was the sound of trickling water: he did not turn round or show any sign.

Val stood there, perfectly still, watching. Then he cleared his throat; but Austin did not show any sign of having heard him: his shirt-sleeves were turned back to the elbow and he seemed to be doing something with a sponge.

" Austin? "

" Damn it," said Austin suddenly; and then, " Come and do this for me."

An extraordinary flush of joy swept through the boy; he came quickly across the floor, still barefooted and in his pyjamas; he then recoiled. A sound broke from his mouth.

For the basin seemed full of blood; a roll of blood-stained bandages lay beside it; and along Austin's right arm, from wrist to elbow, on the inner side, ran a long, deep furrow that dripped blood as he looked.

"Blast it all," snapped Austin again. "Can't you be some good? Look how I'm bleeding."

With a huge wrench at himself, Val gathered his nerves together, and bound them tight by an action of his will. He came round behind his brother, took the sponge from his left hand — the sponge that was all clotted and stained with crimson — wrung it out, dipped it again, and then holding Austin's right hand, squeezed out a flood of cold water on to the wound. He could see now that the furrow was not all: just above the elbow a spot of blood lay welling, and from behind the elbow something dropped steadily into the water.

"That's no good," snarled Austin. "Get some more bandages — quick. There" (he jerked with his head). "Get some handkerchiefs out of that top drawer and tear them up."

Val flew across the room, flung open the drawer, and snatched out the handkerchiefs. He looked hopelessly round for scissors, saw them, snipped the hem of each handkerchief and tore them across.

(11)

As the clock was striking half-past seven, Val, kneeling by Austin's chair in which he had made him sit down for the slow process of bandaging, tenderly pulled down the shirt-arm, unfolded the cuff, and fastened it with its link. Then before he laid the hand down along the chair-arm he kissed it.

" Don't be a blasted fool," said Austin explosively.

They had not spoken one word yet beyond those necessary for the manipulation of the arm. Austin had flatly refused to have a doctor in the first five minutes. Val had not suggested it; but the other had suddenly cried out that he would not have one.

While Val had been working: fetching vaseline from his own room; flinging on a few clothes and dashing down to the porter to send him to a chemist for something that would stop bleeding; and then washing and washing, and untying and bandaging and untying and bandaging again — while all these external things were being done, an interior process was also going on: his pride, it seemed, was melting, his bitterness of self-reproach going, and he appeared to himself to be becoming humble and simple — as a girl might be towards a lover who had suffered in her behalf. It had been as a sort of climax of this process that, in a passion of love and sorrow towards his brother, he had kissed his hand. And now Austin's sharp sentence set all his nerves jangling and quivering once more. It appeared to him from his brother's tone as if there were to be no smoothing over of the wrong by caresses. He stood up, ashamed and angry.

"Look here," said Austin, "we must have a talk. Sit down; give me a cigarette first. And ring for coffee."

"I'll go and fetch it," said Val.

In five minutes he was back again with the tray: he poured out a cup for Austin, and held a match for him to light a cigarette. He set the coffee on his brother's left hand, that he might help himself.

"And look here," said Austin, "first you'd better hear the facts. Then you can settle what you're going to say to the others. I needn't say I shan't be down to breakfast!"

His lips writhed in a kind of painful smile. Then he finished his coffee and leaned back smoking.

"Well," he said, "I went to the place. The others drove up just behind me. When they wanted to know why you weren't there I told them you were ill. I lied freely. There was nothing else to be done. They tried to sneer at that; and Don Adrian

What's-his-name began to make himself offensive. But I soon shut him up by telling him I didn't see what he'd got to complain of: he'd behaved like a dirty blackguard and had been properly chastised; and it was a considerable honour to him that we consented to meet him at all. You were ill, I said; and I had insisted on your remaining at home. And I had come to take your place. Would they kindly begin therefore at once, or I should be obliged to slap him on the only other cheek he had left. . . . It seemed to me the only way out of it. . . . Well, they agreed at last, and we fought; and he gave me this in the first go off. I must say they behaved decently after that; especially the doctor-chap who acted as my second and tied me up. They wanted to kiss and make friends. And I did shake hands with them. And then they put me in a cab and sent me away."

He stopped.

" I feel vile," he said; " I think I'm going to faint."

Val sprang up and ran for the sponge; he tore open Austin's collar and bathed him, face and ears and breast. Then Austin opened his eyes again.

" All right," he said. " Sit down. Now what are we going to do next? We shall have to tell the girls something."

Val opened his mouth to speak, but closed it again.

"I can't possibly come out of my room to-day," went on Austin, not noticing; "and I very much doubt whether I'll be able to travel to-morrow. I don't see how it's possible to stop their knowing. But I'm perfectly willing to say that I insisted on going instead of you; or that you were, honestly, taken really ill in the night. Lord knows I don't want people to say more unpleasant things than they need. That'd be no consolation."

He paused again.

"Which is it to be?" he said. "Whichever you like. Only we must stick to it like death, even at home."

"I shall tell them the truth," said Val in a low voice.

"Don't talk blasted rot," said Austin. "What good would that do? Someone would be sure to talk, and then the whole thing 'ud get out. I don't want one of us to be pointed at as a coward. Look here; you *were* ill, you know. You looked perfectly ghastly."

For one instant even then Val hesitated; he saw one more escape beckoning to him; he perceived in that intensity of thought to which by now every fibre of him was screwed up, that here once more was a way out, as there had been in the other matters — the fight at Eton, the riding of Mention, and the climbing in Switzerland. Even Austin said that he looked really ill. Then he crushed down the temptation.

" That was sheer funk," he said. " I was not ill. I was a coward. I shall tell them the truth."

Austin moved irritably in his chair.

" You seem to me to be simply thinking of yourself again. Can't you for one instant, by way of a change, think of the rest of us? Do you suppose we want all this to get out? It wouldn't be pleasant for us to be pointed at, and to have it said that you were a coward. We hang together, you know; you can't get over that."

Val stood up.

" Look here, Austin. Are you well enough for me to leave you for five minutes?"

" Yes. Why?"

" I'm going to tell them now," he said; and went quickly out before Austin could speak again.

(III)

May was lying in bed, beginning to wonder whether it really was true that a maid had come in, drawn the curtains back, and told her it was half-past seven. Surely the maid must have been before the time — twenty past at the most — and it would be scarcely fair to take advantage of that. In that case she would have been deprived of ten minutes' sleep, unjustly, and it was really almost a duty to

set that right. So she argued, with that singular
logic which prevails at such seasons.

The room she was sleeping in was typically hotel.
It was extremely comfortable and expensive, and, on
the whole, rather repulsive; it had, that is to say,
not the faintest suggestion of homeliness. The only
really comfortable object that met her eye was her
own trunk and the half-open door of a cupboard
that contained dresses and boxes. A small heap of
things — a large Roman leather photograph frame,
a tattered chasuble rolled up, some coffee-coloured
lace, a bronze statuette of Antinous, and a small box
full of moonstones — lying in a huddle on her table,
represented her efforts last night to put together her
locally coloured purchases, for packing.

She presently began to argue that no sounds yet
proceeded from Gertie's room, which communicated
with hers. The door was closed, and it was barely
possible that in spite of the silence Gertie might be
getting up; but it was not likely. And it would not
be kind or tactful to be down to breakfast before her
friend. The boys would most certainly be late too:
they always were; and Val had once said that it
annoyed him to see everybody else breakfasting
when he appeared. By the way, Val wasn't well
last night; and he would therefore be more certain
than ever to be late. By the way, she wondered how
he was this morning. Austin had said it looked

rather like a feverish cold last night — not serious.

"Come — er . . . *Avanti!*" cried May suddenly, pulling the bedclothes up to her chin. (Was it conceivable that this was the maid after all? In that case, she would have ten minutes' good ——)

Then Val appeared, closing the door behind him.

"Val!"

He did not speak for an instant. He looked odd somehow. Certainly he was dressed; but his hair was tumbled . . . he looked as if he had slept in his clothes.

"What's the matter?" asked May, sitting up suddenly in bed.

His lips opened, but he did not speak. She was frightened.

"Val! What is it? Are you ill?"

"Look here, May. Don't be frightened. Nothing's wrong; at least not very. But, first, will you ask Gertie to come and speak to me now — now and here. Promise? Then I'll tell you."

May slipped out of bed, and stood, gone pale in an instant, looking curiously frail and childish in her white nightdress and bare feet. Her hair fell in a twisted coil over one shoulder.

"Yes," she said breathlessly; "I promise. Oh! Val, tell me."

He hesitated again; and she could see the struggle in his face.

"Very well, then," he said almost harshly. "Austin wants to see you. . . . He's not very well. He's . . . been wounded . . . in the arm. No; it's not serious. He . . . he fought a duel, instead of me, this morning — an hour ago. I was a coward and wouldn't go. . . ."

She stood, swaying. He came a step nearer.

"Say what you like to me afterwards — but ——"

Then the door from Gertie's room opened, and she came in, fully dressed.

"Why, May ——"

Then she, too, stopped dead, and her eyes grew large and apprehensive.

"Val. . . . May. . . . What's the matter?" The boy nodded to his sister.

"All right," he said. "Go. . . . He's in his own room."

She seized her dressing-gown and slipped it on: pushed on her slippers. He opened the door for her. Then he closed it after her and turned to Gertie.

"Gertie," he said, "I've come to tell I'm a cur and a coward. I was challenged to a duel last night — by that Italian. I accepted; that's why I went to bed early. And when the time came I behaved like a cur. I wouldn't go; Austin went instead; and he's been wounded in the arm. . . . That's all."

He stood a moment longer looking at her. She did not speak or move. Then he turned and went quietly out.

CHAPTER VIII

(1)

THE door closed behind the steward's-room boy, and the Powers and Dominations faced one another across the decanters placed, according to immemorial custom, exactly half-way between Mr. Masterman and Mrs. Markham. There were also present on this occasion Mr. Simpson, own man to General Medd, a tight-lipped clean-shaven man; Miss Ferguson, lady's maid; and old Mrs. Bentham, once nurse to May and the boys. The gentlemen were in evening-dress, since they had just come down from the dining-room, leaving the footmen to finish the clearing away; and the ladies in black silk, with Mrs. Markham and Mrs. Bentham in caps as well.

It is exceedingly difficult to say how stories come downstairs from the upper department with what is, on the whole, such extraordinary accuracy and detail. It is certain that the General, Lady Beatrice, and Miss Deverell believed that they had behaved with unusual discretion. May's first letter had been received yesterday, and her second to-day at noon;

272

her parents had hardly, even by now, taken in all the facts; yet the story was known by now, in its main outline, by all these distinguished persons in the steward's room. Deep melancholy had reigned at the high table of the servant's hall during supper, almost as if there had been a death in the family. After the cold meat, the aristocracy had risen and filed out in silence, to eat their second course in the " Room "; and, even during this second course, little had been said, and nothing whatever about the subject that lay so heavy in the air; until, the last public ceremonial having been performed, the nuts and sweet biscuits placed in position, and the decanters arranged, James, the steward's-room boy, withdrew, closing the door softly behind him, before speeding on tiptoe down and away to the pantry to discuss what was up.

Mr. Masterman made a gesture towards the decanters. Mr. Simpson poured out a glass of sherry and held it a moment before the hanging-lamp. Then he drank it off, and set down the glass again.

Mr. Masterman began by observing that it was a sad business. Then, after a pause, he related the outlines of the story.

The difference of manner and behaviour of servants when in the presence of their employers and when in their own company is very remarkable. Upstairs they are superb actors, intelligent only as regards their duties, blind and deaf and dumb, it seems, to all else: they are that which they are trained to be, and nothing more. And even in such families as the Medd where they are promoted by long service to a higher and more confidential position — even here the invisible line is rigid and unbending: they may grieve over certain kinds of sorrows, such as a funeral; they may smile and make speeches on occasions of family rejoicing; but never for one single instant are they themselves. Downstairs, however, the world is completely different; the masks are laid aside, and they actually form opinions for themselves, and express them in a manner to which their upstair bearing affords simply no key at all.

There was Mr. Masterman, for instance. Upstairs he was a bent, grey-haired retainer, hurrying, rather pathetic, kindly, trustful, and obedient, ruling his inferiors, it seemed, without effort or difficulty, guiding them as a wheel in a machine guides the other wheels, inevitably and mechanically, a sympathetic echo to his superiors, doing the right thing always, seeing nothing he was supposed not to see, venturing only very occasionally, with an incredible humility, to the tiny sentences of intimacy to which he had become entitled by his long service. Downstairs he was a wise old man, with a very strong individuality of his own, a very great obstinacy in his own opinion, a scathing tongue towards the footman, and a superbly overwhelming silence towards the other under-servants.

He gave his opinion now on the Rome incident, when he had just touched upon the facts of the story; and it was, on the whole, a very fair and generous opinion. Young Master Val was only a boy yet, after all; Mr. Austin was a man; and boys could not be expected to do what men did. It was regrettable, of course, that such a call had been made upon Master Val; but the boy was not to be blamed by those who understood.

Then Mrs. Markham spoke. To her the prominent feature of the story was the murdering proclivity of Papists. Nothing else appeared to her of importance; she was unable to concentrate her mind upon the parts that the young gentlemen had played. For the whole story was just a confirmation of all that she had learned from her uncle who had been butler to an archdeacon. She referred to Guy Fawkes and the fires of Smithfield with an amazing bitterness.

Miss Ferguson was sure that it was all Mr. Austin's fault for leading Master Val into mischief. She was sure that it was only right that Mr. Austin should suffer for it. She was sure, a great number of times, of a great number of things that were not particularly to the point.

Then Mrs. Bentham announced her views. She was of the finest type of the finest servant in the world — the old nurse. She held, now, a rather nondescript position in the household, with two rooms of her own in a wing. She "mended" for everybody: she put things away very carefully in tissue-paper, and then forgot where she had put them. She was loved by the Medds one and all, who made her valuable presents on her birthday, and kissed her continually: she was respected by the upper servants and reverenced fearfully by the lower; for she had her dignities by sheer force of personality and of an uprightness whose besmirching was simply inconceivable.

The first article of her creed, or rather the first axiom of her philosophy, was that no Medd could ever do anything wrong or unworthy, except in such small matters as not "changing their feet" when they came in, or sitting up too late at night; and it was in accordance with this creed that she expounded her views. She was sorry that Mr. Austin had fought, but he knew best; there must have been some necessity. Master Val was quite right not to fight. Why should he fight? There remained the party whom she called "Them out there," which included the Pope of Rome, the King of Italy, France, to which she had paid two visits with the

Family about twelve years before, and the vague mass of foreigners behind and beneath these three; and for " Them out there " she had not a word to say. Obviously they "were in the wrong," since they had come into conflict with the Medds. She would be glad when the young gentlemen were safe home again.

Then Mr. Simpson spoke, after a short pause.

Mr. Simpson, when off the stage, was extremely like a great many of his typical employers. He was sharp, disdainful, decided, and rather pitiless. Upstairs, of course, he was perfection; he was silent, capable, self-effacing, and extremely competent.

He summed up therefore, in a few biting sentences, the opinion which would be held on such behaviour by the majority of sensible, pitiless men of the world. Young Mr. Austin had only done the right thing under the circumstances; young Master Val? . . . Well! Mr. Simpson sneered unpleasantly.

Then Mrs. Bentham fell upon him. She announced that it was disgraceful to speak of the young gentlemen so. Master Val was all that Master Val should be. When Mr. Simpson had been a little longer with the Family he would know better than to speak like that. Mr. Simpson sat silent, twisting his sherry-glass, suffering a little indulgent smile to twitch his brown cheek from time to time. Miss Ferguson began to be sure again of a number of things.

Mr. Masterman broke in at last in a suitable pause. He said that the least said the soonest mended. After all, it was impossible to judge fairly on such slight information. Above all, no word must be spoken outside the " Room." The story must on no account get into the village.

He passed the sherry down to Mr. Simpson again and suggested a night-cap to Mrs, Bentham. Then he stood up: it was time to take the candles upstairs and set out the tray in the smoking-room.

(II)

Mrs. Bentham, after her night-cap — one single glass, ordered by the doctor — climbed upstairs and came into her sitting-room panting a little, both from the exertion and from the last ripples of indignation. It seemed to her disgraceful that a man who had been only three years in the Family should dare to talk so of her young gentlemen.

Her rooms, communicating by a passage and a baize door with the boys' wing, were one of the minor sights of the place, though in a purely intimate and personal way. From ceiling to floor the walls were covered with photographs and pictures — in the bedroom of persons, in the sitting-room of places. It was the Medd family, almost exclusively, whose representations hung in the minor-room — General Medd, from a daguerreotype of him as a subaltern, in a small brass frame, to a huge photograph of him as a general covered with orders, on a charger; Lady Beatrice in frocks and frills, in her drawing-dress, on horse-back with hounds about her; Val and Austin from baby clothes upwards; May in swings, May in sailor-costume holding a rope against a stormy sky — these and countless others plastered the walls. The sitting-room was less intimate but more splendid. Interiors of cathedrals in carved frames; views of Egypt and Exeter and Swansea and the Houses of Parliament; these disputed the walls with hanging bookcases containing pious literature, and huge presses filled with treasures and stuffs long since vanished for ever from the keeping of their owners. A large sewing-table stood in the midst, piled with stockings and linen, with a small tea-table beside it at which, on rare occasions, Mrs. Bentham would entertain to tea Miss May or Master Val. Mr. Austin had given up coming during the last year or two, though he always kissed her courteously and affectionately on leaving or arriving at Medhurst. There were two large easy chairs, subscribed for by the children; and the carpet had once covered the floor of Austin's room at Eton. Little precious things stood on the

mantelpiece and on the tops of the bookcases —
small inlaid boxes, spectacle-cases and scissors too
grand to be used — gifts made her on the occasions
of birthdays; and, in the drawers of the presses still
other gifts reposed, too splendid even for exhibition
— embroideries from Egypt, silver-mounted frames,
and even a jade-handled umbrella, still in its outer
case.

Mrs. Bentham — called Benty — was a worthy
occupier of such glories. Her philosophy has
already been described, and it extended even to the
Supernatural. Heaven, so far as it represented
itself imaginatively to her at all, consisted entirely
in the eternal possession by her of those she loved —
(and, indeed, it is difficult to construct a better
picture) — The Medds and she would dwell together in a celestial group, crowned and palmed,
no doubt, according to tradition, but together. She
would entertain them to tea through all the æons;
and they would come and sit with her in her Man-
sion while she mended their haloes. . . .

She had painful matters to think of now, more
painful than she had dreamed of allowing downstairs; so she took her seat in one of the easy-chairs,
and inspected a pair of socks through her spectacles;
and meanwhile she began to think.

It was not, even now, that she allowed the possibility of Val's having been in the wrong, but it was a sore matter that anyone should think him to have been so. Far away at the outer doors of her consciousness hammered questions and doubts, while she sat within severe and determined, adoring the Family images with resolute faith. Master Val had done perfectly right, she told herself; he always did, except in such minor matters as have been mentioned. And Mr. Austin had done right too. The one had not fought when it was apparently his business to do so; the other had fought when it was not. And both were right.

So she sat and darned, bending her fine old sunken eyes over her work, her lips tightly compressed. She made a splendid and romantic figure here, in stern black, her shoulders covered by a lovely black knitted shawl, clasped at the throat by an enamelled brooch with the number of her birthdays on it in blue against gold. It had been the gift of Austin and Val and May to her last June.

She finished the sock at last — it was one of a basketful of Val's which she had collected before he went abroad — and, as she laid it by, heard the rustle of silk, the thud of a stick, and, as she rose to her feet, the voice she knew so well.

"May I come in, Benty?"

She made haste to push her footstool forward to the other chair as she called out in answer. Lady Beatrice limped in.

Her mistress came in sometimes like this, before going to bed, for a gentle gossip in the firelight. But she looked rather drawn and preoccupied this evening as she smiled at the old nurse whom she had known for twenty years, and she sat down without speaking. She leaned her stick against the wall and sat staring into the wood fire for a minute, without a word. Then she suddenly bent forward and took one of the old wrinkled hands into her own.

"We're in trouble, Benty," she said.

The old woman's face twitched and stiffened.

"It's . . . it's about Val," said the boy's mother.

For tactful discretion towards those whom she loved Benty was unrivalled. She knew perfectly well that nothing must be said about the conversation itself in the " Room." Indeed the conversation was not altogether right, but she had felt herself unable to check Masterman. But in any case it must not be mentioned now. The story had leaked out chiefly through Simpson's having been in the dining-room when he was supposed not to be there. Masterman also had heard the end of a conversation, and the facts, as has been said, had been put together with sufficient accuracy.

"What's the matter with him, my lady?" she asked, trying not to let her voice tremble.

"We . . . we're afraid he hasn't behaved well. He . . . he let Austin . . . run into danger instead of him. And . . . and I must tell you, Benty, because Austin's been hurt."

The old lady looked at her miserably. It was frightful to her that a Medd should accuse a Medd. How could both be right? And yet both must be. Lady Beatrice misunderstood the look. She tightened her hand-clasp a little.

"Don't look like that," she said. "Austin's not in danger now. He was wounded in the arm, in a duel which . . . which I'm afraid Val ought to have fought instead of him."

Benty looked suddenly defiant.

"How could that be, my lady? Master Val knew better than to fight a duel."

"You don't understand, my dear ——"

"And him only a boy," burst in Benty resolutely. "How could anyone expect —— "

"Benty, you don't understand. Of course duels are very wrong. If they had both kept out of it, it would have been different; but it looks as if they had to fight, and ——"

"And Mr. Austin took Master Val's place. And

quite right too. He's the elder. It's his place."

The other was silent. It was balm to her to hear such pleading; it was what she had tried to say gently downstairs half an hour before; and yet she had known it was disingenuous while she had said it. But it was pleasant to hear another say it too. She began to look into the fire again, and to stroke the old hand that lay between her own.

"Don't fret your mind, my dear," went on Benty, thoroughly roused by the perilous position she felt herself in, and beginning herself to pat back with her other hand. "Master Val's done nothing but what a young gentleman should, and so's Master Austin. If they will go out to these foreign parts they'll be bound to get into trouble, and what's more proper than that Master Austin should take the brunt of it." (Benty was proud of this phrase, even while she used it.) "Master Val! why, he's only a boy. Don't you fret, my lady . . . there! there . . ." (for her mistress had suddenly bowed her head on the kind old hands.) "There! there. Sit up, my dear. It's time you were in bed."

For a minute or so the two sat in silence. Lady Beatrice had recovered herself almost instantly, and leaned back, with just the glimmer of tears still in her eyes, soothed and healed by the warm, familiar old presence, with its amazing charity and

loyalty. She knew that Benty would never understand; that she would simply refuse to understand;
and, after all, it was a pleasant and perhaps a wise
philosophy — this refusal to judge, this fidelity to
principles, this denial of facts which appeared to
conflict with those principles. She half envied
this creed of utter faith, and yet she thought it was
not for her. She herself must deal with things in
the world: it was not possible for her, she believed,
to remain always in the atmosphere of this room, to
live by faith, hope, and charity, and nothing else
at all. She stood up painfully at last, helping herself by her stick on one side and Benty's firm hands
on the other.

"You're a dear," she said, and kissed her.
"Now I must go to bed."

"Is the master much upset?" asked the old
woman anxiously.

"Yes, he is," said Lady Beatrice.

(III)

Benty still pottered about uneasily for a few
minutes, after she had seen her mistress to her room-
door. She had promised to go in half an hour to
"tuck her up." But she could not settle down again
to the socks. She went through them indeed, ruthlessly, pressing her knuckles inside the foot of each

to detect the better any incipient thinnesses; she counted them twice to see that the tale was correct. Then she wound up her gilt clock, a gift of the General. Then she went into her bedroom to see that the clothes were properly turned down. (It was the stated duty of a lower housemaid to do this for Mrs. Bentham every night, as well as to make the bed in the morning.) And then once more she sat down before the fire, with her old hands clasped.

There was a long frame above the mantelpiece, containing, as in a gallery, the photographs of General Medd, Lady Beatrice, Minnie, who had died in infancy, then Austin, then May, then Val; and lastly, by a peculiar privilege, the severe countenance of Miss Deverell. She looked up at this once or twice, and particularly at the two boys — Austin, aged sixteen, in a collar much too high for him, with a markedly intellectual brow, from which the hair had been, by the photographer's directions, carefully brushed backwards; and Val, aged thirteen, in an Eton suit, leaning on a balustrade, with Swiss mountains in the background.

And meanwhile Benty went through her little conflict once more.

The doubts and questions which, half an hour ago, had been merely battering at her outer gate, were now clamorous and articulate. That Simpson should " pass remarks " was one thing; that a Medd,

and she the mother, should "pass" them was
another. It was bitter to Benty that Lady Beatrice
should, all unknowingly, have joined forces with a
cynical manservant, who had no real reverence for
the Family at all. So Benty fought desperately. . . .

It is at once a gain and a loss to simple and un-
educated people that they cannot, usually, stand
outside and regard themselves. They have extraordinarily little power of self-criticism — even of
self-observance. But it was pure gain to Benty
now. She fought for her boy instinctively and
quite unfairly; she seized every advantage, she dis-
ingeniously rejected every suggestion on the other
side. She insisted that Val was a boy; she refused
to allow that he was becoming a man. She insisted
that duels were wrong; she rejected the inevitable
conclusion that Austin ought not to have fought
(for she was determined to vindicate him, too, as
well as Val; since both were Medds).

Benty's great word was "proper." It connoted a
thousand shades and *nuances;* its fabric was established convention; but it was embroidered over with
religion, and fine instinct, and violent, loveable preju-
dice; and before she could be satisfied, she must
range everybody with Medd blood under its sanc-
tion. "The master" must be right in being upset;
"the mistress" in being distressed; Austin in fight-

ing; Val in not fighting. And everybody else must be wrong, " Them out there," and Simpson, emphatically Simpson, down here.

Well; she won of course. Charity prevailed over just criticism. She stormed off her guns of disapprobation at the enemy; they were not doing or saying or thinking what was " proper," and she clasped all the Medds, one and all, to her heart. " My Family, right or wrong."

A great peace descended on Benty, and the enemy retired. Visions moved before her of the young gentlemen and Miss May coming home again. Everything would be all right then. Master Val would come and have tea with her; and she would tell him to take off his shoes and warm his feet on the high fender, as he liked to do. Charity would materialise itself and become finally victorious, in little kindly acts showered upon the wounded. They would be healed and made whole.

Before she went to " the mistress " she did an unusual thing; she leaned forward and gently kissed the photograph of the sulky looking boy who leaned on the balustrade in the presence of the Swiss mountains.

(IV)

" Benty," said Lady Beatrice, regarding her over the edge of the bedclothes. " Were they — Masterman, I mean — saying anything about what I told you, in the ' Room '? "

Benty, with a stern face, was shaking out the stockings which Miss Ferguson had placed in a manner displeasing to her, and affected not to hear.

" Benty — were they? "

" Eh? my lady."

" Were they talking about it downstairs? "

" How should they be doing that? " demanded the old lady in sudden indignation. " Why you only told me this evening; and it isn't likely that I should —— "

" Then they weren't? " persisted the other, who had an uneasy sense of having seen Simpson just too late, while she and her husband were talking. Besides, it appeared that Benty herself had been strangely quick in understanding the situation just now.

Benty paused. Then with immense emphasis, she lied.

" No, my lady. And, if they did, I'd soon put a stopper on them."

Lady Beatrice sighed with relief and laid her head back.

" Kiss me, Benty," she said three minutes later, as the old nurse finished with the stockings, and said, " There! "

CHAPTER IX

I

THE little sleeping compartment for two was
dim and ghostly looking within as the Rome
to Paris train de luxe ten days later ran mile after
mile through the southern plains of France as the
dawn began to come up, and its light filtered in
through the drawn flapping blinds, to mingle with
the shaded glow of the lamp in the roof.

Val turned over once again, and rested his cheek
on the edge of his upper berth, looking down into
the compartment beneath. He had been awake
since three o'clock, and had now given up all idea of
sleep. He just lay, listening to the measured beat
of the train sounding above the steady roar of the
wheels, to the flapping of the blind, to the long, far-
away scream of the engine as it tore through sleeping stations, to the banging of a door left unfastened
somewhere down the corridor — he lay there listening and thinking.

Now, however, he opened his eyes, and began
mechanically to study the bird's-eye view of the compartment behind him — the heap of Austin's clothes

on the cane-seat by the window, a couple of Italian newspapers on the floor; his own overcoat and hat swinging from the peg by the window, an open ciga-rette-box that he had hidden for Austin a few miles out of Modane, and produced again afterwards; and, finally, the edge of the red coverlet from the berth beneath where Austin lay sleeping. And as he saw this he leaned over yet further to see whether Austin's bandaged arm, now, however, al-most healed, were lying as it should, in the sling across his breast. The doctor had said it must not be knocked against anything.

Then he lay back again in his own place and re-mained still.

Ten minutes later he roused himself with a jerk and sat up. His tweed suit was hanging at the foot of his berth, and he kneeled forwards to get his leather letter-case out of the breast-pocket of his coat. Out of this he drew a folded paper, and then lay back again to read it through, as well as he could in the dim light, for perhaps the fiftieth time. It was written in a strong, but rather school-girlish handwriting.

" I have thought over everything you have said; and my answer is what it was at the beginning; and nothing you can ever say or do again can make any difference. I cannot marry a coward. When I made our engagement I thought you were a brave man; and I certainly shall never forget that you once saved my life. But that can make no difference now. When you had a *real* test you failed and you allowed your brother to take your place. I need not say how sorry I am to have brought all this trouble on you; but perhaps it is best so, as it has showed me what you really are before it was too late. Marriage without love would be bad enough; but marriage *without respect* far worse; and I could never respect a coward. As for our engagement, I trust to your honour never to tell anyone that it ever existed. If I think it right I shall tell May or your mother myself; but I don't see that I need.

"Of course, we shall have to be friends, in a way, at any rate so long as we are in Rome, and until we get back to England.

"GERTRUDE MARJORIBANKS."

He read it through slowly, all the cruel phrases, the hints at melodrama, the sensible, reasonable sentiments, half-childish, half-womanly, even though he knew it practically by heart. It was the last communication he had had from her about the affair. There had been two or three interviews first, and, finally, a week after the duel, and three days before the doctor would allow Austin to travel, she had written and put this note on his table. He had not answered it.

If his state of mind must be summed up under one word one would say that it consisted of dreaminess. There were moments and even hours when he felt desperately inspired to do some really great thing to prove his courage; there were other moments when he was shaken by a passion of despair. But both these were passing; there seemed to him for the most part now to be nothing anywhere but dreaminess; there was no good in anything anywhere; nothing mattered. He had lost not only the respect of everyone else, but, what is infinitely worse, his own self-respect as well. It was no good twisting and shamming and excusing any more. He was found out; and he had found himself out. . . . A huge gulf separated him from his kind. Gertie was gone, as irreparably as if she were dead; May seemed to stand off from him, almost as if she were frightened of him; Austin, with his pain and his gallantry, accepted as a matter of course all the infinite attentions which Val gave him, and once or twice even had snapped at him rather brutally, once telling him that " he might be a bit more thoughtful under the circumstances," once that he " wished he wouldn't come bothering, but would leave him alone." And, as for his parents at home, well, his chief misery on this journey was the thought that every mile brought him nearer to Medhurst. . . . They had both written to May, but Val's name was not mentioned in either letter. One single figure glimmered with hope, and that was Benty.

He had found himself out then. But he stood now at a point from which this was more wretched than to be found out by other people.

(II)

" Val! are you awake? "

He leant over the edge instantly.

" Yes. . . . Can I do anything? "

" I wish you'd come and look at this string; the knot's got behind my neck."

Val threw his legs over the side and dropped to the ground. Austin drew his breath sharply.

" I wish you wouldn't do that," he said. " I asked you not last night. It jars me."

" Sorry. Let's see the knot."

" Gently! " said Austin presently, " you touched my wrist."

" Sorry. Is that all right? Anything else? "

" What's the time? I suppose you couldn't get some coffee."

" I'll go and see. I think it's about six."

In ten minutes he returned with a tray.

" You've been a long time," said Austin.

" I thought I'd better take some to the girls too."

Austin said nothing, and Val poured out the coffee and held the saucer for him.

" That's better," said Austin more graciously, leaning back at last. " And now, if you'd give me a cigarette ——"

This was done, and Val drank his own coffee, put the tray on the floor outside, and prepared to climb back to his berth.

" Do you want to go to sleep again? " asked Austin.

" Not particularly. Why? "

" Well, we might have a talk. The girls will be up soon, and we may not have another chance."

" All right. Wait a sec., and I'll put on a coat."

Then Austin settled himself down for a lecture.

It must be confessed that Austin was not wholly miserable at the turn things had taken. Certainly he had suffered considerably; his wound had given him really severe pain for some days, and when Val handled him clumsily it still hurt a good deal. And he was sincerely upset at the blow to the family honour; it seemed to him appalling that his brother should have behaved like a cur. And yet there were consolations. It was pleasant to be treated as a hero and adored like a god by Gertie and May, by Gertie especially; it was pleasant to be travelling home to

parents who, though they would certainly find fault
with his discretion, as their letters had hinted, would
equally certainly respect him in a new kind of way
altogether. To have fought a duel at all was not
without distinction; and lastly, and perhaps chiefly,
though mostly subconsciously, it was pleasant to
know that Val's relations with him were finally
decided henceforth and for ever; no longer could
there be any question at all as to which ruled and
which served. He himself had behaved as a model
elder brother; Val had already shown by his attentions and his humility that he knew the duties of a
younger, and recognised their obligations.

It was with all this behind him therefore that
Austin settled down comfortably for his first deliberate lecture of Val.

"Look here," he began, "you won't mind my
saying this first of all — that I think you look after
the two girls a little more than they like. May said
something to me yesterday after lunch, when you'd
gone. You don't mind my saying that?"

"Please tell me."

"Well, you know, they're both awfully upset just
now. And it looks rather as if . . . as if you
were trying to propitiate them. . . . Just leave
it alone a bit; it'll come right. At least . . ."

Val was silent.

"You don't mind my telling you?"

"No. Thanks very much."

"I mean things like taking coffee in to them. They'd much rather ring and ask for it themselves. Honestly, I think you'd better keep rather aloof than otherwise."

Val nodded.

"Well, but," went on Austin, "what I particularly wanted to talk about was what was to happen when we got home — what to say to them, and so on."

"I ought to be back at Cambridge. Fall term began last week. I rather thought ——"

"Oh! but you mustn't shirk coming home. You must face the music."

"I didn't mean I wasn't coming home," said Val humbly. "I only meant that it couldn't be for more than a day or so."

"Well," interrupted Austin rather irritably, "that makes it no better. Whatever has got to be said will be said at once, I imagine. I hope you aren't expecting them to behave as if nothing at all had happened."

"No; I wasn't."

"Well, the point is, what line are we to take? Lord knows, I don't want a fuss. The point is, is there any way we can tone the thing down a bit?"

"I propose to tell them the truth."

"Good God, Val! You seem unable to think of anybody but yourself, even now. Hasn't it occurred to you that this will be about the most ghastly blow to father that he's ever had? I wasn't thinking of you, my good chap, but of him. The point is, can we say anything that'll make it less ghastly — that you were really ill, for instance? I don't think you realise in the least that honour and courage and that sort of thing is about the most —— What's the matter?"

"Nothing; go on."

Austin looked at him with a touch of uneasiness. Val had flinched just now, flinched as from a blow in the face; he looked, even now in this half-light — for he had omitted to turn back the shade of the lamp — curiously pale and worn. Austin determined to be less rhetorical, but felt he must continue to be explicit.

"Look here, Val; I know this isn't easy for you. But you really must face things. You know father's ideas. Do you remember that jaw he gave us both before we went to school about standing up . . . and so on? Well, we've got to get this thing through as easily as we can for his sake and mother's. And I think the illness line is about the best."

"I am afraid that's no good now," said Val almost soundlessly.

"What? I can't hear."

"I am afraid that's no good now. You must remember that May and Gertie know the whole thing."

"I know. You would go and tell them outright. And I begged you not to."

"Well, it's done now."

Austin was silent a moment.

"What have you to suggest, then?" he snapped at last.

Val stood up, feeling in his coat pocket for his cigarette-case. (Obviously this was to soften the situation, thought Austin.) And as he put his cigarette between his lips he answered.

"I have nothing whatever to suggest, except the whole truth. I propose to tell that, without modifications; and . . . and to face the music, as you said. It's no good, Austin; he's got to be told. Of course, I'm perfectly willing that anyone else should tell him who wishes to. I'm not — er — exactly keen on doing it myself. I imagine he knows the outline?"

"He knows that you . . . that you refused to fight at the last moment, and that I had to instead, of course."

" Well, those are the facts, aren't they? "

Austin was silent. Secretly he knew it must be so; that the facts must come out. And he shrank from that, even now.

" Look here," he said, " I'll take you at your word. May and I will tell him. We'll do what we can, for everybody's sake. But I'm afraid you must be prepared for — well — remarks."

" I suppose so."

" There's one other thing," added Austin presently. " It's about Gertie. You remember we had a row about it before. Well, look here, have you — er — any secret understanding with her? One or two things ———"

" Do you mean am I engaged to her? "

" Well, yes, or practically engaged, without any actual promise, you know."

" I am not," said Val. " There's not the faintest understanding of any sort or kind."

" Well, that's all right. Because I was going to tell you that it really won't do, now at any rate. People under a cloud mustn't ——— Eh! what's up? "

" I burnt my lip," said Val.

" Well, then, that's really all . . . Val? "

" Yes."

" I'm afraid you're feeling pretty beastly about all this ———"

He did not finish his sentence. Val was gone out into the corridor, leaving the door open.

Austin snorted to himself.

"What a chap!" he said aloud.

(III)

It was already dark when the boat express from Folkestone drew up at the little wayside station to let the Medd party disembark. It was one of the Medhurst privileges — understood rather than actually stated — since the line ran for a couple of miles through an outlying tongue of the estate. It was not used often, of course; but a telegram had been handed to Austin on the quay at Folkestone, telling him it would be so to-night.

There, too, the brougham waited at the foot of the steps that led down from the high platform, its lamps blazing, and its two horses stamping and tossing their heads after the long wait, ready to take them over the fourteen miles to Medhurst. A cart was drawn up behind the brougham for the luggage.

Val dawdled at the carriage door, pretending to oversee the taking out of the hand-luggage, in reality strangely unwilling to see even one familiar face; and by the time that he reached the head of the steps, the girls were already at the bottom, and Austin was going down gently and carefully on the arm of Simpson, his father's own body-servant. This was an enormous distinction. Usually one of the younger footmen would have been sent to meet such a party.

Three minutes later Austin was in his place, propped by cushions, with Gertie beside him and May opposite. Then Val climbed in. Simpson shut the door, mounted beside the coachman, and the brougham moved off.

The day had passed for Val like a terrible dream. They had lunched in the restaurant-car shortly before reaching Paris; had driven straight across Paris and caught the boat-train at the Gare du Nord. The Channel had been wet and stormy; but they were up to time. But the chief horror of the day, to him, had been the sense of a gulf that deepened and widened between him and the others, as every mile brought them nearer home. He had taken Austin's hint, and had attempted no more officious services; for he perceived that his brother had been perfectly right, and that it had been from a vague sense of propitiation that he had done so much already. And others had met him at least half-way. No one except Austin had spoken to him at all; and indeed they had hardly talked among themselves, at any rate when he was there. And he had only been with them at meal-times, or when they had to change carriages, and for a few minutes on the boat. From Folkestone they had travelled together, because there was a reserved carriage.

It was the actual increase of a sense of alienation that was weighing on him so terribly; for he felt it to be a symptom of the kind of reception he would have at home. If, even after ten days, Austin and May could treat him so, what might he not expect at Medhurst? . . . except . . . except perhaps from Benty.

And now there was dead silence in the brougham. Five minutes after starting he had touched Gertie's foot with his own, and she had withdrawn it without a word; and this afforded him a theme for further meditation.

Then Austin, in despair, had said something about the rain that was now coming on again more heavily than ever; and May had answered him with almost hysterical effusiveness. And then again silence fell.

"Val."

"Yes."

"Was my little brown bag put into the cart, do you know?" pursued Austin.

"Yes. At least, I saw it taken downstairs all right."

"Oh, thanks."

And then again a long silence, broken only by
the beating of the rain against the windows, and the
steady cloppetty-clops of the horses' hoofs over the
splashy roads.

Perhaps three or four other sentences were uttered during the fourteen-mile drive. Once May
leant forward and asked Austin whether his arm
was all right. Once Gertie, in answer to another
question from May, said that she must go home to
her own people in two days at the latest. Once Austin wondered aloud whether there would be anyone
staying at Medhurst; and May said she thought not.
And that was all. The intensity of the silence deepened every instant; it seemed as if it were only
when this became unbearable that anyone spoke;
but for the last three miles they gave it up; and all
four sat absorbed in the silent darkness within here,
thinking, listening to the beat of the rain and the
cloppetty-clop of the hoofs, and again — thinking.

The brougham drew up at the lodge-gate; and it
was then perhaps that the boy's anguish drew to
a point. For he had always remembered this pause
— the sudden cessation of hoofs and wheels, and
then the faint creak of the harness and the jingle of
a chain as a horse tossed his head, or the faint swing
of the carriage — and then the footsteps across the

gravel and the sound of the unlocking of the gate —
remembered it from his old schooldays, when the
pause seemed intolerable to his impatience to be
home.   Whereas now ——!

It was a mile's drive to the house from the lodge;
first through rhododendrons and along the swan-
pond, then upwards gently through the woods till
they came out on to the grass where the rabbits fed
on summer evenings, then up again to the top of
the hill, whence the descent went down to the great
house dreaming among its trees.

Still no one spoke.   But as the carriage topped
the hill, Gertie leaned forward suddenly, as if to see
the lights of the house; the glare from the carriage-
lamps on her side fell full on her face; and Val,
taken unaware, saw even so the look of strain in
those beautiful eyes and the downcurved mouth.
She leaned back almost instantly; but as she did so,
glanced at Val, and their eyes met.

The carriage passed straight on along the front of
the house, as was the custom on wet nights.   Val
saw the grey terrace slip past in the lamplight; but
it was not until at last the wheels stopped at the
south porch that he remembered that it was in this
porch, closed on the night of the ball last Christmas,
that Gertie and he had sat and kissed.

Yet even this memory was not so poignant as the

present fact that faced him; it was but an ironical background to the meeting with his father and mother that was now imminent; and he sat, his heart hammering him sick, not daring even to lean forward into the glare of light that now poured out of the open door.

The carriage-door too was open now; he perceived that without moving his eyes from the ground. Fortunately he sat on the further side. . . . He heard voices talking; and then the carriage creaked as Austin was helped out.

"Gently now, Simpson," said his father's voice, sharp and anxious. . . .

There was a pause. Then May was out; and he heard his mother's voice murmuring something. Yet still he sat motionless. And then Gertie slipped across and was gone. Yet still he sat motionless.

"Master Val, sir," said a voice.

He looked up, and old Masterman was peering in. He raised his eyes over the man's shoulder and saw that the doorway was no longer darkened. Yet still he gave them a moment or two to get clear of his presence, and he pretended to search under the seat for something.

"I'll take everything out, Master Val."

"Ah! it'll be in the cart, I expect. . . . Thanks."

He went slowly up the two steps into the porch;

and then he could see that the brightly lit corridor beyond was empty. Then he heard the swing door into the hall bang, and knew that the way was clear up the back stairs. They had gone, all of them, leaving him.

When he reached the head of the back stairs he stood and listened; but there was no sound anywhere in the great house; then on tip-toe he ran, like a hunted creature, along the passages, through the upper swing door, along the gallery, down a couple of stairs, and so to his own room in the north wing. He caught a glimpse of an old capped face peering out from beyond the baize door that led to Benty's rooms, but he would not see her and ran on.

There he locked the door, and stood listening again. . . . He was only a boy.

(IV)

The stable clock struck ten before he was disturbed. He had heard the bell for the servants' supper soon after he had reached his room, three-quarters of an hour before. Then he had washed, and changed his shoes. He was almost grateful to find hot water ready for him, and shoes and socks set out before the fire. He wondered whether Charles, the young footman, had done it on his own responsibility, or was it Benty, perhaps. Then he had sat before the fire, motionless, thinking.

Somehow, the reality was a hundred times worse than the anticipation. He had rehearsed, of course, scene after scene — each of which had ended in his being turned out of the house. He knew, in a way, that this was ridiculous; yet his imagination was not fertile enough to picture any other way in which his father could adequately deal with the situation. And it had been even a relief to think of himself as an outcast; for suicide or death from exposure had formed the sequel of his interior drama. But the reality was worse. He was to be treated physically with ordinary kindness — he was to have hot water, and a fire, and the curtains drawn; and yet he was, morally, to be treated as if he did not exist. The others must have finished supper by now; and the shameful story must have been told in full. It was all known by now . . . in detail.

When the tap came at his door he started up.

" Yes. Who's there? "

" It's Masterman, Master Val."

He unlocked the door and stood there, barring entrance, still holding out of sight in his left hand a small packet slung on a string, which he had taken from round his neck as he changed and had been holding almost unconsciously ever since.

" Her ladyship says, will you come down and have supper at once, please, Master Val. And when

you've had supper, her ladyship says, will you go
into master's study."

Val nodded. He could see that the old man was
puzzled. Or was it, perhaps, that he too had been
told, and that they were laughing over the story in
the servants' hall.

"I'll come down. . . . Have the others
finished?"

"Yes, sir. They're all in her ladyship's room.
Miss Marjoribanks has gone to bed."

"Very well. I'll come directly."

When the footsteps had died away again and he
had locked the door, he went to the fire once more
and stood there motionless. He had come to his
tragic little determination during the journey across
France; he had almost carried it out on the boat,
but it had seemed to him more judicial and more
final to finish the affair at home. So he had taken
off his little packet of Gertie's photograph and her
letters, and held it now, looking at it. . . .
. Then he kissed it suddenly and passionately.
Then he dropped it carefully into the red heart of
the fire.

"They're all in her ladyship's room," the old man
had said just now. As he left his room at last the
words came back to him.

He could see all so well — his mother in her
chair, his father standing on the rug, Austin perhaps
on the sofa, and May beside him.   Austin would be
telling the story.   .   .   .

Down in the dining-room three people had
supped; the fourth place was still untouched.   They
had expected him to sup with them then!

There was some soup — growing cold.   He ate
some of this, glancing over his shoulder at the door
as he helped himself from the sideboard; he did not
wish to be taken unprepared, and he moved his
place round to where he could watch this door.
Then he ate something cold and drank a couple of
glasses of wine.   And all the while he listened, and
the moment was come.

Yet for a while he still sat, fumbling his bread and
staring with sick eyes at the portraits that watched
him.   There were half a dozen rather inferior portraits here — inferior, that is, compared with the
priceless collection in the great hall.   Four were
women, but two were men, and these two were
soldiers; the one young and smooth-faced, in
breast-armour: he had fought at Naseby, and died
there, aged nineteen; the other in flowing wig and
scarlet, with lace at his wrists — this one had been
one of Marlborough's captains, who had fought at
Blenheim and been wounded.   .   .   .   It seemed
horrible to Val that these should be hanging opposite

him; he remembered his father telling him their stories more than once, when he was a child. . . .

And then, unconscious that he had made any decision to move, conscious only that he rose up from table, as might a machine, he went to the door, opened it, passed out, crossed the length of the hall with his head lowered and his eyes upon the floor, put his hand on the handle of the study door, went in without knocking, closed the door behind him, and stood looking at his father, who was looking at him.

(v)

His father was in the tall chair by the fire, facing him, with his head on his hand. Another chair stood drawn up on the hearth-rug, evidently by design, and, without a word, the old General signed to this.

" There," he said.

Val went straight to it and sat down.

It is hardly possible to say that he was suffering consciously. In mental pain, as in physical, there comes a point beyond which reflection on the pain (which is the essence of suffering) becomes impossible. It was in this state that Val sat and faced his father; he could even notice how the green light from the shaded lamp at his father's side glimmered

on the silver hair above the old man's ears; how the
long knotted hand that lay on the little table beneath
the lamp writhed itself into lines and shadows as the
fingers contracted and relaxed. Even the old familiar fear of his father seemed gone — absorbed in
a vaster emotion. . . .

Then his father cleared his throat and began to
speak; and again Val was more conscious of the
huskiness of the tone than of anything else. Another part of him than that of attention received
and stored every word that he listened to.

"I'm not going to say much to you, sir. I have
decided to do you the honour of thinking still that
there is no need. It is rather of the future that I am
going to speak."

He stopped and swallowed in his throat.

"Your mother and I have talked the matter over.
We knew, of course, all that happened, from the
letters; and we have just heard the last details.
Your brother has said all that he can for you; he
has told us that you seemed really ill; he has done
his utmost to defend you. How far all this may
seem an excuse to you, I do not know. I cannot any
longer pretend to understand you or your code.
May too has pleaded for you. And this is our
decision.

"Henceforth I do not wish one word spoken on

the subject to any living being. When I have
finished what I have to say to-night I shall never
refer to the subject again to you or anyone else.
Neither will your mother nor Austin nor May.
May is now with Miss Marjoribanks, telling her our
decision, and asking her to observe the same condi-
tions. And I expect you — in fact, I order you,
now, to do the same. You are not to discuss the
matter with anybody — not even with Austin. So
far as speech is concerned, the matter is finished.

"As regards action, I shall do what I think right.
I do not mean that I shall exclude you from the
house or take you away from Cambridge. Things
will go on as before in those ways. I shall not disgrace you publicly. But if, at any time, you have
reason to think I am treating you unfairly, or showing any want of confidence in you, you will kindly
remember the reason. Do you understand?"

"Yes."

"Have you anything to say?"

"No."

"You will leave here to-morrow by the nine-four-
teen train, and go straight up to Cambridge. You
will breakfast alone, therefore. When we see you
again at Midsummer we shall take up our old life
again with you so far as that may be possible."

He paused.

Then he called out aloud, sharply:

" Beatrice."

The door leading from his study into his wife's
morning-room was pushed open behind him, and
Val saw his mother come in. She came steadily
forward, upright and magnificent, but her hand on
her stick shook a little. Val too stood up, and
remained waiting.

" Beatrice, I have told him. From this time
onwards no one will mention the subject again. He
must redeem his honour as best he can."

The old man turned again to Val.

" Good night," he said. " Kiss your mother."

And then her arms were round the boy, and he
burst into sudden uncontrollable weeping.

PART III

CHAPTER I

(1)

THE street of Medhurst Village resembles that of the mean average of English villages throughout the land: that is to say that it has specimens of the architecture of about eight hundred years, from the Norman church on the left, in the middle, to the corrugated-iron roofs of the twentieth century covering the ricks, in the suburb on the right. It can look, therefore, exceedingly beautiful or exceedingly dreary, according to the place where one stands to view it.

On this June morning it ought to have looked exceedingly beautiful to Lady Beatrice Medd as she stood in the gate of the Home Farm, looking up past the church, with her Bath-chair, drawn by an Egyptian donkey, waiting behind her. Only she was thinking about something else.

The village ran at the bottom of a shallow valley. Behind Lady Beatrice and the farm-yard were the kitchen gardens, the glass houses, and the park. Opposite her was the village inn, and the Medd Arms swinging from an iron scroll-work bracket

317

that was hung in front; and through the open doors
she could see the June flowers in the garden beyond;
and down, away to the left, ran the street — here a
row of " magpie " houses, dating from Tudor days;
there a red-brick Queen Anne house, standing back,
with a little strip of greenery in front, as if in a
mood of staid and modest gentility, with a roof like
that of a chapel appearing behind; then a row of
thatched cottages, half hidden under the giant
flowers that towered before them. All this was on
the opposite side of the road from the Home Farm;
on this side, the churchyard wall began immediately,
over which looked the church-tower, like a tall, high-
shouldered man, peeping. And then the road
curved and disappeared towards the school and the
farmer's house and the vicarage. The June sun lay
hot and bright on road and house and trees and
flowers.

Lady Beatrice, it has been said, was thinking of
something else than the view. Besides, she had
seen it a thousand times before. It was her custom,
once or twice a week at least, if the weather was
respectable, to come down here in her donkey-
carriage, and talk to the bailiff, or inspect the orchid-
house, or visit the school (which, by the way, she
almost entirely financed). She loved the leisurely
sense of business and responsibility that it all gave

her; and there was often, honestly, something for her to do. This morning she was undecided. She had told the schoolmistress on Sunday that she might be looking in to-day; yet she felt disinclined to go. Two or three ideas floated through her quiet mind; and, meantime, she stood, her parasol resting on her shoulder, watching the infinitesimal drama of the village street.

First there came a tight-breeched cyclist, crouched like a great ape over his low handle-bars, striding up past the church; he eyed the great lady standing there as he came near, seemed inclined to ask her a question, and then thought better of it. He dismounted at the inn opposite and went in; and presently could be descried in the dark little open-windowed parlour on the right, tilting a long glass to his mouth. Lady Beatrice hoped he was enjoying himself. . . .

Then out of the inn door came a fat white dog that reminded her of dear Jimbo, long ago laid to rest under the cedar in the garden, with a Latin inscription, designed by Professor Macintosh, over him. This one came out with the same assured and proprietary air, barked sullenly once at Lady Beatrice, just to tell her he was there, and then lay down on the cobble-stones in the shadow, to keep an eye on her. She could hear, all across the road, the grunt of pleasure (or was it rheumatics?) with which he plumped himself down. Probably he had been disturbed by the tight-breeched cyclist who was now sitting in a chair and smoking.

Then came a procession of fowls round the corner of the inn, through an open wicket gate. Obviously they were doing wrong, for they walked with an air compounded of expectancy, timidity, and defiance. A cock came first, fiery-eyed and high-stepping, once or twice stooping hastily to pick at the ground, and immediately straightening himself, as if he were some great man caught in a moment of weakness, and challenging criticism; he was followed by four homely hens, who picked with more *abandon* and eyed the world with less. She saw the cock pause suddenly in his progress with uplifted claw, and then dart back to lead the retreat, as a girl came out of the inn door and seized a birch-broom to demonstrate with.

The girl then bobbed to Lady Beatrice and went to shut the gate.

" Good morning, Alice."

" Good morning, m'lady."

" Father and mother well? "

" Yes, m'lady; and thank you."

Then the dog barked again; and the Vicar came out of the churchyard gate on the right, with his

coat-tails flying behind him. He had just finished
reading the Morning Prayer and Litany, and was
preparing to go to the school. (Morning Prayer
and Litany were at eleven, on Wednesdays and
Fridays, Lady Beatrice remembered.) He took
off his hat.

"Good morning, Mr. Arbuthnot."

"Good morning, Lady Beatrice."

He was a pleasant, fervent man who worked hard,
and thought the Lady Bountiful a little unsym-
pathetic. He himself was Oxford and Cuddesdon;
and she was of a strongly Evangelical stock. He
was exceedingly active, and read Matins and Even-
song every day, and had a Guild of St. Mary for
females and a Guild of St. George for males, and
suffered secretly and intensely from the presence of
Father Maple in the village. He had had a list
of the vicars of Medhurst Village, from Thomas
de Hoppe of 1493 down to James Arbuthnot of
1891, engraved in brass, and erected in the church
porch, soon after Father Maple's arrival, without
the least hint that anything whatever had been
tended to break the line about the years 1540 or
1560 A.D. He spoke of him always as the "Roman" priest, or when he was not quite well, as the
"Romish clergyman." But he was a good-hearted
and sincere man, and did his best under discourag-

ing circumstances. And he never was uncharitable or bitter, beyond the requirements of strict *odium theologicum.*

"I've been thinking how nice the village looks this morning," said Lady Beatrice, who had not previously thought anything at all about it. "I suppose you are on your way to the schools?"

"Well, I generally go about this time."

"Will you give me your arm as far as that then? I said I would look in myself this morning."

They talked, as they went slowly up the street, about this and that and the other. Lady Beatrice said that she really thought that it was time for Alice-of-the-Inn to go out to service; it wasn't good for young girls, etc., etc. And the Vicar said that he had been speaking to Mr. Jeaffreson himself (tenant of the "Medd Arms") only last Friday on the subject, and that that parent of Alice had given his formal consent; but that Mrs. Jeaffreson still remained to be persuaded. Perhaps Lady Beatrice herself would, etc., etc. It was just that pleasant, kindly, paternal talk of the Great Powers who were beginning to wonder how much longer their absolute domination would continue.

Then they reached the school door. As they entered a loud female voice cried, "Stand"; and then, "Say, 'Good morning, my lady; good morning, sir.'" . . . And so the Great Powers were

saluted; and both sides were pleased: the one by a
sense of fitting homage and respect, the other by a
visible reassurance that there were such things as
Dominations and Authorities still in existence, who
walked with men.

(II)

She came out alone, ten minutes later, assuring
the Vicar that she could get back unaided, and went
slowly down the street. When she came opposite
the church she hesitated. Then she turned and
limped in.

Churches on weekday mornings are apt to look
chilly and unreal, even rather repellent; there is a
curious smell about them too, reminiscent of re-
straint and of Sunday mornings; and the Prayer
Books in the pews look desolate. One is tempted —
I do not know why — to be profane and worldly
when one finds oneself alone in one — to mount the
pulpit and gesticulate in dumb show, to pretend to
go to sleep in a pew, and to behave generally like
a vulgar boy. (Probably it arises from a sense
that the tables are turned, and that for once Solemnity is at one's mercy, instead of the other way
about.)

Lady Beatrice, it need hardly be said, did none of
these things. She limped up the aisle into the Medd
chapel, and sat down in the dusky, smelly splendour,

beneath the banners and the hatchments. She had
not come to pray; but she had an idea that she
could think here more detachedly than at home.

It was about ten minutes before she moved, and
then it was with a sudden start at the sound of a
piano. Very delicately and sweetly the music came
in here — some grave and humorous gavotte by a
German master, scholarly, melancholy, academic,
and yet with soft laughter in it too. Little positive
phrases asserted themselves solemnly, then turned
head over heels, chuckled, and vanished. It
sounded like a light argument by wits round a
dinner-table in the open air. The wind was very
still in the village this morning, and the music came
in, obviously from the Queen Anne house just opposite, as clear as if played in the churchyard itself.

She listened, charmed in spite of herself, fixing
her eyes on the communion-table, gay with its brass
vases, its painted brass cross and candlesticks hung
with pious emblems on shields. Overhead a few
scraps of really old glass — a broken crucifix, two
headless saints, and some detached black-letters —
pieced together reverently by the modern successor
to Thomas de Hoppe, let the sunlight through.
The other windows were not so fortunate. Opposite the entrance, for example, a green Elijah in
a blue chariot, ascended amid purple flames, resembling streams of cherry sauce, towards a heaven

that consisted entirely of Gothic crockets and pinnacles.

Still she listened, and still the music went on.
She began mechanically to read some of the inscrip-
tions with which the chapel walls bulged so thickly.
Here was an urn and a broken column, and a list of
virtues: she had smiled before now at the sentence
with which it ended: "In short, he was endued
with every virtue that could grace the Christian
or adorn the man." (That was old Christopher
Medd, who had a family of seventeen children —
"ob. 1734.") There was a brass to Anthony
Medd, who had fought and died at Naseby; there,
a plain marble slab to John Valentine Medd. . . .
She looked at them, listening to the music. Then,
as it ended, she got up and went out, passed across
the street, and rang the bell at the Queen Anne
house.

"Is Father Maple at home?" she said.

Lady Beatrice Medd was honestly, except for her
very distinguished appearance and her history, not
a very interesting woman. She was as good as
gold; she was conscientious and domestic, rather
religious in her own way, perfectly honourable, perfectly fearless. But her worst enemy could not
have called her subtle, nor her best friend, imaginative. She had instincts which she usually followed,
and gravely justified to herself afterwards. She

had her joys, which she took tranquilly, as of right; and sorrows, which she bore stoically, like a very intelligent animal, without resentment or indignation. In a word, she was an absolutely perfect success in her station. Certainly she had rather dull things to do; but then she was rather dull herself, to compensate.

It was one of those above-mentioned sorrows and one of those instincts that sent her across now to Father Maple's house. She would probably not have gone if she had not heard the piano and known it to be his; even though the idea had crossed her mind as she left in the donkey-carriage this morning that she might perhaps look in and ask him to dinner.

It was a very pleasant room into which she was shown by the Irish housekeeper — a long, high room, lined with bookcases, carpetless except for a big mat before the fire-place, with a writing-table between the windows, and a full-sized grand piano in the very middle of the floor. Another little bookcase stood close beside this, with tall shelves filled with music.

"I thought his reverence was here, m'lady. . . . He must have been after stepping out into the garden. I'll get him."

Lady Beatrice sank down into a chair. Through

the windows she could see the side of the tall red-brick chapel, that was an object of such mysterious wonder to the village and of such Christian dislike to the Vicar. In very sardonic moods he called it a " schism-shop."

Then the tall window-door was darkened and the little priest came in in his cassock.

First she said, " How do you do? " and then she said she had just looked in to see if he would come to dinner on Thursday. No one would be there, she said, except themselves and her son Val, who came down from Cambridge on that day. And then she said how very nice his music sounded as she sat in the church just now; and what was it that he was playing?

He answered all these remarks suitably: said that he would be delighted to dine on Thursday; and showed her the manuscript from which he had been playing, saying that he had copied it in the British Museum the other day, and believed it to be by Sebastian Bach. He sat down even at the piano, and played a phrase or two over again. She liked him, as she watched him with his serious face and grey hair.

And then she suddenly began her real business.

" Father Maple," she said, " you'll think it very extraordinary of me, but as a matter of fact I want to consult you very much about my son Val."

He made a little murmurous sound of encouragement as he wheeled round on his music-stool.

" I know Roman Catholic priests are supposed to know a great deal about human nature and young men and so on. . . . Well, have you heard anything about our trouble? " (She was in for it now, and plunged boldly.)

" Yes," he said.

"Oh! . . . Well, I suppose somebody was certain to talk. It's perfectly true, I'm sorry to say. And I can't tell you how strongly his father feels about it all. May I tell you all, from the beginning? "

" Please do."

So she related the story quite adequately, calling Val " poor boy " two or three times, describing the treatment that her husband had decided upon, and ending with her own bewilderment as to what was to be done next. For it seemed to her that Val's letters were very odd and unlike him; they came punctually, but there was no regret in them, and, it seemed, no real affection. He related the most ordinary things of Cambridge, and that was all.

" And I'm not at all sure," she said, " of what's to be done next. His father won't speak of it even to me. I don't think that anything that has ever happened has affected him so much."

Father Maple was quite silent for a minute, and

she wondered whether she had done right in coming to him. But he had learned two things since he was a priest: first, that priests are told things which no one else in the world is told; and second, that those who give such confidences in nine cases out of ten do not really want any advice at all — they come simply to relieve their own minds. He waited, therefore, simply to see whether she really wanted him to speak. Then he spoke quite simply.

"I think your treatment of him is very severe, you know."

"Severe! Why ——"

"I mean that you are forbidding him the one thing that might relieve the strain. To forbid him to talk about it is to drive him back into himself. And I do not see what comfort he is to find there."

"Well, perhaps that is so," she murmured.

"I don't at all mean that it's necessarily the wrong treatment," he went on, smiling. (He was right round on the music-stool now, with one darned elbow resting on the edge of the open piano.) "You see I hardly know your son. But it's heroic treatment. If he's really fine clay inside, he'll respond, no doubt. But if not — one hardly knows."

"Ah! yes; if not. That's what I want to know." He evaded.

"Really it's impossible to tell."

"Well, make a guess at what might happen —
the worst, you know."

He looked straight at her, and she noticed the
keen, kindly brightness of his eyes.

"If you really want to know — well — I should
think he might go to the bad — or to despair, which
is the worst."

It suddenly came over her how very odd this all
was — this sudden plunge into intimacy. But the
man was as impersonal as a doctor; he seemed quite
at his ease, and to think it entirely natural to be
consulted and to talk like this. She made an effort
to respond.

"I see; thanks very much. Then you think it
dangerous not to allow him to talk?"

He seemed to hint at a shrug with his eyebrows
and shoulders. Then he smiled again, and she
noticed his white, even teeth.

"Yes, it seems to me dangerous, but not necessarily fatal."

"I wish you'd notice him on Thursday, and let me
know what you think. I meant to talk to the Vicar
about it, but somehow I've not had an opportunity.
And then the Vicar knows him almost too well
to judge."

"Certainly. I'll have a talk with him if I can.
But, you know, one evening ——"

She stood up, and he handed her her stick.

"Thank you so much, Father Maple. I'm so glad I came. . . . Then, on Thursday."

She smiled genially and impulsively as she gave him her hand, with all her great lady's air back again.

(III)

Again the feeling that it was all very strange and unconventional came on her as she sat in her donkey-carriage, going slowly up the park and along the garden paths, with the old groom at the donkey's head. She had talked to Father Maple about a dozen times in the whole of her acquaintance with him, and never until to-day had she even dreamed of consulting him about any intimate matters. And yet she was astonished at the way she had felt at her ease with him. She supposed that the reason was that he had not looked surprised, had not hummed or hawed, or put on a professional air; he had been as natural as a surgeon consulted about a rickety child.

And, ah! the rickety child in question!

She could hardly tell when her anxiety had begun, nor even her reasons for it. Yet from the first moment, when she had come in at her husband's call and seen the boy standing there, white and set-faced, a spring had been tapped in her which she scarcely suspected her heart contained — a spring of extraordinary compassion. Her old pride in him was gone, struck dead when she had first read May's letter; all those attributes which by training and birth she had associated with manhood were no longer his; yet in their place she was conscious of an emotion which she had never felt towards her other children. She had been perfectly loyal to her husband's plan — of which, indeed, she had approved — and never in her letters to Val at Cambridge had she allowed any unusual emotion to show itself; she wrote of the surfaces of things, of the prospects of the young pheasants, of a fall May had had out riding; and she had received in turn the same kind of letters back with disconcerting promptness. She would probably have snubbed him had he broken the contract, but she was inexplicably troubled by the fact that he had not. . . . She was just normally unreasonable and inconsistent.

It was this compassion that had made uneasiness possible, so soon as she was able to readjust herself to these new sentiments; and it was an uneasiness for which she could find neither remedy nor explanation. Neither remedy — since she did not dream of speaking to the old General; he felt it all too cruelly; he had sat motionless, evening after evening, for these two months, pretending to read books on things just like Afghanistan, but again and again, she knew very well, thinking of the son who had disgraced him so intimately. Nor explanation, since there was nothing that was not dutiful and ordinary in Val's letters. It was this uneasiness, then, that had gradually melted her reserve and driven her to the very last man to whom, a year ago, she would have thought a confidence possible.

Even now she wondered meditatively at herself. She did not know why she had chosen him; she supposed it must have been the cultivated discreet air of him, or perhaps his music, or perhaps his kindly bright eyes. She felt she had been vaguely disloyal to the Vicar. She must make up for it. Should she ask him, too, to dinner on Thursday? . . . No; some other day . . . next week . . . or the week after.

May met her by the gold-fish fountain under the further cedars.

"What a long time you've been!" said the girl.

"I went into the schools with Mr. Arbuthnot," said Lady Beatrice.

CHAPTER II

(1)

BENTY was in a state of intense and radiant excitement on the day that Val came home. Five minutes after she had risen from the breakfast-table in the "Room" she was beginning to pull the mattresses off Val's bed, in order to give them one more entirely unnecessary warming; and for the rest of the morning the baize door between her rooms and the boys' was continually being pushed open and banging gently again behind her, as she went to and fro bearing sheets and blankets and baskets full of mended socks and shirts.

She could not, of course, for one instant have analysed her own feelings precisely. She was always delighted when any of her "children" came home, especially Val; but there was a sense in her, this time, that a particular effort was demanded — she did not quite know why.

A rather ominous silence had prevailed on the subject of the crisis ever since Val had departed for Cambridge a little over two months ago. On the same morning the "mistress" had paid her another visit, and had managed to get into her mind the idea that no one was to speak of the matter any more. This was good, thought Benty; and yet she was not satisfied. She had not seen Val at all during the twelve hours of his stay, except for a moment, and as he passed her in the passage; and it appeared to her that the situation was not yet as entirely devoid of bitterness as she would have wished. A good deal, she thought, depended now on the way Val was greeted when he came home, and, for her part, she would do her best.

Val's brougham could not possibly reach the house before twenty minutes to two; but by a quarter past one Benty had made her excuses in the " Room " and was busying herself in one of the spare bedrooms whose windows commanded a view of the drive. At twenty-five minutes to two she had given up even the pretence of occupation, and was honestly staring out with puckered eyes for the first glimpse of the carriage over the slope of the hill. She had to watch ten minutes before she had her heart's desire, and could get away to her baize door, whence she could command Val's approach to wash his hands.

" Eh-h-h," she cried, with lifted hands and radiant face, as he turned the corner from the stairs and came upon her suddenly.

"Why, Benty!" said Val, and kissed her twice.

Her boy did not look very well, she thought; but for no consideration imaginable would she have said so.

"Now, Master Val, there's some hot water ready. You must wash your hands and brush your hair before you see your mamma."

Val smiled properly in answer to this old gambit; but his face grew grave again too quickly to please her. And he said nothing at all about his mamma, as he generally did.

"There," said the old lady, pushing his door open. "And I've put you out your old brushes, till your bag's unpacked."

She hung about outside until he came out again, for her strategy was not finished; and as soon as he reappeared was on him again.

"There'll be company at tea," she said.

Val's face changed swiftly.

"Will there? I say, Benty, shall I come to tea with you?"

Her old face broke out into wrinkles of pure joy.

"Eh! if you would!" she said. "If your mamma wouldn't ——"

Again came that swift and anxious gravity, all the worse, since he smiled simultaneously.

"Oh! they won't mind," he said, "they'll like it."

"Nay now, Master ——"

Val took her hands again and pressed them.

"I must go down to lunch," he said. "I'll be with you by five. Give me another kiss, Benty."

(II)

She pondered over it all as she sat over her work that afternoon, so far as it was possible within the limitations of loyalty which she observed so strictly and conscientiously. No one must be blamed — that was quite clear and certain; every Medd must be right; and yet it was perfectly obvious that there was something wrong; and there seemed to her no solution except the practical one of going downstairs about four o'clock and making the steward's boy polish her silver teapot, milk-jug, and sugar-basin — another set of gifts at the end of her twenty-five years' service — under her own eye. Then she went on to the still-room, made her selections and issued her orders; and by twenty minutes to five all was in place, and the teapot stood ready downstairs to be filled and brought up instantly by the still-room maid as soon as the nursery bell rang twice, together with the buttered buns already warming at the fire.

It was a delicious room, this, in summer, for it looked out from beneath the eaves on to the south gardens, and the surface of the great cedar fans, from beneath which came already the sound of talking from the " company "— one of the usual parties of friends' friends who had come over to see the house. Beyond the terrace on the further side of the cedar lay the meadow-land sloping down to the village, now all alight with summer glory of green and gold; and across this, walking slowly and alone, came presently the figure she longed for, with his hands in his pockets and a white hat on his head. . . . She felt uneasy at seeing him alone on this the day of his home-coming. . . . Never mind, he. would soon be up here at tea with her. As she heard, a minute or two later, the baize door swing, she rang the bell twice, according to arrangement.

He looked curiously weary and miserable, even as he came in, and began the elaborate humour that most delighted Benty's heart. He said, as in duty bound, that he hoped he. wasn't going to be given dry bread because he was two minutes late; that he wasn't going to change his feet however much Benty might talk; and that he hoped she had been a good girl all this long time that he had been away and not able to look after her. She made the proper responses and ejaculations as she poured out the tea, and put the buttered buns where he could reach them without stretching; but she was more than ever convinced that something really was wrong and that the situation was not what it should be.

Then, as at last he drank his last cup of tea and

took out his cigarettes, he opened straight on to the subject himself.

"Benty," he said, "I'm a naughty boy, and my papa and mamma aren't pleased with me. Did you know that?"

Benty's face became suddenly distressed.

"Nay now; don't talk like that," she said.

"But it's true," said Val. "And I mustn't talk about it. I'm forbidden: So you must be very kind to me to make up."

"Nay now ——" she said again.

"The less they see of me the more they'll like it," went on Val, with a kind of resolute bitterness. "They've made that quite plain already. Oh, no; they haven't said anything, of course; but I know how it is. So I shall come up and see you very often indeed, Benty; and you'll give me tea and be nice to me, won't you? . . . Shall we run away together, and go to Gretna Green?"

"Now, Master Val ——?" began Benty, not in the least amused; but he interrupted her.

"My dear," he said, "it's perfectly true. Now I'll bet you a penny that nobody asks me whether I'll ride. They haven't yet, and they won't. You'll see. . . . What time are the horses ordered?"

"Masterman was saying, at half-past five."

"Well, there's five minutes more yet. Now you'll see."

"But they don't know where you are," complained the old lady, half rising. "I'll be off and ——"

"No you won't," said Val very deliberately. "You won't move. They'll be able to find me perfectly well if they want me; and, besides, the horses must be ready by now, and I haven't heard a word."

"What have you been doing this afternoon?" asked Benty, anxious to change the subject.

Val smiled with that same disagreeable irony he had shown before.

"I ate my lunch like a good little boy," he said, "and everyone asked me whether I had had a good journey and what time I left Cambridge. And then I went into the hall and we all drank coffee; and then my mamma asked my papa what time he would have the horses, and he said five; and then she said that he'd forgotten people were coming; and then May dropped the sugar-basin. And then I began to look at the *Illustrated London News;* and then everybody went away; and so I went away too. And — let's see, what did I do next? Oh, I went up to my room and filled my cigarette-case; and then I came down to the hall again, and nobody was there. So then I went out and began to knock the croquet-balls about, and nobody came. So then I went down to the farm to see whether the dogs were all right, and I took them for a run. And then I came back, and the company were under the cedar; so I went and said, ' How do you do?' like a good little boy; and nobody said anything; and then I came up here. . . . Rollicking afternoon, wasn't it, Benty? Everybody so jolly pleased to see me, weren't they?"

His tone cut the old lady like a knife. He had raised his voice a little at the end, and the bitterness broke out undisguised.

She began to rebuke him.

" Nay, Master Val — then why didn't you go and talk to them yourself? I'm sure Miss May would have been only too pleased ——"

" Oh, yes; she'd have come and played croquet with me if I'd asked her. But that's just exactly what I wouldn't do. And they'd all say how nice it would be if I went downstairs now and ordered Quentin and went out riding; but that's just exactly what I'm not going to do. If they don't choose to ask me ——" He broke off.

" Master Val ——"

" Look here, Benty; it's just half-past. And you and me'll go and peep from the windows in front and see them start. Come along, old lady."

He jumped up and took her by the arm.

" Nay now ——"

" Come along!"

Together they went, she gently protesting, he

hurrying her away, through the baize door, down the passage, and round to the right to the same room from which, before lunch, she had watched for his arrival. He shut the door carefully behind them.

"Now, then; behind the curtains," he said. "They mustn't see us."

"There," she cried, peeping as she was ordered. "There's Quentin all ready for you, Master Val. Now be a good boy and go downstairs."

"I won't," he said. "Ah! they're coming out."

From beneath, as they looked, advanced first the General, and then May holding up the skirt of her habit, across the paved space and to the head of the steps, where the three horses were being led to and fro. Masterman was already in waiting there. The distance was too great for them to hear through the closed window anything that was said, but it was obvious that a conversation was being held; and presently the butler came hurrying back to the house as the General went down the steps.

"Let me go, Master Val," cried the old lady. "The master's sent for you. Let me go and tell Masterman." He let go his clasp on her arm.

"Don't you bother, Benty; I'll go and tell him myself."

"Nay now ——"

"You be quiet," said Val, and went out.

She followed him, and stood listening when she saw him bend over the banisters.

"No — I'm not ready," she heard him say. "Tell the General I didn't know he was expecting me; and that I'm not dressed."

She heard the murmur of the butler's voice from below.

"I can't," said the boy again. "Say that I haven't got my things on. . . . Or . . . or . . . wait; no, say I'll come after them. Tell them not to wait. Tell the man to keep Quentin at the steps."

As he straightened himself again, the old nurse was at his side.

"That's right, Master Val," she said. "And now you'll go and have a nice ride. How'll you know which way they've gone?"

He smiled.

"I'm going a nice ride all by myself," he said, "in exactly the opposite direction."

(III)

"That's right, my boy," said his mother, five minutes later, as he came to the hall door in his breeches. "They left a message to say they were going over the Hurst. How was it you weren't ready?"

Val paused. The "company" was now being

conducted over the house, and was ranged in a line below the famous portraits.

" I didn't know what time anyone was going out," he said, " till too late."

She looked at him uneasily. He was so exceedingly calm and self-possessed, on the one hand; and she, on the other, was perfectly aware that he had not been definitely asked whether he would ride when the arrangements had been made. She had meant to ask him herself, later; and had forgotten.

" Well, make haste and catch them up."

Val made no answer, but moved on to the door, taking his whip from the rack as he did so. Just as he went out he turned again.

" Was it the Hurst, you said, mother? "

" Yes, my boy: make haste. . . . Have a nice ride."

She turned again a moment or two later, in the midst of her discourse on Anthony Medd, surprised at the noise of hoofs on turf, plainly audible through the open windows, for the way to the Hurst lay round by the stables; and there was Val, full gallop up the front, riding, as he had said to Benty, in exactly the opposite direction.

(IV)

Benty was, of course, at the same window soon after seven o'clock. She had gone to and fro on her business, very heavy at heart, since Val's little scene with her, first clearing away the tea-things, and then paying more than one visit to his room, to reassure herself that all was as it should be and that Charles had done his duty. Then she had taken a piece of mending to the bedroom window again, telling herself that she could see better there than in her own room.

She had not long to wait. Somewhere out of sight came the sound of hoofs, first on turf and then on gravel. Then she saw a groom run out from the stable shrubbery, and simultaneously Val come into sight and pull up. A minute later, as he was coming up the steps, again came the noise of hoofs, and the two other riders came down the slope. Val paid no attention; he walked straight on without turning his head, and vanished into the house.

Benty bundled her mending under her arm and hurried out. She felt discomfort all around her and within her: she wished to reassure herself by another word or two with her boy.

As she reached the passage, whose banisters on one side stood out over the inner hall, she heard voices below.

"Yes; they're just coming, mother. . . . No, I missed them. . . . Yes; I went the other way over the Hurst; and thought perhaps I'd meet them. But I didn't."

There was silence, and then the sound of a closing door.

Benty hurried on, and was outside Val's room as the boy came up.

"Well, did you have a nice ride?" she asked timidly.

"Lovely!" said. Val. "And all by myself. Come in, Benty, and I'll tell you. . . ."

"But you didn't go the right way, Master Val," she said when they were inside the room.

Val closed the door and looked at her. His face was a little flushed with the exercise; but there was no buoyancy in his eyes — only that same suggestion of bitterness under his half-lowered eyelids.

"I went over the Hurst," he said, "exactly as I said I would. And I went the opposite way. And when I heard them coming, I rode into the bracken and hid till they'd gone by. That was why we didn't meet. Wasn't it a pity?"

CHAPTER III

(1)

"**F**ATHER MAPLE, my lady," announced Masterman.

The priest came forward into the great hall, where the light of the setting sun lay splendid on the stamped leather and the banners and the lower edges of the gilded portrait frames, a slender, unimpressive little figure; and Lady Beatrice rose to meet him.

"My son Valentine," she said. "I think you've met before, though."

A tallish, pale boy, looking younger than his years, bowed slightly from the shadow behind her without moving, and almost immediately the General came in.

"And we hope you've brought some music," added his hostess, smiling.

It appeared that he had. It was in the porch with his hat and stick.

It was a curiously constrained dinner, thought the priest, who was observing, according to request, with

347

all his power. Val never spoke at all unless he was spoken to, and then quite shortly, though adequately, hardly lifting his eyes; and the General seemed to talk with an effort every time. It was the father somehow, even more than the son, for whom the priest felt sorry. It was as if a kind of vicarious humility or shame had fallen upon him: his solemn, genial assurance was absent, and he spoke as a man might speak who was under a cloud and was never unconscious of it for an instant. Just once or twice a gleam of interest shone under his hairy eyebrows — a pin-point of light — as, for example, when he talked politics; but it died again, and he applied himself gravely to his plate once more. The other two were scarcely better; for it was, the priest reflected, Val's first evening at home since his ignominious departure for Cambridge nearly two months before. Lady Beatrice, under all her self-possession, was ill at ease; she tried to draw Val into the conversation far too pointedly, and he answered more and more shortly each time; and May was spasmodic and nervous. (Miss Deverell, I forgot to say, was also present, with her usual air of discreet severity.)

It was a relief to everyone when dinner came to an end. The General asked the priest and Val whether they would take any more wine in such a manner that it was practically impossible to say

yes, and suggested going after the ladies immediately with an air of undisguised satisfaction.

"We can have our cigarettes in the hall," he said.

As they went out under the gallery the priest
turned to Val.

"Just back from Cambridge, aren't you?" he
said.

"Yes," said the boy.

"I'm a Trinity man myself," said the priest.
"Letter M, Great Court."

The boy nodded and smiled with a deliberateness
that was almost insolent.

And then, five minutes later, Lady Beatrice asked
Father Maple to play.

He went to the piano in a very serious frame of
mind. For he could see the stress under which
the whole family lay, and he could not see the
issue. It was his business, as it is of every priest,
to be an expert in human nature, and he understood perfectly that there were elements here that
might lead to a really grave catastrophe. By
heredity, by instinct, by training, this group of persons was infinitely sensitive to certain things, among
which honour and courage, and their opposites,
lay supreme. And it was exactly in those points
that their sentiments had been outraged by one of
themselves. To live wildly, to be dissipated, to
gamble, to idle, even to be overbearing and oppres-

sive — all those sins could be condoned; they passed
and left no irremediable stain behind. Some of
these Medd worthies looking down from the walls
had set startling examples in those aristocratic
vices. The young man in the dining-room who had
fought at Naseby looked no better than he should;
and here in the hall was the portrait of the notorious
Mrs. Anthony Medd, who had occupied a more than
doubtful position in the Court of Charles II. Yet
their portraits hung there, and their histories were
told without any very overwhelming shame. But
this was quite another matter. If Val had been
ruined at cards, or had run away with somebody
else's wife, it would have been sad, but not tragic.
But to have shirked a duel, however foolish or indiscreet the fighting of it would have been, was in
a completely different category. And, as a crown-
ing touch and as a final complication, the boy himself, it was obvious, had all the sensitiveness to his
crime which his father had. If he had been cal-
lous or ill-bred, if he had been just selfishly calculating or prudent, the priest would not have feared
so much. . . .

It was with the consciousness of this that he went
to the piano, and, as is the result always with certain
natures, his nerves were strung up, rather than en-
feebled, by the fact. The instant he touched the

piano, with those few preliminary chords with which
a perfectly competent player begins, he was aware
of it; and in that moment came to him a determination to use it, and to find a way to this boy's confidence by that which is, perhaps, the most subtle
road of all. He laid his music-sheets aside and
settled down to play to Val. . . .

(II)

He had been playing about ten minutes when he
saw the boy move.

Up to that moment he had been aware of a tense
atmosphere such as he seldom won even with such
a tiny audience as this. He did not look up from
the piano, but he perceived in the semi-darkness of
the hall that the four figures within his range — the
husband, the wife, the daughter, and the shadowy
companion — remained entirely motionless, each in
its place — the old man on this side of the hearth
and the three women on the other. He had not
seen where Val sat down; but he noticed now the
figure of the boy pass from the window-seat at the
further end to that which was nearer the piano;
and thenceforward saw the blot of his head against
the darkening sky outside. There were no lights
here; the sun had not long gone down, and, as he
was extemporising, he had himself blown out the
two candles on the piano.

Up to the moment when Val moved, the player had been doubtful, wooing, so to speak, enquiring, asking, wondering whether the language in which he pleaded would be understood. But now all doubt left him; he knew, by that strange intuition that lives only on the plane of art, and which is as certain in that realm as are the senses of sight or hearing in the physical order, that he had established communications. Whether or not those would lead to anything was another matter; whether, when his artistic oratory was done, any answer would come he did not know; but this at any rate he determined — that he would finish what he had to say. It might very well be that the soul of this boy, harrowed by eight weeks of miserable isolation, and now wrenched and torn again by his return home, and the countless associations he met there, and the reality of his disgrace — it might very well be that the answer would come, and that the boy would understand that here at least was one who understood.

So he gathered up his strength.

Up to now he had played plaintively and caressingly, with infinite pathos, seeking to draw tears and soft sounds; it was sentimental, he knew, but sentimentality in disguise, for it was by this alone that he had thought he could find his way to the strange mixture of commonplaceness and distilled refinement which he perceived to be the fabric on which these souls were built. But now he threw aside sentiment and sought strength. . . . The great chords crashed on. . . . He was amazed at his own fire: that soft tingling began in nerves and sinews, that electric pulsation ran up every fibre, connecting heart and brain and fingers, by which the artist knows that he is transfigured; his contractions and limitations passed away; and he felt himself pouring out from wires and keyboard and feet and hands, out into the solemn gloom of the hall, and into those beating hearts, that tremendous passion of which the artist and the orator alone know the secret, and the priest the source.

So he played, and ended. And Miss Deverell sniffed, distinctly, in the silence, after a decent pause.

It was a full minute before any moved or spoke. He heard a sigh and a rustle; and then he himself spoke, with a deliberate offhandedness.

" And now I'll play the gavotte you liked the other day, Lady Beatrice."

(III)

He came and sat down when he had done, and drank his coffee, which had grown cold. He had not an idea as to what would happen next; and he had determined not to risk anything by intrusion. Meanwhile he answered questions.

"Yes," he said, "I studied at Leipsic and Dresden for ten years. . . . Liszt? Oh, yes; I knew Liszt very well. In fact I very nearly ——"

He stopped.

"Yes?" asked May breathlessly. (She had moved her seat to be near him.)

"I nearly took up music as a profession."

"Why didn't you?"

"I became a Catholic, and then a priest," he said simply. "I wasn't ordained till I was forty, you know."

"And you gave up your music?" cried May.

"I gave it up as a profession," he said. "But I still get a good deal of enjoyment out of it. I am afraid I still play for two or three hours a day."

"But ——." And she stopped again, amazed.

Val had showed no sign; he still remained in the window-seat, silent. Yet all the while that the priest was talking he was more aware of the boy's presence than of the three with whom he talked. The two women were voluble; even the General pulled his long chair a foot or two nearer to listen to the musician's account of his Leipsic days; but the boy's silence talked more loudly than them all. It seemed to the priest as if he knew exactly what

was passing behind the heavy curtain — the world
of misery and shame that trampled so ruthlessly on
hope; the voice that cried, Rise and begin again,
and the louder voice that proclaimed that it was too
late, and that the thing was done, and that an end
held more hope than a new beginning. For he had
watched the boy's face at dinner, and had seen how
every delicate fibre had withdrawn itself inwards,
only to find that the worm that dies not is more
agonising than the fire which is not quenched; he
had seen that the torment within had been sub-
stituted for the disgrace without. He had said that
a boy in such a position might go to the bad, or,
what was worse, to despair; and he had learned
that it was to the worse of those that the move was
being made. . . .

"And you have never regretted it?" asked May
presently.

He smiled.

"Priests dare not, anyhow, regret their priest-
hood. And even if that were possible, it's foolish to
regret things that are passed. There is always a
best to be got out of them."

(It was a sententious remark, and he knew it.
But he made it deliberately.)

May sat back and was silent; he understood why.
And then Lady Beatrice began.

It was when he got up at last to go that he had his first opportunity of speaking to Val. He looked at his hostess carefully as he shook hands, and that lady was quick enough to understand.

"Val," she said, "see Father Maple to the door. I don't want your father to go out. He's got a touch of cold. (No, my dear, I insist.)"

The boy came forward quickly and silently from the window-seat — he had not spoken one word since the priest had sat down to the piano — and the two went out together to the porch.

"What a heavenly night!" said the priest.

He stood breathing in the heavy, fragrant night-smells of summer. It was a clear night overhead, but the dew-laden grass suffused the atmosphere with vapour, and the stars shone dim and soft. The great trees at the head of the slope opposite stood motionless blots against them. Somewhere in the gardens behind a nightingale began to sing.

"You won't walk with me as far as the garden gate, I suppose?" said the priest.

"Why, yes," said Val.

All the way down through the gardens the priest talked on indifferent matters, with pauses, trying to put the boy at his ease and to give him an opportunity of speaking if he wished. But Val answered in monosyllables, and only just enough for courtesy.

Once or twice the priest thought that the other's silence was trembling on the edge òf speech; but nothing happened.

At the garden gate he said good-bye.

" Look in any time you like," said the priest. " I'm nearly always at home."

" Thanks very much," said Val, with a complete dispassionateness that told nothing.

As the priest went on he listened for footsteps going back to the house, but there were none. Val was either still standing looking at the night, or had turned off across the wet grass for a lonely stroll.

When Father Maple reached home he wrote a little note to Lady Beatrice, and set it out on his table to be taken up in the morning.

" DEAR LADY BEATRICE,

" I must thank you very much for a charming evening.

" Your son walked with me a little way homewards; but he was quite loyal to the conditions that have been laid on him. I still hold (since you are kind enough to allow me to say so) that these are very severe; and I should strongly advise your giving him to understand that he will not be transgressing them if he talks the matter over confidentially with someone whom he trusts, and who is not intimately concerned with the story itself — the Vicar, for example. It is always dangerous to hammer down the safety-valve, I think.

"Yours sincerely,

"ARTHUR MAPLE.

"P.S.— Please don't dream of sending an answer to this. It needs none."

He wrote this rather slowly, in his pointed small handwriting, hesitating now and again for a word, but with a kind of even decisiveness. He then read it through and sealed it and put it ready.

Then he took up his office-book and sat down in his deep chair by the lamp.

CHAPTER IV

(1)

TRAGEDY and small ignominious infirmities are, unhappily, not incompatible. If, on the one side, monumental sufferers could stride always in the limelight to the sound of muffled drums, without fear of the toothache or a cold in the head; or, on the other, if persons with the gout were immune from the great passions, the parts of both would be comparatively easy to play. But real difficulties begin to enter when the parts are mixed; when the gentleman with a bad liver loses his only son, and, still more, when the tragedy king breaks his bootlace. For the whole focus is in an instant changed; the bereaved invalid is crushed by a sound for whose magnitude he was not prepared, and the purple-robe hero becomes as irritable and peevish as anyone else.

Something of this kind happened to General Medd within a week of his son's return from Cambridge.

Now certainly General Medd was a sufferer on the large scale, and there was something magnificently pathetic and solemn about the way in which he bore himself. His very proper pride had been wounded

359

in its most delicate spot; that which was the main-spring of his life, his central ideal, his most intimate and living gospel, had been smirched by his own son. It perhaps seems ridiculous to those who have not his ideals, yet it was a fact that, for him, however absurd it may appear to a democratic and common-sense age, the whole fabric of the whole of the nobility of life rested on honour and courage. It seemed that nothing was left that was worth having if these were gone. Austin, no doubt, was a con-solation; he might be a prig (as his father secretly suspected), but he was a straightforward and coura-geous prig; yet, after all, Austin had only done that which it was his duty to do, and Val had failed in the first and most elementary obligation which a gentleman could have.

It was this sense of outrage, then, that he carried with him always; and though he observed the condi-tions which he himself had made as loyally as was possible, the very sight of Val brought the outrage up again to the raw and sensitive surface. If Val had not returned for six months or a year after his crime, perhaps his father would have learned to manage his emotions more adequately.

The first little outbreak came about in this way.

The successor to Jimbo was a Scotch collie, mid-dle-aged when he arrived, and now approaching senility. Yet he was not so old as not still to attempt sometimes to go out with the riders, though he usually dropped behind discreetly after a mile or two and returned home at his own pace. And on a certain evening in June, feeling, I suppose, particularly buoyant, Laddie accompanied his master with a great deal of shrill barking and rather stiff careering all the long way round the woods as far as the further end of the village street, there intending, it appeared, to leave them unnoticed and to slip up home by the farm and the gardens. His master knew his little ways by now, and was too tactful to interfere with them.

Accordingly, as the three rode down by the school, intending to strike across the village and up into the wooded country beyond, Laddie began, with a show of intense absorption, to smell some palings which he knew perfectly by heart already.

" He's beginning to hedge," said May, smiling.

" Don't notice him. He's had quite enough exercise for to-day," said the General.

So Laddie smelt and smelt, edging nearer by every apparently unconsidered step to the route homewards, as the three passed on; and it was certainly his intention, upon their return an hour or two later, to greet them at the steps of the house with gestures and cries of mingled relief, love, and reproach. But they had hardly turned up the lane

out of sight before a lamentable clamour broke out
behind them, and May wheeled her mare round on
the instant.

"It's that hateful retriever of Palmer's," she
cried; "he's at him again."

Now the General had been aware when he awoke
this morning of an evil taste in his mouth, and on
examining himself in the glass had detected a certain
tinge of yellow in his eyes which caused him to
avoid ham at breakfast, and to take a little sharp
walking exercise after breakfast, swinging a heavy
stick. But the liver, even when treated so promptly
as this, is not always submissive, and all day long the
old man had found it necessary to curb his tongue
on matters which seemed to him very significant and
tiresome.

He too swung his horse round now sharply and
irritably.

"Go and kill the brute!" he snapped.

Val had turned with May, for he was exceedingly
tender to animals, and by the time that the other two
had ridden up was already on the scene.

It was not a very pleasant sight.

The big retriever, who was a born bully, resenting,
it would appear, Laddie's air of suspicion with
respect to the railings within which he himself
happened to live, had dashed violently out of the
half-open garden gate and discharged himself, a

thunderbolt of black hair, white teeth, and blazing eyes, against the collie, whom he had bitten badly once or twice before. Laddie had responded gallantly, but too late; and by the time that his master came up he was down on the ground shrieking and struggling, with the big black brute striding over him, endeavouring, to the sound of really terrifying snarls, to get his teeth firmly and deeply into the throat. Laddie was making great play with his frilled hind-legs, scratching and kicking upwards; but he was at least five years the senior, and had, besides, been taken at a disadvantage.

"Good Gad! he's killing him," cried the General. "Separate them, Val . . . quick."

Val was off his horse in an instant, even before his father had finished speaking; but it was not easy to see exactly what to do. The retriever was leaping from side to side, snarling like a demon, pivoted, as it were, by his teeth in the other's ruff. Laddie was shrieking, as only a collie can; and a cloud of dust rolled and bellied out, now hiding, now revealing the twisting, tearing bodies beneath. Mrs. Palmer herself had run out of the cottage, and was lamenting with upraised hands the unseemly spectacle. The noise and confusion were bewildering.

"Get at them, Val," roared the General, with the note of anger very audible.

Yet still the boy hesitated. Honestly and sincerely he did not quite know what to do. To seize the retriever would not be easy, and he did not know where to seize him; to snatch at Laddie might only make matters worse.

Then, as he hesitated, came a roar from the General:

" You damned coward! "

And a hatless figure rushed past the boy with up-raised hunting-crop. Whack followed whack, now on the retriever, now on the unhappy Laddie; but the fury of the onset was so great, and its general moral effect so stupendous, that the retriever sud-denly dropped his hold and fled with a howl of pain and dismay. Laddie leaped to his feet, and, with his tail between his legs, fled in the opposite direction, his shrill, hysterical bark dying away at last in the friendly shelter of the Home Farm gate.

The General turned on his son in a flare of rage.

" Afraid of a couple of dogs, are you? "

Val looked at him, white as a sheet. If he had been conscious of deliberate cowardice he would have felt it less; but, on the contrary, as he had sprung off his horse, he had driven down by an act of the will the perfectly natural hesitation that every living being would have to interfere too suddenly; and he had not thrown himself into the fray simply because he was honestly doubtful of what was best to do.

And, on the other hand, his father, brooding (as he had) day after day on the cowardice of his son, was perfectly certain that here was one more instance of it; and his excitement and the state of his liver had compelled him to express his opinion with a force which he would otherwise have avoided. So the two, father and son, eyed one another, both alight with emotion and hostility. May looked at them both with dismay, and Mrs. Palmer went discreetly indoors again.

Then Val went to his horse, mounted, and rode homeward after Laddie, leaving the two silent.

(II)

The next incident of importance with regard to the development of Val took place in July.

The father and son had never mentioned the dog-fight affair to one another. The General had discussed it with his wife, and had come to the conclusion that possibly he had been a little hasty in expressing an undeniable truth; for he entirely rejected the mother's theory that perhaps Val had really not known what to do. And Val discussed it with nobody. May had attempted it, but he had silenced her.

His mother had passed on Father Maple's suggestion as if it came from herself. She had told him, after a good deal of hesitation, that promises of silence (she specified nothing further than this) did not apply to spiritual advisers (wondering at her own Jesuitry as she said it); and that if Val cared to talk over his affairs with Mr. Arbuthnot or . . . or with anyone else, she was sure that he would not be breaking any pledges he had ever made. Val had met her suggestion with a polite air of interest and silence.

Then, about the middle of July, the second incident took place.

There was a week-end party in the house. This year the Medds had not taken a house in town, as they usually did — the doctor had said that the General would be better in the country — and instead they entertained people from Fridays to Tuesdays about twice a month.

At this week-end there were several old friends, among whom, as an intellectual giant, towered Professor Macintosh. The Merediths too were here; Austin; and finally Miss Marjoribanks, who, having steadily refused to come before, for reasons not given, consented at last to visit May, on condition that there were plenty of other guests. May imagined, very naturally, that her hesitation rose from her remembrance of the Rome affair.

It was actually on the first Friday evening that the thing happened.

The smoking-room at Medhurst opened out of the billiard-room in the north wing; and hither, when the ladies had gone to bed, proceeded Professor Macintosh, in all the glory of his velvet and frills and skull-cap. He found the Merediths, father and son, already there — the father, with his hands behind his back, circling slowly round the room, looking at the pale-coloured sporting engravings; and Tom, seated in a long chair, earnestly and silently smoking a briar pipe. (Tom was one of those people who only do one thing at a time, and do it very seriously.)

Sir James Meredith privately thought Professor Macintosh an ass, and at the same time a rewarding ass. He enjoyed, in fact, helping him to say characteristic things, which he would recount to his friends afterwards. This time, however, the Professor needed no assistance.

"Sad thing about this boy, isn't it?" he began briskly, even before he sat down. "And got very interesting. It's a case of what we scientific gentlemen call a freak."

This was a very promising beginning, thought the lawyer. It was always amusing when the Professor spoke for his supposed colleagues. But he had not an idea to what he referred; so it pleased him to rally him on his absentmindedness. (Sham geniuses always respond to that, as flowers to the sun.)

He turned from his coloured engravings and sat down.

" You thinkers and students always begin in the middle," he said, with an air of humorous respect. " May I ask what you happen to be talking about? "

The Professor beamed. (He found this rallying line very pleasant.)

" Why, about young Valentine. One of the keepers was telling me about it before dinner. A new man, I think. I haven't seen him before."

" What's young Valentine been doing? " asked the lawyer. (He glanced, as a mere precaution, at the billiard-room double doors. They appeared to be closed.)

The Professor told him, fitting his fingers together as he had once seen Dr. Huxley do, and wearing an air of intense and yet detached scientific interest. It was especially interesting to him, as a sociological student, he said. Here were the Medds — good old family, with medieval instincts; the strain was very pure; and here, suddenly, had appeared a freak — a boy with the heart of a rabbit. He wondered whether the alien characteristic had come from Lady Beatrice's side. He would look into Lady Beatrice's ancestry. Of course he said, too, some kind things; he remarked how distressing it all was — particularly as it had got out somehow into the village, probably through a servant's talking — some servant who had known of Austin's wound and had, perhaps, overheard something he should not. At any rate, the new keeper had told him a story that hung together very well, and it seemed to him to fit in perfectly with little things he had noticed. Of course the General knew nothing of the talk of the village; and ——

At this moment the General came in from the corridor, with Austin; and the lawyer instantly remarked:

"Yes, I think these engravings are originals. . . . I've just been looking at your engravings. They seem to me capital."

The General made a suitable remark. Then Sir James got up.

"Excuse me. May I shut this door?"

He went to the billiard-room doors and closed them. But he first glanced into the room. It was empty. And yet just before he spoke there had been a sudden vibration of the doors, as if the further one, opening into the corridor, had been opened. But the room was empty. Therefore someone had left the billiard-room immediately after the General had come into the smoking-room. This was logic. . . . But of course it might have been a servant.

The lawyer sat down, and was rather silent. And Val did not appear.

(III)

The Professor, of course, was a great deal too much emancipated to go to church. When you have reached a position in the scientific world sufficiently eminent to justify your wearing a crimson skull-cap and a frilly shirt, you need no longer consider conventions; and there is, of course, no reason, beyond that of convention, why you should go through the wearisome form of addressing a Being whose lowest form is a kind of jelly on the seashore and whose highest development is yourself. Self-communing becomes the only intelligent method of adoration.

But the Professor observed the Sabbath, for all that. He said that the instinct of those old nomads was remarkable; and that the brain and body were none the worse for one day's rest in seven, and that he, for one, deplored the modern rush and lack of repose.

So when the party assembled in the hall on Sunday to walk down to church — Sir James, as usual, presenting a perfect model of a God-fearing English gentleman — the Professor took occasion to pass through in leather slippers, with a thin, voluminous grey plaid over his shoulders, and to announce that he proposed to go and sit in the summer-house above the cedars until worship was done. He also displayed a green-covered work on Parasites, which he intended to study.

At about twelve o'clock he closed his eyes, the better to think over what he had been reading. The summer air was hot and enervating, the splash of the fountain at the foot of the slope was soothing, the hum of the flies about him almost somniferous: so it was possible that he dozed. He had not read a great deal about Parasites, for he had been rash enough to take with him as well, after the church-party had gone, a number of the *Pall Mall Magazine* which he had not previously read, and this now lay, face down and opened, upon his knees, upon a fold of the grey plaid. . . .

The next thing of which he was aware was that the door of the summer-house was darkened, and with the natural genius of a great mind he concluded that someone was standing in it. So he opened his eyes, simultaneously snatching away the *Pall Mall Magazine.*

Then he saw that it was Val.

" Can you give me ten minutes? " asked the boy, who seemed breathless, as if he had been running. (He appeared to pay no attention to the *Pall Mall Magazine.*)

The Professor sprang up.

" Why, certainly," he said.

" Do you mind just coming up into the woods? I think the others may be coming here."

The Professor ingeniously enfolded the magazine, which he had been holding out of sight, under the grey plaid, presenting only for view the green book on Parasites, and the two went together through the little swing-gate by the summer-house, up into the fringe of the woods, that here encroached right down on the garden fence. Then they sat down, oddly enough in the very place where Val three or four years ago had lain and dreamed of prowess and nobility.

" Look here," said Val abruptly, " I must ask you two or three questions. Do you mind? I don't believe any more in all that down there "— (he jerked his head towards the village and the squat Norman tower)—" and I want to know what scientists think."

" But, my dear young man ——" began the Professor reprovingly.

Val turned a white face on him.

" Please don't jaw about that," he said. " I know you don't believe it either. . . . Well, but this is what I want to ask you about. You know I heard everything you said in the smoking-room on Friday night."

" Eh ——" began the Professor.

" I was in the billiard-room. I heard my name, and then I listened on purpose."

" You did very wrong," exclaimed the Professor energetically. " And I'm not at all sure ——"

" You can't tell my father, anyhow," said Val. " You see, he thinks nobody knows except himself and the rest of us. So let's leave all that. What I want to know is whether it's my fault, and whether I could ever get over it? "

The Professor's mind whirled wildly a moment or two. He was not accustomed to human problems, and knew nothing whatever about them. He was accustomed to treat of human beings merely as a development of protoplasm, and to consider that which was not protoplastic, so to speak, as negligible. He was a kindly old man in his way, very complacent and positive. But even without those qualities he could see that the boy was badly upset. So he attempted to soothe him.

" Look here, my boy," he said. " Better leave all those problems alone. Just do your best; don't be too hard on yourself, and don't think too much about it all. We've all got our flaws somewhere, and it's no good taking them too hardly."

" You mean that these flaws are incurable then? That we can't change ourselves? That's just what I want to know. I'm born flawed, and I can't alter it? "

"Of course we can do something by effort," said the Professor judicially; "always supposing that there's sufficient impetus from outside forces. But we've all got our limitations, and it's far wiser to recognise them. No one can possibly blame you for being what you are — no philosopher, that is; I think none the worse of you, I assure you, my boy, for not . . . not having as much nerve as your brother, for instance. We're all the creatures of our descent, our education, and so on. Scientists are beginning to think that we're practically formed when we're two or three years old. Every year that passes after that makes us less and less plastic. At least that's what Science tells us."

"That's exactly what I wanted to know," said Val quietly — "what Science says. Then . . . then I must make the best of myself? I can't be blamed for what I do?"

"Not by a philosopher," said the Professor. "Of course uninstructed people ——"

The boy jerked his head. The look of strain in his eyes became more set and fixed each instant.

"I don't mind about them," he said. "I want to know the facts. . . . And then there's one more thing. . . ."

"Yes, my boy," said the Professor encouragingly. He was delighted to find so apt a pupil.

"It's about the life after death. What does Science say about that?"

The Professor paused. He wished to be perfectly fair.

"If there is a life after death," he said at last, "it falls outside the purview of Science. Science deals with physical phenomena; with the body, the mechanism of the brain, and so on. She knows nothing of the soul; she deals only with that which, if there is a soul, is merely its instrument."

"She knows nothing of the soul," repeated the boy. "That means that Science does not recognise it as a fact; that there is nothing to show that there is such a thing. Is that right?"

The Professor bowed his head.

"That is so," he said. "Certainly there are certain claims made by non-scientific people which, if they are facts, cannot at present be explained by Physical Science. But that does not prove that they will not be explained some day; if, that is to say, they really are facts."

Val lifted his head impatiently. He had been staring steadily down, frowning, with pressed lips, at the moss and dead leaves beside him. He had been quite quiet and quite business-like throughout.

"Well," he said, "to be short — Science says that there's no evidence that there's a soul, or a life after death. Is that right?"

" That, I think," said the Professor solemnly " is a fair summary. But ——"

The boy got up, heavily, but with a determined, final kind of air.

" Thanks, very much," he said. " That's all I wanted to know. . . . I think the others are coming."

(IV)

It was a curiously trying week-end for Gertie Marjoribanks. But she had seen that she must face sometime a meeting with Val on their new footing, and had determined to get it over. To have delayed much longer would have been to have aroused suspicion; and if there was one thing of which she was vehemently and energetically ashamed, it was of that boy-and-girl engagement into which she had so sentimentally entered last Christmas, and so courageously broken off again at Easter. She had quite decided by now never to tell anyone about it — not even May.

Her feelings towards Val were remarkably keen, and their sharpness when she had first set eyes on him after her arrival had surprised even herself. She hated, as she confessed to herself when she went upstairs to dress for dinner, after shaking hands with him in the hall, the very sight of him. It seemed to her that he belonged now to a part of her life for which she had nothing but resentment and shame. It was abominable to her to remember that they had kissed one another. . . .

For the reaction was complete. She had taken him on a certain valuation, and in the enthusiasm of his service to her in the woods between here and Penshurst, had, so to speak, abandoned herself altogether to her feelings. He had stood to her for her perfect knight; he was to be her defender, her Percival, her king. The blow he had struck for her in Rome, on the steps of the Pincian, had been magnificent in her eyes; and it had reached a transfiguration when, to the gaiety of the hidden band in the hotel, she had raised to him her tiny glass of Chartreuse. So far she had flung the whole of her schoolgirl idealism into the fire, and it had blazed into glory, filling her world with flame. . . . He had been to her Lohengrin in silver armour, Caruso in tights — her gentle, perfect knight. And then, with a crash, her world had tumbled; and to her rather theatrical but sincerely passionate nature, it seemed that the intolerable shame had enveloped not him only, but herself. Exactly at that moment when heaven should have opened, the earth had opened instead; and there, in the pit, lay she and he.

So she had set herself during these two months to climb out. It was a consolation that someone had fought for her; but she could not allow herself to dwell on this until she was again on safe ground. It was not until she had built up her world once more, until she had scoured by resentment and interior fury the last remnants of Val from her soul, that she could dare to see him again, or to talk even with Austin. And when she had seen Val again, in the hall at Medhurst, standing a little apart from the others as he ought, and had taken his hand and let go of it again, it required all her powers of will and energy not to show her loathing for the boy who had failed her so cruelly.

It was a terrible pleasure to her to notice his isolation: she saw that he had no place in his home; that the deliberate kindness of his mother emphasised his loneliness all the more; that the silent overlooking of him by his father must surely keep the wound open. She took a certain pleasure even, when she had recovered herself after the first shock (for she had distinctly a touch of tiger-blood in her nature), in talking to him rather ostentatiously, in a very clear and distinct voice, in order to show to him and to herself her sure, supreme detachment.

This lasted for forty-eight hours; and then on the Sunday evening, for the first time, compassion made itself felt — a little cloud of it, like a man's hand.

Sunday evening in summer has a peculiarly sentimental effect upon young persons, especially if they

have been to church; and Gertie, who was a little
dévote sometimes, had not only been to church with
May, but had assisted in the singing of "Hark!
hark, my soul!" after the sermon, and had been
played out of church to the strains of "O rest in
the Lord."

Then she had come up to cold supper, and had
drunk a little Moselle. Then she had put a filmy
wrap about her head, and gone out with Austin into
the gardens at the back of the house. (Austin, she
had noticed, was quite polite always to Val; but
occasionally did not seem to notice that he was
there.)

It was a delicious evening, warm and perfumed,
and a belated nightingale (perhaps the same that
had sung to Val and the priest three weeks ago) was
recalling fragments of his old early-summer song.
Again, too, the stars were dim and soft — a whole
vault of them, set in grey velvet. The tall trees
were motionless, and the flower-beds gave off the
cool reflex perfume that comes from such after a hot
day.

They went across the lawn under the cedar and
down upon the first of the terrace walks that fall
towards the village; and there they stood presently,
leaning on the stonework, without speaking. Behind them, beyond the huge cedar, glowed the tall
windows of the house, open to catch the evening air,

and now and then a spoken word or two came to them.

This was a most fitting scene for the close of Sunday: the emotional effect of the evening service was not yet exhausted in the girl's mind; everything seemed to her to-night very holy and peaceful and complete. . . .

Presently she lifted her arm from the cool stone and began to go slowly up towards the end of the terrace furthest from the house, and Austin went with her. Their thin shoes made hardly any sound at all on the paved walk; but just as they got near the end Austin made a remark. She answered it; and at this instant reached the end, just in time to see Val, perfectly recognisable in the twilight, moving quickly away from a seat just below the balustraded end of the terrace. He was going with quick, noiseless steps on tiptoe, obviously unaware that they were so close, and, equally obviously, intending to get away round the shubbery before he was seen.

It was then, for the first time, that compassion laid a finger-tip on her heart. The boy had slipped out, she saw, immediately after supper, and had come out here alone, to brood. He had found, he thought, a safe refuge; and there he was now, stealing away into the dark for fear that he should interrupt or be interrupted.

She said nothing; nor did Austin till they reached
again the further end of the terrace.

Then —

"That was Val, wasn't it?" she said.

"I think so," said Austin indifferently.

"Does he . . . does he feel it all very much?"

"He's got to," said Austin briefly. "It's his
best chance, poor brute."

CHAPTER V

(1)

"I'VE got to send into East Grinstead," announced Lady Beatrice at breakfast on the
following Wednesday morning. "Does anybody
want anything? The dog-cart's going at eleven."
There seemed no demand.

Everybody had gone away yesterday. Even Austin had gone. Gertie had been loudly reproached
by May, but had declared an uncancellable engagement to be photographed, and she had travelled up
to town, under Austin's escort. The Professor had
gone. He had sought out Val once more before he
had left, and had endeavoured to impress a more
genial and human philosophy upon him than that
which had been propagated in the summer-house on
Sunday; and had been surprised, and a little ag-
grieved, by the boy's apparent lack of interest. And
the Merediths were gone — all three of them; Tom
and his father still preserving their air of imper-
turbability throughout, treating Val with exactly the
same friendly but detached air as that which they

had shown before the Professor's disclosures.
There were left then at Medhurst, once again, the
General, Lady Beatrice, May, and Val. (I forgot
to add Miss Deverell.)

At about half-past eleven Lady Beatrice thought
to put into effect a decision she had arrived at two
days before — namely, to have a good talk with Val
herself. She had perceived, unmistakably, the
aloofness in which he had walked during this week-
end; and, as Gertie had seen, had rather increased
the boy's embarrassment by trying to draw him into
public conversation. He had been polite, but impenetrable. So that, now that the guests were gone,
it seemed to her a good chance to find him and to
say a word or two. . . . The sense of burden
was increasing on her with every day that went by.

About half-past eleven, then, she took up her stick,
and limped through the hall and up the staircase
that led to his rooms. The fine weather had broken,
and since breakfast a steady rain had been falling.
She was almost certain, then, of finding him upstairs
in the room that he and Austin still called their own.

She came down the passage, tapped (as her custom was), and then, hearing no answer, went in.
Val was not there. But she stood, looking about her
for a minute, before ringing to make enquiries.
The room was as she had always known it, rather
untidy, very boyish, and with an appearance of try-

ing to be a caricature of a real smoking-room. A couple of small books lay in the seat of a chair; and she glanced at them. They seemed to her very dull. One was by a man called Haeckel; and another by a man called Laing. Then she rang the bell and sat down.

It was a fairish long wait before anyone came, and she was just going to ring again when Charles, the footman, came in.

"Do you know where Master Val is?" she said. "Please find him, and say I'm up here."

"Yes, m'lady."

Charles disappeared, walking a good deal quicker than he had come, and while she waited she again looked at the books by Messrs. Haeckel and Laing, and found them duller than ever. There were disagreeable diagrams of man-like monkeys, or monkey-like men — she was not sure which, as long Latin names were printed beneath them — on several of the pages. Then Charles came back.

"Please m'lady, Master Val's gone in with the dog-cart."

"Where? To East Grinstead?"

"Yes, m'lady. He came down to the stables just before it started."

She lifted herself out of the chair. (Charles, the footman, handed her her stick deferentially.) It was no good waiting then.

"Let me know when the dog-cart comes back," she said. "You needn't say anything to Master Val. I'll speak to him myself."

"Very good, m'lady."

But she was quite unconscious of the depth of her own uneasiness until she ran into Val in the hall just before lunch, and was aware of a perfectly clear sense of relief at the sight of him. He was just hanging up his cap on the stag-horns near the door.

"Why — where have you been, my boy? I was looking for you."

"Been to East Grinstead," said Val steadily.

"But you didn't tell me —"

"No. I only thought of it after breakfast. There were one or two things I wanted to get."

"And you got them all right?"

"Yes, thanks," said Val.

"Well, come along in to lunch."

And she took his arm in friendly and maternal fashion to help her along.

(11)

About seven o'clock the same evening she sought him again, once more painfully picking her way up the slippery stairs. She would have half an hour or so before the dressing-bell rang; and she preferred to find him, as it were informally, rather than make an appointment.

And the last stimulus she had received, causing her to come up this evening rather than to wait for to-morrow, was a short conversation between herself and Miss Deverell.

"Jane," she had suddenly said after tea when May and the men had gone, "Jane, I'm not satisfied about Val. There's something the matter with him."

"I think so myself," said Miss Deverell drily (who of course had been told of the disaster, and had made no comment on it).

The other jumped. (One never got accustomed to Miss Deverell's characteristics. The suddenly startling little sentences that she fired off half a dozen times a week were always unexpected.)

"Oh! you think so too?" said Lady Beatrice rather feebly.

"The boy is unhappy," pursued Jane energetically. "But I am not his mother."

"I'll go and see him."

"I think you had better."

Here then she came.

This time she was more fortunate. Val's voice answered her tap, and he sprang up from the deep chair as she appeared.

"Doing anything important, my son?"

" No, mother."

" Just sitting by yourself? "

" Just sitting by myself," repeated the boy in a perfectly even tone.

She took care not to look at him particularly as she slowly sat down; but she was none the less conscious that something was seriously the matter. It was not exactly depression that she perceived; rather it was a tense kind of excitement. His face was quite resolute; his voice quite steady; and there ran through both a sense that something was tight-stretched somewhere. There was no longer that miserable sort of laxity that she had noticed before, nor that subtle tone of self-defence that had been apparent a good many times in public. Rather there was a ring of confidence in his voice . . . and yet that same barrier of secretiveness hid its meaning from her. It seemed to her rather unwholesome.

" Tell me about Cambridge," she said. " Have you had a nice term? "

Val paused a moment. Then, with complete self-possession, he proceeded to give her the kind of account of the term which a nephew would give to a maiden aunt, without the humour. It was quite intelligible; it was full of information; and it was perfectly superficial. He allowed no emotion to appear; he did not permit the smallest chink of light to penetrate his own feelings. He spoke of his lectures and the Lent vaes. . . .

"Oh, yes," said Lady Beatrice inattentively. "And what do you want to do during the vacation? Wouldn't you like to go away somewhere — with Austin, or one of your friends?"

Again came that deliberate little pause.

"I hadn't thought of it," said Val. "I rather thought of stopping here — altogether."

And then she couldn't bear it any longer. It was intolerable to her to sit here and be excluded from him so completely. A wall was between them, and she could see neither over it nor through it. Only she was aware that he was suffering behind it; and a rush of tenderness surged up in her.

"My boy, what's the matter with you?"

Again there was a moment's silence. She had stretched out one jewelled hand towards him in an unconscious gesture, as if to invite his own to be laid in it; but he did not move. Indeed, she thought for an instant that he was going to give way; the sense of strain grew tighter than ever. But it did not break.

"Nothing's the matter," he said.

"Listen, my boy," she began hurriedly. "I understand perfectly that you're unhappy. And of course I know why. But I did just want to tell you this — that nothing you've ever done or not done can make any difference to me. You mustn't think hardly of your father; he's a man, you know, and thinks slowly. But he's very fond of you. . . . That's why he feels as he does. We're all fond of you, Val."

Val swallowed in his throat. And then the bitterness burst out: he clasped one hand tightly with the other, and began to speak. An appalling venom was in every phrase, and his face worked.

"Fond of me, is he? Really! And he called me a coward before the whole village. That's what he thinks of me! Really! I don't see how he can be fond of me if he thinks that. . . . And he hasn't withdrawn it, or said he was sorry. . . ."

"Val!" (She was sitting upright now, terrified and amazed.)

"He treats me like a dog . . . a cur. And I dare say I am one. I know I am one. . . . Have I ever denied it? Well, I didn't ask to be born. It's not my fault. . . . But don't let's pretend he's fond of me. . . . How could he be?"

"Val! Val! . . ." (Her voice was imploring, not shocked.)

"Then why can't I be let alone, to . . . to return to my own vomit, as the Bible says? I only ask to be let alone, to go my own way. I'm not doing any harm to anyone, am I? . . .

except by being alive. And that ——" (He broke off.) "Well, why can't I be let alone? I've been keeping away as much as I can. . . . I don't think I've bothered anyone much. . . . And you will try to drag me into things, and make me talk . . . and try to pump me. I won't be pumped. I'm a beast and a cur, am I? Very well; then let me behave like one . . . and . . . and keep to myself. Father and you have got Austin, haven't you? and May? What more do you want? Why can't I be left alone?"

"Val, you oughtn't to speak to me like that."

"Who began it? I didn't. I haven't come whining to you, even if I am a cur! But even rats turn, you know, in a corner."

"Oh! my boy, I didn't come up here to bother you ——" wailed the mother.

He drew a sharp breath; and his passion seemed to pass.

"Very well, mother; I'm sorry. There, will that do?"

"I didn't come up to bother you. I had no idea you were feeling like this. I thought you were just unhappy, and hurt perhaps . . . perhaps . . ."

Her beautiful eyes suddenly ran over and her voice choked.

"I'm sorry, mother," said Val, steadily refusing

to look at her. "I'm a beast . . . I know that well enough." She was relieved by her tears, and she looked up at him, with her eyes still swimming. He was sitting hunched up in his chair, his hands clasped round his knees; his face was colourless and fallen. But there was not the faintest sign of softness there. He had pulled in his horns; but his shell was still impenetrable, and she perceived that he meant to keep it so.

"Val, I won't trouble you any more now. You're feeling it all too bitterly. But, my boy, do remember that I care, dreadfully. I've been miserable about you."

He remained expressionless.

"I wonder whether you wouldn't like to talk to someone else. There's Father Maple . . . if you don't care to talk to the Vicar. He's a good man. I'm sure he is. And he'd understand."

"Thanks very much," said Val, resembling a pool in a dead calm, after storm.

"Well, will you? I could send a note down. Or you could go yourself, to-morrow morning?"

"I won't forget," said Val dully.

She stood up. He gave her her stick, as he would give it to a stranger. Again that wall was between them; but she was thankful for it now. She must try to forget, she told herself, the glimpse she had had of what lay beyond. He would quiet down presently. . . .

" Give me a kiss," she said, trying to smile.

He kissed her, and his lips and eyes were like stone.

(III)

She had reached the top of the stairs, that night at bedtime, with Miss Deverell beside her, when she paused.

" Go on, Jane," she said. " I want to go and speak to Val a moment."

Dinner had passed off quietly enough. She had said a word to her husband about the boy when they were alone together in the hall before going in, but he had shaken his head, with grim lips, without speaking. But she had understood from his silence that she might speak to the boy as she liked. At dinner she and May had done most of the talking. Val had sat at the lower end of the table, next Miss Deverell, and had answered shortly but quite adequately, when he was spoken to. Before the candles and glasses were brought in he had slipped off, and had gone in the direction of his rooms, without wishing anyone good night. And now she too was going to bed, and thought she would like to say a

word to him first, to reassure herself rather than
him. She intended to speak about Father Maple
again in the morning — not to-night, for fear the
boy should think himself persecuted.

Her heart beat a little apprehensively as she
tapped at his sitting-room door. There was an instant's delay before he answered. Then she went
in; and he was just rising from the writing-table
in the window, and closing the big leather blotting-
book.

"I came to wish you good night, my son."

She went up to him slowly, leaning on her
stick, as he stood with his back to the writing-
table, as if guarding it. She noticed that he kept
one hand upon the blotting-book as he leaned
towards her.

"Good night, mother," he said, and kissed her.

But somehow she did not feel as much reassured
by the sight of him as she had hoped. He was
quite quiet; but the excitement she had seen blaze
out three hours ago was still there, somewhere
far down beneath the surface. It glowed there, like
life in a sleeper.

She looked round the room, as easily as she could,
with an air of interest.

"It's rather shabby, Val," she said. "I wonder
whether you'd like new curtains. Aren't these your
Eton ones?"

"Yes."

"Wouldn't you like some new ones? And perhaps a carpet?"

"Oh! these'll do very well," he said.

"That's the list of the Boats, isn't it?" she asked, going up to the framed paper on the wall by the fireplace.

"Yes."

She looked down the list. There was his name. Medd *mi.*— the third in the list of the St. George; as he had pointed it out to her proudly six or seven years ago. It had meant a lot to him then.

"How pleased you were," she said, turning to him and smiling, "when you first got into the Boats."

"Yes."

"What's this?" she said suddenly, looking curiously at another object under a glass dome.

"Which?"

"This, under the glass."

"Oh! that's a bit of stone off the top of the Matterhorn."

She smiled.

"I remember," she said. "Austin brought it back with him, and showed it us in the dining-room. Do you remember? May's got another, in her room."

"Yes," said Val.

"How sorry you were not to be able to climb it too. . . . Val, wouldn't you like to go out again some day, and do it?"

"I'm afraid I haven't the head for it," said Val grimly. "Besides ——"

"Yes?"

"Nothing."

"Think about it," she said. "Perhaps your father would let you go this September. You and Austin might go, if he can get away. You'd like that, I expect. Or perhaps Tom Meredith would go. He generally goes about then."

She was doing her utmost to lift the level to a less tragic point; for it was nothing short of tragedy that was in the air of this room — a boy's heroics, no doubt, yet as overwhelming, subjectively, to the boy as calf-love itself. She was trying, then, to be natural and ordinary and friendly; perhaps that would keep him better than explanations; those before dinner, at any rate, had not been very successful.

"Well, good night again, my son," she said, as she went at last across the floor. "Sleep well."

"Good night, mother," he said. "I'll try . . ."

Outside the door she paused and listened. But there was dead silence, except for a sudden gust of rain below against the passage window. It had been raining off and on all day, and now that night was come the wind seemed getting up too.

She went noiselessly down the passage, scarcely using her stick. She did not want him to think she had been listening outside the door. As she reached the end she turned again in the dark shadow, and as she did so the door of the sitting-room she had left opened suddenly and swiftly; a head was thrust out, then withdrawn; and she heard the key turn in the lock. . . . At any rate he had not seen her.

(IV)

She found it hard to sleep that night.

Soon after the stable clock struck twelve she heard her husband come up to the dressing-room next to hers, where he slept, and softly push open the door between them, as his custom was, in case she called to him in the night. But she did not speak; he was apt to be upset if he found her awake so late.

She had said her prayers as usual, with Dr. Ken's evening hymn at the end: —

"Teach me to live, that I may dread
The grave as little as my bed.
Teach me to die. . . ." And so on.

She remembered how she had felt the irony of this in the first days after her accident, when she had feared her bed at night considerably more than she hoped to fear the grave, when the time came. And now as she lay in bed to-night, looking out at the tall old walls about her, just visible in the glow of the night-light, at the rows of photographs over the mantelpiece, the gleaming points on the dressing-table, the tilted, ghostly-looking, full-length mirror by the window, she hoped that her son was long ago in bed and sleeping off his pain. " I shall be better in the morning," she had said to herself over and over again during these same weeks of pain.

And so her thoughts turned and twisted, formed into little vignettes of illusion and dissolved again, uttered themselves in little audible sentences and were silent again; and through them all moved Val — Val looking at her; Val asleep, as a little child, in the old night nursery, twenty years ago; as she had seen him when she had stolen up after dinner in her jewels; Val's voice speaking words she forgot again as soon as she heard them; and lastly, once Val's face, very close to her own, enigmatic and terrible and grey, with burning eyes and colourless lips. . . .

This woke her in earnest. . . . And she heard three o'clock strike.

But by half-past three she was asleep and happy.

(v)

Benty, too, had had rather an uncomfortable evening.

First, there had been a remark or two at supper from Masterman to the effect that Mr. Val looked melancholy-like. But Benty's severity of aspect, and of a single sentence that she uttered, had been such that Val had been discussed no more.

Immediately after supper she had gone straight upstairs to her own room, and after two or three minutes' listening at the baize door, had stolen through and into the boy's bedroom. She had no idea what it was that made her uneasy, yet the fact was undeniable that all day there had rested on her a certain weight which, very prudently, up to now she had attributed to a touch of indigestion. By now, however, indigestion or not, the mood had deepened to positive apprehensiveness, and yet she had not an idea as to what it was that she feared.

The bedroom looked all right. Certainly Charles and the housemaid had done their duty with admirable promptness. The day clothes and the boots were gone, and the bed was ready, with the sheet turned down and a light quilt laid over the foot. She lifted her old bedroom candlestick this way and that — for, as a true Conservative, she never used any other light unless she was obliged — and peered about. Then she went out, and into the sitting-room.

Now, of course, as a sensible old lady, she did not for an instant give any countenance to superstition, and yet, if she had only formed the psychological habit of reflecting upon her own consciousness, she would have known that her own uneasiness took the absurd form of feeling that there was something sinister in the atmosphere of these two rooms, and, indeed, to some extent, in the whole house. She went so far practically as to lift her candlestick again in every direction and to peer into the dusky corners. Then she went to the writing-table, but all that lay there that was in the least unusual was a little pile of paper laid on one side ready to the hand. But there was nothing written on it.

She felt guilty, somehow, with all this poking and peering. . . . Then she heard a step somewhere in the house, and fled out briskly, down the passage, and was standing, holding her breath, on the other side of the baize door, to hear her boy go down into his room, and shut the door.

Ten minutes later she came out again.

In the meantime she had gone to her room and had busied herself with ordinary familiar affairs, putting away her mending and her work-box, and seeing that the windows were properly secured against the rain and wind. Then suddenly she had taken up her candle once more and stolen out.

It took her a full minute to make up her mind to the very ordinary act that she proposed to perform: it was only to look in on her boy to see if he had everything he wanted and to wish him good night. She did this almost two nights out of three if he came up early enough, yet it seemed to her to-night to be an unusual effort. . . . Then she compressed her lips resolutely, went up to the door, and tapped.

There was a pause before he answered, and it seemed to her old ears as if there were a rustle of paper. Then he called out, and she tried the door. It was locked; she waited. Then he opened it and confronted her, and as he saw who it was, the rigidity of his face softened.

"Why! Benty. . . ."

"I came to wish you good night," she said.

"Come in a minute, but it must only be a minute."

Benty was no detective beyond the point to which unreasoning love could bring her, but it was obvious that Master Val had been writing. The chair was half wheeled round, and a pen laid on the blotting-paper began to roll down the slope as she looked.

"Now don't sit up late at your writing, Master Val. Go to bed like a good boy."

He said nothing. He stood regarding her, with his shoulders against the mantelpiece. She peered about, uncomfortable under his long look.

"Go to bed, Master Val, won't you?" she said.

He put his hands suddenly on her shoulders.

" Old Benty! " he said. " Give me a kiss, my dear, and then go to bed like a good little girl."

His voice trembled a little. Then he kissed her slowly and deliberately on either cheek.

" My dearest boy! " she murmured.

" Say ' God bless you,' as you used to, Benty."

" God bless you," she said, frightened at his burning eyes and pale face.

At the door she turned and nodded again.

" There," she said. " Now have a good sleep."

And she went to her room, still uneasy, telling herself he would be better in the morning. Ten minutes later he heard her ladyship's stick on the boards.

CHAPTER VI

(1)

WHEN Val had peeped out to see whether his mother was listening, he had locked the door and gone back again to the writing-table.

Then he opened the blotting-book, slipped out three or four sheets, and sat back to read them over. He must not lose the run of the sentences. Then he leant forward again; and for nearly an hour wrote steadily, with many pauses, again leaning back from time to time to consider what phrases to use.

A little before twelve he finished. He folded the sheets, placed them in five envelopes, already directed, sealed them carefully, and then went and propped them in a row on the mantelpiece, just below Austin's paper of " Pop " rules, framed in light blue ribbon.

Then he sat down on the couch opposite, and looked at them a long time without moving.

Half an hour later he got up and went to the corner cupboard, and lifted out from it a big cardboard box full of old letters; and for the next hour, sitting on the floor, he went through these, reading some, tearing up some, laying some in a little pile to be replaced. Then he carefully tied up with tape those he meant to be kept, and emptied the waste-paper basket full of fragments into the fire-place. Then he set a light to these and watched them burn. . . .

About two o'clock he got up again out of the long chair where he had been lying with his eyes closed, and stood a moment or two on the hearth-rug. There was a long, low looking-glass below the " Pop " rules; he caught a glimpse of his collar and white shirt front in this; and he leant forward, his hands on the shelf, and for a minute or two stared steadily into his own reflected face. He saw there his eyes, unnaturally bright, rimmed with dark lashes, his compressed lips, the pallor of his skin. He was in a state of intense interior excitement by now, as the time he had fixed was very near; and he began to wonder, as people will in such moments, as to his own identity. . . . When he was quite a child, he remembered, he had been tormented by such thoughts. " It is I who am thinking," he had reflected, in childish wordless images, " but I think that I am thinking. Therefore the ' I ' is be-hind my thinking. But I think that I think that

I am thinking. Therefore the 'I' is behind the
thinking that I am thinking." . . . And so the
" I " receded indefinitely, behind ring after ring,
after consciousness. . . . Then what is the
" I "? Is there anything behind all this? Is there
more than a series of husks of consciousness? Is
there any kernel at all? . . . So he pondered
now, intent and maddened by his own intentness.
Whatever " I " is, it is beneath the face whose reflection he stared at, beneath the convolutions of the
brain, beneath the processes of the brain, beneath the
pure thought that emerges from such processes, beneath even the infinite series of the consciousnesses
of self. Or is there nothing behind all these? Is
self merely the coincidence and sum of the
whole? . . .

Then he tore himself away suddenly, as the intricate thought whirled in his brain with an almost
physical vertigo, and leaned with his back to the
glass, looking out over the familiar lighted room,
perceiving that it was simultaneously more familiar
and near than ever, and more infinitely apart and
remote. It was the nearest expression of himself
that he had ever made — of himself mingled with
Austin. Right up from the little box of broken,
dusty butterflies which he had collected before he
went to school at all, to the new rook-rifle he had
bought last Christmas — all resembled the case of

a caddis-worm, sticks and pebbles gathered in a day of life. And now he was going to split the case and climb up through the dim and mysterious atmosphere to another state of existence — if, that is, there would be anything that could climb when the half-assimilated particles were dissolved. . . .

The rain spattered suddenly against the shuttered windows, driving his thoughts instinctively to the safety and shelter he enjoyed here — the protected sleeping house, all at peace in bed, his parents, May, the servants; and out there the stables, the horses, the coachman's house, the grooms' lodgings. For an instant he looked down on it all, with the roof off, and in each little closed compartment lay a little body coiled up asleep. And his eyes suddenly filled with tears of self-pity. He was to leave all this — all the people who did not understand him, who had snubbed him and repudiated him. . . . He was going to show them whether, after all, he was such a coward as they thought; when the morning came, and all the little people awoke and came running in here, they would know whether he had been a coward or not. They would find his little caddis-case lying here; and they would find his last words too, his forgiveness of them all, his serenity, his sorrow — all written out and fastened up carefully in those envelopes behind him — the envelopes addressed to his mother, to Austin,

to May, to Benty, and to Gertie, but none to his
father! . . . They would know in the village
too, where they had discussed him and laughed at
him; that new keeper would know, the one who
gossiped about him, and was so respectful to him in
his presence. . . . And Benty? What would
Benty say and do?

Then the clock struck the half-hour, and he
started upright. It was time. It must all be over
by three o'clock. That was the time he had fixed.
He went straight out of the room and passed into
his bedroom.

(II)

In the corner of his bedroom nearest his bed was
a little badly carved oak cupboard. He unlocked
this with a key on his watch-chain and took out a
cash-box. Then again he unlocked this (his hands
had suddenly begun to shake, so that the compart-
ments clattered as he handled it), and opened one
little lid. Then out of this he drew first a phial and
then a small graduated medicine-glass.

He had bought both these this morning at East
Grinstead. He had had a little trouble with the
poison, and had been obliged to explain elaborately
that his father wanted it for killing a horse. General Medd had sent him in on purpose, in order that
there might be no difficulty; it was for an old horse,

which they did not want to shoot in the usual way.
It was quite a good lie; it ensured that the dose
would be certainly fatal, and it had seemed so unusual as to be quite convincing. The chemist had
let him have it then — arsenic or prussic acid, or
something — he had forgotten — after making him
sign his name in the book. And the graduated
medicine-glass he had bought with a vague feeling
that he would like all his instruments to be new and
unsullied and his own; he shrank a little from using
a glass belonging to the house.   .   .   .

Of course other methods had occurred to him.
He had contemplated jumping off the top of the
house, or shooting himself with his new rook-rifle;
but he had feared the noise and the uncertainty of
the second, and his own nerve in the first. Poison
was much better; surely no one, he had thought,
so desperate as himself, could shrink from a little
medicine-glass filled with colourless liquid.

With these in his hands then, he went back again
on tiptoe into his sitting-room; again he locked the
door; then he sat down on the sofa and contemplated the little dark blue phial with the staring label
and the innocent little glass beside it. He thought
the phial looked disagreeable; he would pour out
the draught at once and put the bottle away. He
had nearly half an hour yet, before all would be

over. So he did this — the liquid did not come as
far up the glass as he had expected, and he put the
bottle behind one of his envelopes on the mantelpiece, where he could no longer see it. Then he sat
down again, staring at the glass. . . .

He started all over as the stable clock struck the
quarter. For an instant he thought that it must be
three, and simultaneously the idea crossed his mind
that if it was three it was too late; he would have
broken his resolution, and would no longer be
obliged to keep it. But the six strokes sounded and
were silent: his honour was still safe.

Then he suddenly reflected that there was no great
hurry. The chemist had told him that the poison
killed practically instantaneously as well as pain-
lessly. He could have a good twelve or thirteen
minutes yet. Yes, he would wait thirteen — no,
fourteen minutes. . . . He took off his watch
and chain and laid it on the table by the glass.
. . . Fourteen minutes. It was no good staring
at the glass. He would lean back and close his
eyes. . . .

Then began once more the conflict which he
thought he had wholly finished with last night by
the beehives, when Gertie and Austin had interrupted him. He had gone through it all then — had

faced the two sides — life with its intolerable shame
and death with its uncertainties. And he had just
chosen death — coolly and consciously — when he
had heard the voices, and started up just in time to
escape being seen. He had known exactly what he
was doing, and he had clenched the decision by a
solemn resolution made, oddly enough, on his knees
by his bedside. Since that time up to the present
moment he had never wavered: the excitement of
the plot, the going to East Grinstead, the explanations to the chemist, the careful and subtle buying
of some rook-rifle targets in case he were questioned
as to what he had bought, the keen sense of drama
as he had seen himself sitting down to lunch for the
last time, to tea, to dinner, his fierce outburst to his
mother, his last good night to her, his deliberate
avoidance of a good night to his father; and then,
above all, the intense shuddering pleasure of the
composition of his letters — his tender forgiveness
of Gertie and the confession to her of his own weakness, his proud and manly farewell to Austin, his
letter to his mother telling her that her sympathy
had all but weakened him in his resolution, his little
note to May, cheerful and resigned, his careful directions about his funeral — no flowers and no religious service unless it were very strongly wished
by his mother — the doing of all these things had
been so absorbingly exciting and inspiring that,

with the exception of one or two bad moments, he had simply not been aware that there was any instinctive clinging to life at all. He seriously believed that the thing was settled.

And now it came back like a thunderstorm; and the figure round which it centred was Benty — Benty in her room over the fire; Benty hearing the news next morning; Benty as she had stood at the door just now after wishing him good night.

Up to three minutes ago he had really been unaware that it would. He had enjoyed keenly, though he did not know it, the contemplating of himself awake in the sleeping house, bent on his desperate act; he had enjoyed, though he did not know it, the formal and judicial deliberation by which he had proceeded to his bedroom and unlocked the instruments of his death, the slow pouring out of the poison and the setting of it before him on the table. . . . But now that all was done, now that no act remained except that to which all his other acts led up, without which they would all be silly and theatrical mockeries, the intoxication of drama and action was gone, and he faced the facts. . . .

If he kept his resolution he would be dead in ten minutes — *dead*. . . . Medhurst would have reeled off from him and vanished for ever — Medhurst, Cambridge, his horse, his family, this room

— every one of those things by which he assured himself of his own identity and in which he expressed it; his own heart which he could hear drumming in his ears, his wet hands that now were knitted tightly one about the other, the pulses in his body — all those things by which he knew self — these would be gone; and he ——? . . .

And, on the other side, he could just go to bed and pour this silly stuff out of the window, take off his clothes as usual and put on his pyjamas and go to bed, and awake to-morrow with Charles in the room and the morning light on the floor . . . and begin again.

And no one would ever know.

But he would have broken his resolution! — that resolution he had made so deliberately, that resolution by which he had demonstrated to himself so forcibly that all the world was wrong about his cowardice and he right.

But no one would ever know.

Besides, had he not already proved that he was no coward? What coward would have done all this — bought the poison, faced death for over twenty-four hours unflinching, made his last dispositions so tranquilly and sincerely? Surely he *had* conquered interiorly, and that was all that mattered! He had meant to die, had done all things necessary for death. He had proved himself to himself! And

if he was no coward interiorly and really, what
would it matter what the world thought? Would
it not be braver? . . . And Benty! . . .
Was it kind to Benty? Would it not be far finer
to live? . . .

He sat up as this brilliant light broke on him. For
a moment or two he saw himself as magnificent and
transfigured — a heart of steel and fire within, yet
misunderstood and misrepresented without; a man
desperately courageous in all that mattered, of whom
the world was not worthy . . . a soul of infinite tenderness as well as of courage.

Then down on him again came a sense that he was
more of a sham than ever — a braggart, a liar, who
posed splendidly when there was no danger, who
failed miserably always when the point came. He
had swaggered about his boxing at Eton, and had
refused a fight; he had talked big about his riding,
and had funked Quentin; he had swung his ice-axe
and rehearsed his dramas of Switzerland, and had
cried out like a woman at the bad place; he had
galloped after Gertie and saved her, but had meant
to draw off if the edge of the quarry came too near;
he had slapped a blackguard's face on the Pincian,
and had let Austin go to the duel in his place. And
now he had written his letters and poured out his
poison . . . and . . . and *was not going
to drink it.* . . .

Then the clock began to chime the four quarters of three.

He started up from the sofa where he had lain writhing and seized the glass. . . . His brain and heart whirled together in inextricable confusion; his visions of himself came and went like flashing light and darkness on a wall. It was three o'clock, and he must do something. It would be too late in a minute. Three o'clock was the time appointed by Destiny and himself.

He ran to the door and unlocked it, sobbing gently to himself; ran out, still carrying the glass carefully, into his bedroom. . . . He must be quick, or *he might drink it* . . . it had not yet finished striking three. The window was open, according to orders, and the blind hung over it; he tore this aside with his left hand, carefully, lest he should spill what he carried in his right, and then he flung the contents of the glass far out into the shrubbery.

He drew back, still shaking all over; consumed with shame, yet desperately intent; plunged the glass again and again into his water-jug, dried it, and set it among some bottles on a shelf above the washhand-stand. Then back through the open doors he ran, snatched the letters from the mantelpiece, tore them into fragments, still sobbing, and flung the pieces among the ashes in the grate —

those letters which he had taken two hours to write last evening.

And then, with a sudden wail, he ran back into his bedroom, leaving the lights burning, tore off his clothes, and crept naked into bed; blew out the candle, and crouched down under the clothes, sobbing and moaning aloud.

He was only a boy still.

CHAPTER VII

(1)

TO be perfectly frank, Father Maple had fallen asleep over his office in the garden. There was every possible excuse: it was a really hot afternoon; his housekeeper, who was a woman deeply Conservative in all matters except Home Rule, had insisted on giving him hot mutton for lunch, followed by sago pudding, in spite of his remonstrances; the flies were so troublesome that he put his handkerchief over the top of his head, and it had slipped forward so as to shade his eyes; and the pages of his book insisted on turning green by way of balancing the glow of the afternoon sun. So, on finishing the second nocturn, he had thought that he would attend better to the third if he closed his eyes for three minutes to rest them, with the result that when the clock from the Norman tower over the way struck four, it failed to disturb him.

It was a pleasant, rectangular, old-fashioned garden in which he sat, with his head bowed on his breast. It was surrounded by a high old brick wall, mellow with age, and covered on its east and west walls with trained fruit trees; the south wall was occupied by the Queen Anne house, with the chapel projecting; and the north by a properly built brick summer-house with a tiled roof, with a shrubbery on either side. The garden itself was just one lawn split into four by paved paths, with a sundial in the middle, and skirted by long and deep herbaceous beds; and the priest had erected a trellis on the top of the wall that divided his own garden from the next in such a manner that he could not be over-looked even by the upper windows. It was a formal but friendly place, exactly appropriate to the formal and friendly house that it served.

It was very quiet here this afternoon. Outside lay the long, hot street, silent and empty. Even cyclists were absent, and there were no brake-parties come over to see Medhurst, as to-day was Thursday, and Tuesdays and Fridays were the only opportunities when the family was at home. A dog or two lay asleep in the shadows, no doubt, sitting up now and again to snap at flies; the farm-yard opposite the " Medd Arms " was empty; the church-yard was as empty as a churchyard ever can be. And it is probable that in perhaps thirty or forty bedrooms all along this street there slumbered per-sons who on cooler days would have been talking or bustling and disturbing the world generally. The hot weather had come back indeed, and was doing its work. And, what is very touching indeed if one reflects upon it (though quite irrelevant to this story), the clergyman was as soundly asleep in the vicarage garden as the priest in the presbytery's.

Almost immediately after the clock had struck four Bridget's figure appeared in the study window. She peeped out under her hand, and immediately disappeared. Simultaneously with her appearance the priest opened his eyes, without otherwise moving, and saw her; and since he knew her ways, called out, before she had time to take any further steps:

" Is that anyone for me, Bridget? "

Bridget reappeared again.

" Sure I was just telling the gentleman that I mustn't disturb your Reverence."

The priest got up, put his handkerchief in his pocket, and went towards the house as Val came out, carrying his white hat in his hand.

" Tea, Bridget," said the priest; and then: " This is excellent. You're just in time for tea."

He observed Val while they had tea, though he scarcely looked at him; and perceived that there was some very particular emotion hidden a long way out of sight, which, if he himself were at all abrupt or careless, might never come to light. He had hoped he would come some time ago; but three or four weeks had passed since the dinner at which he had met him, and the boy had not come. He conjectured then that something had happened since then, that was the cause of this visit.

The priest had a great theory about the sequence of events. He held that things happened or did not happen — things, that is, in which free-will integrally came in — according to the movements of a kind of under-world in which free-will played a very large part. (Prayer, of course, is one manifestation of all this.) For instance, it had become plain to him that he himself must make a big attempt to get at the boy whose mother had been so confidential, and that he must get him to come spontaneously: it would not be of the smallest use to ask him outright. So he had set to work on the night of the dinner to communicate with the boy without the boy's knowing it; and so certain was he that he had succeeded, that he was really astonished that the effect had not followed sooner. However, it seemed to have worked at last; for here was the boy. And the fact that he held such a theory, and habitually acted on it, made him quite extraordinarily confident and self-possessed, now that it had been justified once more. . . . He gathered, however, from the abruptness with which the boy had turned up, that something rather important had happened to precipitate the process. (I do not know whether all this is in the least intelligible. At any rate, it was what the man held.)

The priest talked of odds and ends for some time, while he handed tea and made suggestions as to various kinds of food. He felt that he must first establish a sense of ordinariness and normality in the boy's mind; and meantime he watched interiorly, with extreme care, the gradual settling down of the other's agitation. Val soon began to answer easily; to sit less on the edge of his chair; and even to begin little new subjects.

"I say, that's a splendid piano you've got," he said.

The priest spoke of his piano; pointed out one or two ordinary devices for increasing resonance; explained that he had as few hangings and carpets in the room as possible, for the same reason.

"What was that thing you began by playing when you dined with us?" said Val. "I've never forgotten it."

"That was what's called extemporisation," said the priest. "You take a theme ——"

"Do you mean that you made it up as you went along?" asked Val, amazed.

"Oh, it's not so impossible as it sounds. You take a theme first — an idea that's to say, expressed in sounds instead of words — an idea that's in-

teresting, you know, and that's capable of development — like . . . like a paradox; and then you
comment on it, and expand it, and draw it out, and
turn it upside down, and alter it — yet it's all the
same main idea. Then you contradict it flatly and
argue it out . . . and finally you make it win,
when you've explained it."

He broke off, smiling, seeing the boy's consterna-
tion. But he had seen, too, that he was not entirely
unintelligible.

"Does that sound quite mad?" he asked.

Val smiled too, rather painfully.

"No . . ." he said. "But it seems to me
extraordinary that anyone can do it — straight off."

The priest checked himself on the verge of another sentence. He saw that the boy had led up to
the taking-off edge. . . . But the moment
passed. Val struggled with himself an instant, and
drew back. . . .

"Shall we go out into the garden? I know you'd
like to smoke. It's very good of you to come and
see me at all."

So once more, in the garden, the priest soothed
and reassured this boy who was shying, like a colt,
at every opportunity. It was a laborious business.
The priest knew perfectly well that the other had
come down on purpose to make a confidence; and

yet that it was quite conceivable that he would go away again without doing it.

And then at last the moment came.

Val, who was obviously not attending in the least to his host's description of the Dresden Kur-haus and its contents, suddenly interrupted.

"Look here," he said. "I've got to be up at the house at six, to go out riding. There's something I want to ask you most awfully: and it'll take rather a long time. . . ."

(II)

It was half an hour before he had finished.

Again and again the priest had to help him out by a question or a comment, to reassure him when he grew too bitter, and finally, to sit without moving a finger or an eyelid, while Val recounted the last scene — that desperate attempt — a sham attempt, as he now saw it to be — to kill himself. It was very delicate work. A phrase too much, or a disdainful movement, or a touch of sentimentality would have upset the balance — the very delicate balance of a soul spinning free at last from complications, on a single line. . . . He had to let his soul come out clear into the open and see facts as they were. And then, then it might be possible to deal with it.

. . . "That's what I've come about then,"
ended the boy, pale and excited. "I didn't know
who else to come to. . . . I felt I must come
to someone who didn't know me. I could tell him
the truth, then. . . . And this is the truth.
I'm simply a coward. It was when you were playing that I first felt I could come to you — I don't
know why. And there it is! I'm a coward. And
I want to know what I'm to do. I hate myself
every time; and I tell lies to myself. And I want
to know, once and for all, whether I can do anything in the world to cure myself. It's no good
telling me to do a big thing: I probably shouldn't
do it. . . . And I want to know what to do."

The priest moved a little in his chair. He had
been listening for the last five minutes without a
word or movement.

"Look here," he said quietly. ("Take another
cigarette.) . . . I take it you've come to me, as
to a doctor? Well, I'm going to answer you like a
doctor. Is that what you want?"

"Yes."

"You want to hear the truth? However unpleasant? Remember, I shouldn't tell you the truth
unless"—(he leaned forward a little)—"unless
I was perfectly certain there was a cure."

"Yes, the truth."

" Very well, then. Now listen.

" First, however, I want to say that you've done a brave thing in coming. . . . No; don't interrupt me. It is brave. It would have been much easier for you not to have come; to have gone on — er — lying to yourself. Particularly as there was no earthly reason why you should have come to me — to me, of all people. You would have easily salved your conscience by going to your mother ——"

The boy started.

" How did you know that?" he asked breathlessly.

" My dear boy, it's exactly what a real coward would have done. . . . No doubt you thought of it; but then, you see, you didn't do it. You came to me. Now listen, please, carefully."

The priest sat back in his chair, hesitated a moment to gather his words, and began.

" The first point is, Are you a coward really? To that I say, Yes and No. It depends entirely upon what you mean by the word. If it is to be a coward to have a highly strung nervous system and an imagination, and further, in moments of danger to be overwhelmed by this imagination, so that you do the weak thing instead of the strong thing against your real will, so to speak, then — Yes. But if you mean by the word coward what

I mean by it — a man with a lax will who *intends* to put his own physical safety first, who calculates on what will save him pain or death and acts on that calculation, then certainly you are not one. It's purely a question of words. Do you see? . . .

"Now it seems to me that what is the matter with you is the same thing that's the matter with every decent person — only in rather a vivid form. You've got violent temptations, and you yield to them. But you don't will to yield to them. There's the best part of you fighting all the time. That's entirely a different case from the man who has what we Catholics call 'malice' — the man who plans temptations and calculates on them and means to yield to them. You've got a weak will, let us say, a vivid imagination, and a good heart. . . . (Don't interrupt. I'm not whitewashing you. . . . I'm going to say some more unpleasant things presently.) . . .

"Well . . . a really brave man doesn't allow himself to be dominated by his imagination — a really brave man — the kind of man who gets the V.C. His will rules him; or, rather, he rules himself through his will. He may be terribly frightened in his imagination all the while; and the more frightened his imagination is, the braver he is, if he dominates it. Mere physical courage — the absence of fear — simply is not worth calling bravery. It's

the bravery of the tiger, not the moral bravery of
the Man.

" And you aren't a brave man — in that sense.
Nor are you a coward in the real sense either.
You're just ordinary. And what we've got to see is
how you're to get your will uppermost.

" The first thing you've got to do is to understand
yourself — to see that you've got those two things
pulling at you — imagination and will. And the
second thing you've got to do is to try to live by
your will, and not by your imagination — in quite
small things I mean. Muscles become strong by
doing small things — using small dumb-bells — over
and over again; not by using huge dumb-bells once
or twice. And the way the will becomes strong is
the same — doing small things you've made up your
mind to do, however much you don't want to do
them at the time — I mean really small things —
getting up in the morning, going to bed. . . .
You simply can't lift big dumb-bells simply by
wanting to. And I don't suppose that it was
simply within your power to have done those other
things you've told me of. (By the way, we Catholics believe, you know, that to fight a duel and to
commit suicide are extremely wrong: they're what
we call mortal sins. . . . However, that's not
the point now. You didn't refrain from doing
them because you thought them wrong, obviously.

We're talking about courage — the courage you hadn't got.)

" Now this sounds rather dreary advice, I expect. But you know we can't change the whole of our character all at once. To say that by willing it we can become strong, or . . . or good, all in a moment, is simply not true. It's as untrue as what you tell me that Professor said — that we can't change at all. That's a black lie, by the way. It's the kind of thing these modern people say : it saves them a lot of trouble, you see. We can change, slowly and steadily, if we set our will to it."

He paused. Val was sitting perfectly still now, listening. Two or three times during the priest's little speech he had moved as if to interrupt ; but the other had stopped him by a word or gesture. And the boy sat still, his white hat in his hands.

"Well, that's my diagnosis," said the priest, smiling. " And that's my advice. Begin to exercise your will. Make a rule of life (as we Catholics say) by which you live — a rule about how you spend the day. And keep it ; and go on keeping it. Don't dwell on what you would do if such and such a thing happened. As to whether you'd be brave or not. That's simply fatal ; because it's encouraging and exciting the imagination. On the contrary, starve the imagination and feed the will. It's for the want of that that in these days of nervous systems and rush and excitement that so many people break down. . . ."

"And . . . and about religion?" asked Val shyly.

The priest waved his hands.

"Well," he said, "you know what my religion is. At least, you almost certainly don't. And, naturally, I'm quite convinced that mine is true. But that's not to the point now. If you really want to know, you can come and talk some other time. With regard to religion, I would only say to you now, Practise your own: do, in the way of prayers and so on, all that you conscientiously can. . . . Yes, make a rule about that too, and stick to it. Make it a part of your rule, in fact. If you decide to say your prayers every day, say them, whatever you feel like. Don't drop them suddenly one morning just because you don't feel religious. That's fatal. It's letting your imagination dominate your will. And that's exactly what you want to avoid."

Val stood up briskly.

"I must be going," he said. "The quarter's just going to strike. Thanks most awfully."

The priest stood up too.

"Not at all," he said. "It's my job, you know."

Val still stood looking at him. What amazed the

boy most was the naturalness and the absence of emotionalism of the whole thing. He had come down here facing, as he thought, a crisis. And to this quiet, small, grey-haired man it did not appear that it seemed a crisis at all; it was part of the day's work. Val wondered why on earth he hadn't been before — why he hadn't known that there were such people in the world. . . . Were all Roman Catholics priests like this? . . .

"Well, thanks again," he said. "By the way ——"

"Yes?"

"Do you think I shall have a chance — when I'm stronger, I mean — to . . . to show —— ?"

"I'm quite sure you will," said the priest. "It may not be a very sensational chance, and perhaps no one will know. But you'll have one, don't be afraid." He paused. "Almighty God doesn't really waste His material, you know."

When the priest was alone he sat down again for a minute or two and remained without moving.

Then he spoke aloud softly — a bad habit he had contracted through living alone.

"And to think," he said excitedly, "that that boy doesn't know anything about Absolution! . . . What a . . . a damnable shame it all is!"

CHAPTER VIII

(1)

IN life, as in rivers, there occur occasionally long flat reaches where nothing particular happens. The water moves, the sun shines, but there is nothing much by which to mark either. And it seemed to Lady Beatrice, as she sat one morning in her room, that she had lately been drifting down such a period. First, they had not been up to town this spring; and even Medhurst, if lived in continually for eighteen months, becomes almost ordinary. For her husband was distinctly growing older: he slept more after dinner; he was more unwilling to go away; and the effect had been that except for ten days in August, when they had gone to Scotland with the boys and May, to a rather dreary house, they had done literally nothing except mind their own business at home.

Interiorly too nothing much had happened. There had been the shock of Val's behaviour in Rome at Easter, and there had been a very unpleasant little scene with him one evening after he had come back from Cambridge for the long vaca-

tion. She remembered even now how badly she had
slept after it. In the morning, however, things had
been all right again; Val too had looked as if he
hadn't slept much. But nothing whatever had
happened, and she had soon lost that feeling of
anxiety of which the affair of that disagreeable
evening had been a climax. She remembered having recommended Val to go and talk to Father
Maple, but was rather relieved now that he had not
taken her advice. One never knew what complications might not arise if Roman Catholic priests
became too intimate. Certainly she liked Father
Maple; he had been up to dine again two or three
times during the summer; but there had been no
further talk between them on the subject of her son.
Besides, Father Maple had been quite wrong in his
hints that the arrangement which they had all come
to with regard to the Rome affair was hard on Val.
On the contrary, it had been admirably successful.
No one ever mentioned it; and what a relief that
was! Such things were best ignored and, if possible, forgotten.

Well, it was now October, and the flat reach was
ending; at least, it was, at any rate, about to turn a
gentle corner. On the eighth she, her husband and
May were to go to Debenham for a week (where her
eldest brother now reigned) for the shooting, leav-

ing Val alone at home. But Val himself was to go
to Cambridge on the tenth, and he was already
shooting here every day, so she needn't trouble about
the boy. On the whole, she was pleased with Val
just now: he was receding, that is to say, in her
mind from that plane on which she had been anxious
about him. Certainly he was very quiet; but young
men were quiet sometimes; and he certainly was no
trouble. There had been no more such painful
scenes between him and his father, as (she had been
given to understand) had taken place over two dogs
that were fighting in the village. He was quiet; he
had none of his friends to stay with him; he
did not talk much in public, but the air of sulking
had quite disappeared now. . . . He was becoming more like Austin, she thought.

So she pondered, sitting back in her chair, after
she had finished interviewing the housekeeper and
writing her three or four letters. And then there
was a tap, and her husband came in.

"About the keys," he said without introduction.
"Masterman had better keep them, I suppose."

She knew him well in this mood. It soon passed;
but it was a little trying while it lasted; for it mani-
fested itself in a strenuous sense of responsibility
and in what a less tactful wife would have called
"fussing" to his face. She knew what he meant.

He was referring to the fact that they were going
away the day after to-morrow, and that certain
precious and almost symbolical keys had to be
placed in safe keeping. They were the keys of such
things as the small plate-safe — the safe, that is,
where were preserved certain pieces of silver connected vaguely with Charles II and the First
Pretender — the glass case in the library, where
were such things as a pair of buckles worn by
George II, a fan of Queen Anne's, a pair of stockings reputed to have been worn by Elizabeth, together with a number of miniatures, enamelled keys,
snuff-boxes and silver coins; and, lastly and chiefly,
the "muniment-room," in the south wing on the
first floor. It was in this muniment-room that the
almost priceless papers of the estate were kept,
together with the relics referred to in the first
chapter of this book — relics which even now must
not be named for fear of incredulity. . . .

"Yes, dear, I suppose so," she said. "Doesn't
he generally have them when we're away?"

"My dear, you forget," fussed the General, with
an air of solemnity. "These keys are always kept
by a member of the family if anyone is here." He
eyed her reproachfully.

She remembered then. It was a detail of the
tremendous Medd etiquette, more rigid than that
of any Royalty, that prevailed here wherever the

" Family " was concerned. She felt a little ashamed of her remissness.

" Val will be here till the tenth," she said, " and I think Austin comes down in the morning to shoot, doesn't he? "

" You think then I can safely leave them with Val? " he asked, as one deciding eternal issues.

" I think the poor boy would be rather hurt if you didn't," she said. " That is, if he remembers."

" Very good," said the General, with the air of one who yields generously against his better judgment, and hurried out of the room again.

It was only for a moment or two that she allowed herself to remain amused. She could see her husband bustling off in his knickerbockers to reveal to Val the responsibility that would rest on him for two days; and then return to his study to complete his other arrangements for the day after to-morrow; his interview with Masterman, his anxious turning out of drawers. . . . Then the purple glory of the Medd pride came down on her once more and enveloped her in its rather stifling splendour.

(II)

She was wrong, however, in one detail. Her husband did not go to Val's room, but summoned him instead in a stately manner, through Masterman, downstairs to the library.

It is difficult to describe the exact state of mind of this old man towards his younger son, since his emotions were so massive and huge as to defy analysis. Two vast principles faced one another within him — principles before which the merely domestic affections and tendernesses crouched like ants before a mountain-range — and those two principles were Family Pride and Disgrace. These two things stood out dominant; and seven months had not yet reconciled them. Val was bone of his bone and flesh of his flesh — a Medd, in fact; and Val had outraged his birth. However, the General's interior arrangements do not matter much. . . . Practically, he treated Val now with a cold courtesy; he never found fault with him (in fact, Val gave him no excuse, and his father was, at any rate, objectively just); and he spoke to him as seldom as he could. He respected the Medd, if he could not admire the Valentine. He was conscious now that he was going to perform an act of great generosity.

"About these keys," he said when the boy came in. "I shall give them into your charge when we go away; and you must hand them to Austin when he comes down on the tenth."

"Very well."

"Look at them. Here they are, these three." (He handed them across the table on either side of which the two were standing.) "They are labelled;

so you will know them again — the small plate-chest, marked ' P.C.'; the glass case in the hall, marked ' G.C.'; and the muniment-room, marked ' M.R.' You understand?"

" Yes."

The General solemnly moistened his lips.

" Very well. I keep them here as a rule, you see." (He indicated a drawer in the table.) " Masterman will have the keys of the house, as usual. But these three I leave in your charge. You understand?"

" Yes."

The General paused. . . . (Yes, he had better say it. Perhaps Val did not quite realise the responsibility.)

" I am doing this, my boy; but not every father would do it under the circumstances. . . . You understand, eh?"

He saw a very faint flush come up on the boy's face.

" Yes, father; I quite understand. Thank you very much."

" Very well. That's all, my boy."

When Val had gone again the General carefully put the keys back in their place, on the little hook that he had had placed in the drawer for their express accommodation, and forgot to lock it up. But he felt glad, on the whole, that he had decided

to confer this honour on the boy. Not many
fathers, he thought, would have done it. . . .
And then he was not sure whether he had not been
a little weak; and he stood staring out at the cedar,
breathing audibly through his nose, as his manner
was when in deep thought.

There was an abundance of things to do always
when the Family left home for a few days; drawers
to be locked up, papers to be put away; dispatch-
boxes, which did not contain anything in particular,
to be moved from the window-seat to the little cupboard behind the sofa. Then there were interviews
with old Masterman — mysterious conversations
about certain bins in the cellar; interviews with Mr.
Watson, the head coachman, as to the use of the
horses and their proper exercise; interviews with
Mr. Kindersley, the head keeper, as to any shooting-
parties that the boys might be allowed to hold.

So the General could not stand still and breathe
through his nose for long; for Austin was coming
down on the tenth with Tom Meredith and another
man; and Mr. Kindersley was in waiting to receive
exact instructions as to which coverts were to be
shot. It was a pity, thought the General, that they
couldn't come down a day or two earlier; then Val
might have shot with them too. But Austin, it
seemed, was unable to get away before the day on

which Val left for Cambridge; and, after all, Val had had several days already out with the partridges; and a boy still at Cambridge mustn't expect to have everything his own way.

(III)

The departure on the morning of the eighth was tremendous.

The Family was going to drive; and the men and the maids were to take the luggage and go round by train. Debenham was not more than fifteen miles by road, and not less than twenty-six by rail, exclusive of the drive at either end. Mrs. Bentham had gone the night before, as an independent and honoured guest, to stay with the Debenham house-keeper for her annual visit.

About nine o'clock, therefore, the wagonette and the luggage-cart drew up at the south porch, and a tremendous scene of activity began. First, great trunks shaped like arks began to appear, inter-spersed with mysterious bandbox-shaped pieces of luggage, sheaves of umbrellas, two gun-cases, and three or four portmanteaux.

Then, as May saw from her window, Masterman appeared, in rigid black as usual, directing with waves of the hand two persons in green-baize aprons in the placing of those articles in their proper positions — first in the luggage-cart, till it appeared imminent that the stout brown horse would presently be lifted from the ground by his girth and suspended in air (May, in a neat travelling costume, watched, fascinated), and then in the front seat of the wagonette.

At this point May's own maid, resembling a thin duchess in disguise, hurried into May's room and distracted her by apologies for leaving out a pair of gaiters. She seized these and vanished again. When May turned to the window once more the company had grown: Mr. Simpson, the valet, dressed in chocolate-brown, with a black overcoat, black hat, and black stick (not altogether unlike a stage detective), was holding open the door of the wagonette for the ladies to mount; Mrs. Caunt, Lady Beatrice's maid, was in the act of ascending; and one of the persons in green baize, cowering it seemed under Mr. Masterman's denunciating hand, was shifting a trunk from the luggage-cart to the already high-piled front seat of the wagonette. Then Fergusson herself came out, carrying a flat parcel — no doubt the gaiters — modestly shrouded in brown paper. . . .

" What a business it all seems — (Good morning, mother) — What a business it all seems, this going away ! "

Lady Beatrice kissed her daughter absent-mind-edly. Something of the solemnity seemed to have descended upon her too.

"Caunt's gone," she said. "And I can't find my spotted veil. She didn't leave it here, did she? She's got no head, you know."

She cast a roving glance round the disordered room and limped out again.

But the departure of the luggage and the servants was a comparatively furtive and ignominious affair, considered alongside of the departure of the Family itself.

The first note was struck at breakfast, at which the ladies appeared in hats, and the General in a grey suit, with spats, carrying an overcoat which he had just fetched from the hall, a pair of field-glasses with case and strap complete, and a small leather-covered box which he called his "travelling case." It was understood by the world to contain a flask of spirits, a horn mug, and a brush and comb. All these things had been set out carefully by Mr. Simpson on the hall-table, in readiness for the journey; but it had seemed fit to the General to bring them in to breakfast.

He shook his grey head severely as he set these down on a chair by the door.

"Simpson's losing his head, I fear," he said. "I found these things on the hall-table."

"Perhaps he put them there," said May audaciously.

The General shook his head again as he went to the sideboard.

"He must have. . . . Miss Deverell, can I give you a little of this cold bird?"

Three-quarters of an hour later the hoofs of great horses could be heard, and the rolling of wheels; and May, in her hat and cloak, playing with the new Persian kitten in the hall, went to the door to look out, just as the carriage wheeled round and drew up.

Already Masterman was on the steps of the terrace, as if by magic (since he had been in the hall, it seemed, not two minutes before) consulting with Mr. Watson, now enthroned on the box-seat, with the two great black horses in front of him, all a-shine with gloss and black harness and great silver crests, held at the head by a groom. The two seemed to be consulting about the weather.

Then various other persons began to appear.

James, the first footman, who was to drive with them, and, apparently, be company for Mr. Watson coming back, since there was nothing else in the world for him to do at either end of the fifteen miles, hurried through the hall to the library and back again twice, already in his long blue coat. Obviously, from the place he went and returned, and went and returned, the General must have rung with some vehemence. Then round the shrubbery corner by the stable appeared two figures — another groom and the "helper"— mere spectators, however, of the Progress, since they stood and eyed afar off.

Then a housemaid, very much agitated, hurried in.

"Please, miss, her ladyship can't find her spotted veil."

"Tell her ladyship that there are two of mine in the top left-hand drawer of the wardrobe."

"Thank you, miss."

Then Miss Deverell appeared like a shadow, as the clock from the stables struck the appointed hour. She was habited, gloved, veiled, and bonneted with extraordinary precision.

"My dear, you have not your fur boa on."

"It's too warm," said May. "Besides, it's packed."

Miss Deverell winked with both eyes two or three times, and sat down on the edge of a chair.

Then Masterman, who had been comparing his watch with the striking of the stable clock, and verifying the time by an apparent appeal to Mr. Watson, came back to the house, and went in the direction of the library with the air of an assured and privileged intruder. Evidently he was going to warn his master that a quarter-past ten had struck.

Then Val appeared, in his knickerbockers, with his hands in his pockets, obviously intending to be dutiful. May remembered that he would be gone back to Cambridge when she returned. . . .

(IV)

May's feelings towards Val went in moods, like layers in a Neapolitan ice. She had been sincerely and deeply shocked that a brother of hers could have behaved as he had in Rome; yet, on the other side, duels were wicked. Again, she was both a Medd and a girl: as a Medd she resented the outrage to the family honour; as a girl she was extremely fond of her brother, who had bowled to her on the lawn so often and taken her birds'-nesting. Again, she was as fundamentally unimaginative as her mother. Sentiment took the place of imagination on the top; and this lack of imagination sometimes made her feel unduly hard on Val; and sometimes obscured the malice of his crime. The result of the whole was that she had certainly drifted a good way apart from Val during these last months; since a boy is naturally intolerant of capriciousness, and May had seemed to Val distinctly capricious. There had been moments when he had leapt, so to speak, at her in kindly moods; established, as he thought, an understanding one evening; and the next morning had found her with the blinds drawn down over her friendliness and a façade of cold dignity presented to him. Besides, he could not altogether forget that nightmare of a journey back to England, when the two girls had nestled together apart and looked at him with something very like repulsion. . . .

" You'll be there by twelve," said Val, leaning up against a sofa, still with his hands in his pockets.

" Not if father dawdles much longer, we shan't," said May ungrammatically.

Then Masterman hurried by again from the library with the same air of agitation as James had worn. Evidently, in spite of the preparations having been begun two days before, they were not yet complete. As he vanished Lady Beatrice rustled in, on her stick.

" Where's your father? "

" I don't think he's quite ready," said May. " James and Masterman seem hunting for something."

Lady Beatrice rustled out again.

" You'll be gone when we get back again," observed May after a silence, for want of a better remark.

" Yes," said Val.

He wandered to the side-table and began to look

at the *Graphic,* replacing his hands in his pockets as he turned each page.

It was instructive to see how his hands came out and his figure instinctively straightened, as there suddenly loomed from the direction of the library the form of the General, arrayed as for an exploring expedition, and moving rapidly and impressively. On his head was his tall grey felt hat, shaped like a cake; over his grey suit a darker grey great-coat, slung with straps; white spats over his chestnut-coloured boots; in his gloved hands on one side a little sheaf of sticks and implements, on the other his " travelling case." He moved rapidly, and there went with him a smell of tweeds and an air of importance.

" Come along, come along," he cried to his daughter. " We're ten minutes late."

Then began the last whirl of the departure, resembling the passing of a tidal wave.

His wife swept along behind him, coming surprisingly fast, with a housemaid plucking at her dress *en route.* Masterman reappeared from a totally different direction from that in which he had vanished. May sprang up and plunged into the stream by her mother's side. James flew through a side door, with his long tails clapping behind him;

the faces of two female servants peeped over the edge of the music-gallery; and Mrs. Markham, the housekeeper, in black silk, was observed to be standing with her hands folded together, at the head of the staircase, as if about to take part in a liturgy.

The travellers were packed in at last in the great landau. Miss Deverell was already there, sitting upright in her proper place on the far side. (She had disappeared from the hall, presumably, soon after her single remark to May; but no one had seen her go.) Beside her now sat Lady Beatrice; opposite Lady Beatrice, May; and opposite Miss Deverell, the General. Masterman shut the door and James climbed to his seat.

"Good-bye, my boy, good-bye," cried the General, waving a gloved hand to Val, who had drifted out behind the surge and was standing now hatless at the head of the steps. "Now we're ready at last."

Lady Beatrice kissed her hand at the boy. (She was ashamed that she had forgotten to say good-bye; but the rush had really been too great.) May nodded and smiled.

"Good-bye, Val."

"All right, Masterman."

There was a stir of the carriage. The great black horses started a little as Mr. Watson's whip drew gently across their flanks, jingled their bits, and moved off. The groom and the helper vanished behind the shrubbery, as they were not in full dress; female faces appeared at windows. Masterman bowed twice, bending at the small of his back.

And so the Progress began, and the Medd Family left its Country Seat.

Half-way up the hill, when the General had done enquiring after his field-glasses, which had slipped round to the small of his back, May looked back at the house.

There it lay, in its solemn splendour and beauty, indescribably lovely, far more an essential of the landscape than the oaks and beeches grouped to show it off; its two wings held out like welcoming arms, its twisted chimneys sending up skeins of delicate grey against the clear October morning sky, its great central block majestic and dominating, rising above the broad flagged terrace and the steps; and there by the doorway, surmounted with carving, stood a tiny, grey, hatless figure in knickerbockers, still looking after them. Masterman had gone; the faces in the windows had disappeared; the shrubbery was deserted. There remained Val for a moment or two.

She looked at her mother. Her mother was pulling the rug straight.

She looked at Miss Deverell. Miss Deverell appeared to be closing her eyes for sleep.

She looked at her father. Her father was straightening the strap of his glasses.

And as she looked back again at the terrace as the carriage topped the hill, she saw the grey knicker-bockered figure go back into the house.

CHAPTER IX

(1)

CHARLES, the second footman, was still young enough to appreciate the absence of the family from home and the presence of one or both of the young gentlemen.

All kinds of indulgences were silently permitted. Shirt-sleeves could be largely worn throughout the day; a neat dark suit was full-dress; there was very little bell-answering to be done, very little waiting at meals. To be sure there were certain other dreary jobs to be performed: furniture had occasionally to be moved about, disused silver to be polished; but even these occupations would be interrupted by surprising and interesting errands ordered by the young gentlemen, such as accompanying one of them to beat for wood-pigeons in the pine wood, or to manage the boat while a little coarse fishing was done. There was an air of holiday abroad even if the day was as full as ever.

On both those days, for example, Charles had a sight of sport. On the eighth, after lunch, Master Val went out after wood-pigeons, and Charles was

448

stationed for the greater part of the afternoon, with permission to smoke, on a charming seat in the sunshine at the north end of the pine wood, with no responsibilities except to keep himself in full sight of the open sky, and to tap occasionally with a stick on the trunk of a tree. This acted as a " stop " to pigeons returning homewards from the beech woods and stubbles, and sent them round instead to the south end of the wood, a quarter of a mile away, whence came gun-bangings from Master Val, who was crouched under a little withered shelter. Charles had ultimately to carry no less than eight dead pigeons home at the close of day, and ate two of them himself that night for supper.

On the ninth he had even greater enjoyments, for Master Val informed him, when he came to clear away breakfast, that he was to accompany him and the under-keeper to certain outlying stubble-fields and undergrown copses, in the first of which a few partridges might be got, and in the second, rabbits, and perhaps a strayed pheasant or two. They did get these animals, with some success; returned for lunch, as the house was not far off; and went out again after lunch for the rest of the afternoon. It was true that Mr. Masterman was a little overbearing and strenuous during the evening that followed, but still a day in the open air was a day in the open air.

When Charles had brought coffee in to Val, who dined, as the custom was at such times, in the " morning-room," he went upstairs to pack the portmanteaux for the journey to Cambridge the next day. Then he went downstairs for supper, at which he ate half a newly killed rabbit, and within an hour was in bed in the men's quarters over the south wing.

Soon after two o'clock he awoke and smelt burning, and, as he sat upright in bed, thought he heard a voice calling.

(II)

At ten minutes to two the same night, Mr John Brent, blacksmith's assistant, was passing the south end of the house, about a hundred yards distant, carrying parts of a very powerful air-gun concealed on his person, a dozen small nets wrapped about his body, and a ferret, with muzzle and line complete, in his huge breast-pocket. He was walking very carefully over the grass in the shadow of the trees, in light tennis-shoes stained black, and was on his way to the coverts over the hill. These were at least a third of a mile from the house, and nearly half a mile from the keeper's cottage.

He kept out a careful look, however, in the direction of the house, since this was the one habitation that he was practically obliged to pass, even though it was almost inconceivable that he should be seen; and it was not unnatural, therefore, that he should notice a peculiar light that came and went oddly in the ground floor of the south wing. . . . At first he thought the phenomenon might arise from the movement of branches between him and an un-shuttered lighted window; so he stopped to observe, himself still in the darkness of the belt of trees he was traversing, since a lighted window might mean danger to himself. . . .

The result of his investigations after two or three minutes' watching was peculiar. First, very quickly he drew out the bones of the air-gun; then he un-wrapped a net; then he took out the ferret and wrapped her up in the net; then he took off the other nets, made a bundle of the whole, and put it very carefully down a rabbit-hole with which he was familiar. John Brent was a good fellow; he had nothing but honour, and even affection, for the Great Powers who provided him so abundantly, though unwittingly, with game; and it was not to be thought of that their House should be afire and he not warn the authorities.

Then, in his tennis-shoes, with a fragmentary explanation of his own presence framing itself in his mind as he ran, he went at full speed across the wet grass, right up to the billiard-room window, whence the light and smoke were now bellying out; and presently, with his hands to his mouth, was bawling aloud, careless of his own personal safety. As soon as a window went up he shouted a sentence, tore round to the front, and began pealing at the bell.

(III)

It is astonishing how quickly a house can be roused where there is a real necessity. In three minutes windows were being thrown up, and Charles was on his headlong way to the stables. In five minutes the stable bell was pealing and horses were being saddled. In ten minutes riders were gone in three directions after fire-engines; in twelve minutes every soul in the house was assembled in the hall, maids in skirts and shawls, men in shirts and trousers — except those who were circulating vehemently round the south side of the south wing, and beginning to organise a supply of water. All lights were turned full on, except in the bedrooms, and the great house blazed among its trees and lawns as if *en fête*. Great shadows wheeled across the grass, and a clamour of shouting and bells filled the air.

It was astonishing too how quickly Val assumed the commandership. He was out of doors and round the corner of the south wing in his pyjamas and evening shoes before Masterman was in the hall, and he was back again issuing orders by the time that Mr. Watson with a troop of stablemen burst round the corner on to the terrace. Val leaped on to the low wall above the steps and began to shout:

"Watson, choose six men and form a line from the well with buckets; throw water from the outside into the windows without stopping. . . . You've sent for engines? That's right. . . . Masterman, go back into the hall and begin to take down the portraits. The maids must help you: we can't spare any men. Pile all the portraits out here, on the terrace — that side. Then go on with the furniture. Oh! by the way, send someone. No Charles! *Charles!* . . ."

"Yes, sir."

Charles thrust up his hand out of the seething crowd. (His face had a smear of black already across it.)

"Charles, go round all the bedrooms — *all,* like the wind, and see that everyone's out; then come back to me. . . . Mrs. Markham. Where are you, Mrs. Markham? . . . Please see that none of the maids go near the fire without leave. Please stand in the hall for the present. James, I want you here. And . . . and William —"
(The footman came obediently out, followed by the groom.) "Stand here: I'll want you in a minute."

"Master Val ——"

"That you, Masterman? . . . I can't hear. Oh! hold your row, you maids. Go back into the hall at once — *at once,* I tell you. . . . Yes: and shut the door. *Shut the door!* I can't hear, Masterman. . . . Go and do as I told you. . . . William. James. Oh! there you are. Where's Charles? . . . Never mind. Come in, you chaps."

Val leapt down again from the wall.

He had his plan clear-cut in a moment or two. That is one advantage of an imagination: its possessor can see a number of things all at the same time.

He had been awakened by Charles, had sprung out of bed entirely alert, and had run straight out and round the house to the billiard-room windows. There he had made his diagnosis from outside, to the effect that the fire had broken out in the billiard-room — the last room on the east end of the south wing — and had communicated itself to the smoking-room next door. He supposed this was so, from the fact that the fire, seen through the shutters, was far brighter in the first than in the second room. (Probably, he thought, a fused wire had started it.) Then he had torn back through the hall, had laid his hand on the billiard-room

door, and then drawn back, startled by the roar of
flames from within. He knew it was dangerous to
create any further draught, and had understood
that all that could be done for the present was to
pelt water into the windows from the outside until
the engines came. Then he had locked the door
and thrust the key into his jacket-pocket. Then
he had run back and issued his orders as the crowd
of servants surged out on to the terrace.

(IV)

Charles came down the stairs into the hall, three
stairs at a time, after accomplishing his errand —
(he had found all the servants' bedrooms empty,
with the exception of one in which the new scullery-
maid was putting on her stockings)— just in time
to see Master Val followed by the two men vanish
through the door into the south wing. He turned
and darted after them, as they bolted into the
morning-room, where Lady Beatrice had a number
of treasures — portraits, silver, furniture. This
was next to the smoking-room, and was, obviously,
the next room to be threatened. But on the threshold Val turned.

"Charles! Oh! there you are. . . . Go up
the back stairs, and see if you can get into the
rooms above these others. If you can, chuck

everything you can out of the windows. Don't be
an ass and throw the china, now. . . ."

Charles was gone, hearing already from outside
the voices of the stablemen, and the crash and hiss
of water as the buckets were emptied into the burning windows on his left. By extraordinary good
fortune the fire had broken out in the wing not fifty
yards distant from the well from which the house
tanks were filled.

The rooms looked strangely quiet and peaceful
after the rush and confusion below, as he switched
on the electric light at the doors. The smoke was
already oozing up through the floors, but the atmosphere was still perfectly bearable. He ran to the
windows and threw them open, and then began his
task — first tearing down the curtains with great
common sense as the most inflammable articles, and
then setting to work to toss out pictures, chairs,
rugs. . . . They were the bedrooms of the
master of the house and his wife.

After a quarter of an hour the heat and the
smoke became suddenly intolerable. He snatched
at a little inlaid desk which he had overlooked and
tried to get to the window. But a great burst of
smoke met him, and he staggered back choking,
dropped the desk and bolted, forgetting to turn out
the lights, that already were shining like street

lamps in a fog. He banged the door behind him, and after a long gasp or two ran downstairs.

" Good Lord," cried Val. " Are you all right? Finished? "

" Pretty well, Master Val. But I haven't —"

" Come and help here. . . . Where are those blasted engines? "

The morning-room was nearly empty. The Persian carpets were gone; the little tables, the cabinets, the pictures, the chairs — all these lay in confusion outside the windows on the trampled grass and the flower-beds — visible in the bright light that streamed out through the open windows. In the same light, growing now a little yellowish and smoky, could be seen the figures of the stable-men outside, passing buckets like fiends. Mr. Watson's voice could be heard shouting directions now and again, but the roar of the fire grew louder and the crackling more insistent.

Master Val and the two men were struggling now with a great black cabinet, certainly not too large to be passed through the wide-flung windows, but apparently too heavy to be moved across the slippery floors. Charles plunged into the group and added his weight.

And then suddenly Charles heard Master Val swear distinctly.

" Good God! I've left the muniment-room."

"Charles! take charge here. When you've got this out, do the best you can ——"

"Master Val. . . ."

But Val was gone.

Five seconds later Masterman, still toiling at the portraits, of which ten or twelve were already down from the walls and piled on the terrace outside, saw him running and dodging the bewildered maids, between the disordered tables and chairs, and disappearing in the direction of the library. He called feebly after him, but there was no answer. The white-clad figure was gone. And then back he came a minute later, and a little bunch of keys clinked from his finger as he ran.

"Master Val ——"

But Val was gone again; and a moment later Charles, emerging from the morning-room, saw him through the thin smoke flash into sight from the direction of the hall, and dash up the first steps of the back staircase that led to the floor above.

He was after him in a second, and had him by the arm at the top of the first flight.

"Master Val. . . . You can't; it's impossible. It's all ——"

"Bosh! let go. . . . *You don't understand.*"

"Master Val, sir."

"Let go, will you."

There was a scuffle. Then the boy tore himself free.

" It's all right, I tell you," he shouted straight in the man's face, and was gone.

" Master Val, you can't. It'll be afire by now."

But there was no answer. Already from overhead came a great gust of smoke, and Charles, staring up with blinded eyes, saw that the ceiling above the top of the stairs had vanished in clouds. But no flame was visible; it did not look particularly dangerous, after all, just yet.

(v)

Mr Watson had worked like a Trojan. He was naturally both stout and agitated; but he had his men in excellent disciplinary order, and for the first half-hour or so had, with his own hands, thrown into the billiard-room windows the water that was passed to him, bucket by bucket, by the six men' behind. One pumped, the rest passed from hand to hand. Then Mr. Watson, exhausted, had taken his place second in the line, and watched the muscular stable-keeper do the work of the actual throwing.

It was, of course, still pitch dark so far as daylight was concerned, but the light from the windows blazed out in all directions on to lawns and

trees and black agitated figures. Charles had
finished throwing valuables out of the first floor by
now, and under Mr. Watson's directions a water-
carrier had been dispensed from his business to remove these out of harm's way, as well as those
from the morning-room. When the great black
cabinet emerged at last and crashed down among
the autumn flowers, Mr. Watson himself lent a
hand to remove it some twenty yards across the
grass.

It was as he let go of this at last, panting and
sweating, that he heard his name called vehemently,
without any prefix.

"Watson! *Watson!*" shrieked a young man's
voice across the din of the voices, the rumble of
furniture, and the roar of the fire.

He looked up, and there, perfectly visible in the
clearly lighted room overhead, where just now had
been shuttered darkness, was Master Val in his
pyjamas, dancing with excitement. His hands
were full, it seemed; the heavy bars of the window-
frame showed like a network against his figure.

The coachman ran up.

"I'm going to chuck things out," cried the voice.
"I want you to watch and guard them."

"Master Val, come down: it isn't safe: the next
room ——"

"It's all right here. Here, catch."

A heavy parcel that crackled as with paper as it fell, crashed through the man's hands and fell.

" Pick 'em up. Don't lose them, for God's sake."

And the figure was gone again.

Then parcel after parcel flew out. The window was some twenty-five to thirty feet high, as the rooms below were built up on a half-sunken basement; and the bundles, each wrapped in a rug or curtain, descended with considerable impetus, now and again accompanied by the crash of glass. While Mr. Watson stooped to pick each up, the white figure vanished again, and was ready once more by the time that the last bundle had been added to the heap.

Then there was a pause.

" Come down, Master Val, for God's sake. The next ———"

Then once more the figure appeared empty-handed, gesticulating.

For a moment the man did not understand. Behind him, in a momentary stillness, he could hear the sobbing of the men's breath as bucket after bucket still passed up the diminished line; then the roar of flame bellowed out again, and drowned the words screamed from overhead. From the bed-room windows, left open by Charles, next to that single heavily barred window where the white figure shook the iron and screamed inaudible words, great tongues of red and orange flame pierced, like crooked swords, the huge volume of smoke that poured up now into the dark sky, alight with sparks and burning tinder. From beyond the house, as each new burst of flame died into comparative quiet, came the sound of the stable bell still pealing desperately, and the voices of shouting men. . . .

Then the terrified, bewildered man understood, and with a loud cry and a grotesque gesture, set off, shouting vague directions to the crowd in general, full speed for the front of the house and the only open door by which he could gain access to the interior of the south wing.

(VI)

It must have been almost immediately after this that the men, still desperately passing buckets from hand to hand, caught a sight of that solitary screaming figure, and understood too.

One at the inquest said that he ran for ladders; but they were all gone from their place in the stable-yard — taken, no doubt, to help in the removal of the portraits; and that when he came back it was all over.

Another said that he made an attempt to fling water — it was the only thing he thought of — but that the window was too high to reach.

A third said that he ran round too, to try to get

up by the back staircase to the muniment-room, but
found it already ablaze. He then tried the front
staircase, and here too, beyond the baize doors that
led through into the south wing on the level of the
first floor, there was just one furnace 'of flame.
Mr. Watson was here, he said, screaming like a
madman. . . . He had to hold him back.

It is plain, however, how the end came; and what
those saw who stood helpless and watched —
the men who dropped their buckets and stared; the
crowd of half-dressed men and women from the
village, who had been surging up for the last half-
hour and now formed a ring of terrified spectators
thirty yards away, on the edge of the south lawn.

Val had stayed too long in the muniment-room,
and on opening the door to escape must have been
met by an outburst of fire. It is probable that
even then he might have escaped, if he had dashed
for it instantly; but he must have lost his head, and
run back, hopelessly and instinctively locking the
door, from a possible to a certain death. For the
bars of the muniment-room windows cut off the last
possibility of life.

There then he stood screaming and crying, shaking at the bars like a savage, in full view of the
crowd. Now and again his figure and his distorted
face disappeared in gusts of smoke from beneath.
. . . But the horror of it all was that he lost all

control over himself. . . . Phrases, fragments of sentences, the names of God and Christ — these were heard again and again by the helpless watchers. Once he disappeared; and all thought that the floor had fallen, for the windows of the morning-room beneath were now merely squares of flame. But he must have run once more to shake the door and scream for the help that could not come. . . . For he was there again at the window a moment later, mad with fear, dashing himself at the bars, wrenching at them. . . .

And then the end came, mercifully swift.

A great crash sounded out above the roar of the flames. A vast explosion of smoke, lit house-high by a torrent of sparks and fire, burst out of all the windows at once. And when it cleared the figure was gone; and the noise of a clanging bell grew louder and louder behind as the first engine from Blakiston came at a gallop up the drive.

EPILOGUE

"**I** HAVE come to ask your reasons for writing as you did," said Lady Beatrice; "I must thank you very much for writing at all. It was kind of you, at any rate."

The priest sat down again in the chair he had left when she was shown in.

She was as pathetic as crape and genuine grief could make her. She had pushed her black veil up, on coming in; and her beautiful, aging face was white and a little thin.

It was three weeks now since the funeral. Up there at the house all still looked desolate. The south wing was now altogether demolished, and a temporary wall of brick was built across the charred end of the great hall and across the passages above. The family was to leave for Egypt in a few days' time, until the work of restoration was complete. It would probably be finished by the early summer. It was known that Austin was to go with them.

" I wrote," said the priest as quietly and naturally as he could, " because I had had three or four long

465

talks with your son Valentine; and I think I may say he gave me his confidence. I understood that it was what you yourself wished him to do."

"Certainly I suggested it to him."

"Just so. . . . So I did not communicate with you. . . . Well, you will forgive my saying this; but you know people will talk; and the explanation given of . . . of various things that have happened — at the funeral, for instance — is that General Medd is ashamed of his son. If I am wrong in that, I have nothing but apologies. But I was informed that this was so; and I thought it better not to shelter behind the plea of gossip, but to tell you outright that there is nothing to be ashamed of."

In spite of the heaviness that lay on her, she was conscious once again of surprise that he was so simple and direct. There was no conventional tenderness in his voice or manner. And she was surprised too that she did not find herself in the least resenting it. She hesitated before answering.

"That is perfectly true," she said; "though I do not know how such things have come to be said. But it is perfectly true that our chief grief lies in our knowledge of how . . . how he behaved in the face of danger. You see it was not the first time. There was that affair in Rome only

this Easter . . . there was his behaviour in
Switzerland. Perhaps he did not tell of that?"

"He told me everything," said the priest.

Her beautiful eyes filled suddenly with tears.

"I am glad," she said. "But that makes no
real difference. . . . It must seem terrible to
you that I can speak of him like this, poor boy!
. . . But it is more terrible to us that he . . .
that he . . ."

"That he seems to you to have behaved like a
coward?"

"Yes. . . . You see everyone saw it. He
. . . he behaved dreadfully at the window.
He . . . he lost his life through it too."

"Have you considered that he did a brave thing
in going up to the room at all?"

"Yes," she said. "But it did not seem to him
dangerous at the time. (I am just saying what my
husband has said to me.) He thought that the way
was clear. . . . Oh! it seems cruel to speak
like this; but you understand, don't you, Father
Maple, that it is just our love for him and our pride
in him ——" (She broke off.) "And then when
he saw the danger he . . . he . . . Ah!
I couldn't say this to anyone else. . . . I
haven't said a word. But you do understand
how . . . how all this hurts us. I . . ."

She covered her face suddenly with her hands.

The priest waited, motionless and silent, till she got her grief and misery under control. Then she looked up again at him, hopelessly.

"Will you listen to me carefully, Lady Beatrice? I wrote that letter to you with full knowledge of what I was doing — that letter in which I said that I considered your son to have been markedly courageous. Will you hear my reasons?"

She nodded. But there was no hope in her face. It was the look of one who felt herself bound in justice to hear the other side.

"Well, I must begin by repeating what I said to your son that first time he came to see me. . . .

"There are two kinds of courage — the physical courage of the brute, and the moral courage of the man. Your son had not the first. He had a very sensitive and imaginative temperament — a very highly strung nervous system. Now at least twice or three times this temperament of his overcame him — in Switzerland and in Rome — to take two instances only."

She looked at him swiftly, with a question in her eyes.

"Yes, and there were other instances. But take those two. . . . Now he was horribly ashamed of it. And the first really morally brave thing he did was to come and tell me. He need not have told me. It required a very high degree of courage indeed to come. He had never been taught to confide in anyone. And he made no excuses. He told me that he had found out he was a coward; and he wanted to know what he was to do. . . .

"Just think over that quietly, Lady Beatrice. There is more in it than appears to you now. The *real* coward goes on making excuses to the end. He made none — at the end."

The priest paused a moment to let that sink in. Then he went on.

"Well, I told him then about the will. He seems never to have heard of it. For instance, I said that a man who did a thing he was afraid to do was a far finer creature than the man who was not afraid to do it. That is very obvious, if you think of it. But the conventional view is exactly the opposite. And the conventional view ruins more lives than all fanaticism put together. . . .

"Well, I gave him a little advice about the training of the will. And then — now we're coming to the point. . . .

"The last time he came to see me he said something that seems to me now very nearly prophetic. I think I can remember his exact words. He said, 'I wish something would happen that I knew was dangerous, but which didn't look dangerous. I think I could do that. Or a thing that I knew really was dangerous, but which I hadn't time to think about.' I asked him why. He said, ' Because I should do that; and then I shouldn't feel so hopeless.'

" Then we went on talking . . . and at the end he said something like this: ' Suppose, after all, when the thing was done — done deliberately, knowing the danger — I collapsed and behaved like a cur again — would that be cowardly?' I told him certainly not. I said that any number of people collapsed when the thing was done; and that the fact that they did showed what a tremendous strain they must have been under, and how splendidly they must have been controlling themselves. . . .

" Lady Beatrice, do you see my point of view at all now?" (The priest leaned forward, gripping the arms of his chair. Underneath his quiet voice and face he was intensely moved.) " I don't think that either you or his father — if you will forgive me for saying so — understood the boy in the slightest. You do not understand how terribly he felt things, how his sensitive nature gave him the most acute pain, how his imagination dressed things up. If he had yielded to all this and given in — even then I could not have blamed him very greatly. But this was exactly what he did not do. He fought tooth and nail against it. And . . . and then God gave him exactly the opportunity he was asking for. He knew the danger perfectly. Why, he said to one of the men, ' You don't understand,' as he ran up. And then, when he had done his work he collapsed. Do you blame him for that? I don't. He had his opportunity at last, and he took it."

She sat still, looking at the priest. Outside the cold November sunshine lay on the garden where Val and the priest had talked together for the last time scarcely more than a month ago; the chairs they had sat in were now locked up in the little brick summer-house at the end. And across the way, over the low churchyard wall, was the long mound, in the shadow of the high-shouldered Norman tower, beneath which lay the body of her son who had disgraced his name. And she did not understand, even now. She saw only a minister of religion whose business it was to console and to say soothing things, not a priest whose business in life it is to understand motive and intention and to interpret events by those things.

She got up, painfully, with the help of her stick.

"Thank you very much, Father Maple. It is very kind of you to have seen me. Our old nurse, you know, said the same ——" She broke off, and then continued, "I will think over what you have said. . . . The poor boy!" (Her eyes filled again with tears.)

But he saw she had not understood. She remembered the external facts only; she had seen nothing of that other realm which he had tried to describe, and not even a glimpse of that blind, lovable charity by which it seemed that even the old nurse had seen so deep.

"You are going to Egypt, I think?" he said at the hall door.

"Yes. . . . We shall be back, we hope, in the spring. They will have finished the building by then. . . . Thank you so much, once more."

THE END

LaVergne, TN USA
24 March 2011
221299LV00005B/8/P